The Valentino Affair

Also by Colin Evans

Blood on the Table: The Greatest Cases of New York City's Office of the Chief Medical Examiner
The Casebook of Forensic Detection: How Science Solved 100 of the World's Most Baffling Crimes
The Father of Forensics: The Groundbreaking Cases of Sir Bernard Spilsbury and the Beginnings of Modern CSI
A Question of Evidence: The Casebook of Great Forensic Controversies from Napoleon to O.J.
Slaughter on a Snowy Morn: A Tale of Murder, Corruption, and the Death Penalty Case that Shocked America

The Valentino Affair

The Jazz Age Murder Scandal That Shocked New York Society and Gripped the World

Colin Evans

LYONS PRESS
Guilford, Connecticut
An imprint of Globe Pequot Press

Lyons Press is an imprint of Globe Pequot Press.

Project Editor: Lauren Brancato
Layout: Kirsten Livingston

Library of Congress Cataloging-in-Publication Data is available on file.

ISBN 978-0-7627-9149-1

Printed in the United States of America

10 9 8 7 6 5 4 3 2 1

I'll never pause again, never stand still,
Till either death hath closed these eyes of mine
Or fortune given me measure of revenge.

—William Shakespeare, *3 Henry VI* (2.3.31–3)

Contents

Prologue

August 3, 1917

The driver squeezed his foot flat to the boards. His boss at the garage had warned him that the client sounded cranky, the way rich folks always seemed when they wanted a cab in a hurry. James Donner knew it didn't pay to keep the well-heeled waiting. The car's engine roared as he gunned it through the wooded outskirts of Roslyn, a sleepy upmarket village on the north shore of Long Island. High-priced real estate flashed by. It was eight o'clock, but it still felt like a Turkish bath. When his destination, a cottage called Crossways, finally came into view, Donner squealed to a halt.

Two women were waiting for him by the main gate. One—small and dark, youngish, probably early twenties—bore the unmistakable stamp of authority. Despite the sticky weather, she was wearing some kind of buckled sweater with big pockets over her white silk dress. Anger pinched her ashen face.

"You seem to be late,"[1] the woman said as Donner jumped down from behind the wheel and threw open the rear door. Donner apologized, explaining that his boss hadn't called him till nearly eight o'clock; he'd driven as fast as he could. The woman brushed his excuses aside impatiently. "Do you know the Ladenburg estate?"

"Yes, ma'am."

"If you get there in time, I'll give you a dollar tip."[2] She climbed quickly into the car. Her companion—a maid, he guessed—had her hands full with a clumsy white English bulldog that she heaved into the passenger compartment before settling alongside her mistress. Donner closed the rear door, then took his seat behind the wheel. As he let the clutch in, the woman leaned forward and asked if he knew the shortcut across the plain to the Ladenburg estate. Yes—but she still insisted on giving him directions.

The day had broiled into the eighties, and the last remnants of the fiery sun were just dropping below the horizon as Donner motored south across the scrubby grassland of Hempstead Plain. Since the declaration of war on Germany four months earlier, rumors had swirled that the plain would double as a training ground for whipping doughboys into shape before they were shipped off to the mayhem of Europe. For now, though, the fields lay open, deserted, desolate.

At age forty-three, Donner was too old for the draft; he fought his battles with crusty passengers. Although the lady hadn't specified what "in time" meant, she kept urging him to go faster. In between spells as navigator, she huddled in deep conversation with her maid. Not that Donner could catch what they said; the roar of the overworked engine devoured every syllable.

Five hair-raising minutes brought them to Whaleneck Avenue, the long arterial road that bisected the island from north to south. Just ahead lay the Meadow Brook Hunt Club, famed for its yelping hounds that pursued Hempstead's dwindling supply of foxes, closely followed by blueblood riders all decked out in their finest hunting pink: a fragment of old England transplanted to the New World. Tonight, a different kind of chase was under way. The woman squinted over Donner's shoulder at the road ahead.

"There!" she said, pointing to a barely noticeable turnoff. Donner braked hard and swung the automobile left onto Valentines Road. Thick trees and heavy shrubbery slowed him to a crawl as he threaded through the shadows, tires crunching the gravel. A privet hedge rose up before them.

"Stop here," the woman commanded. In the distance—about two hundred feet away—lights flickered. The woman let herself out of the vehicle. "Wait here, and look after the dog," she told him. "I won't be long." She and the maid hurried off across a well-manicured lawn toward the lights. The murkiness swallowed them whole within a few strides.

Donner watched them go, then turned the car around and switched off the engine. The dog lay curled up on the backseat, almost asleep. The cabbie reached inside his pocket for a pack of cigarettes; he no doubt had time for a quick smoke before she returned.

A full moon crept across the purple sky as Donner shifted stickily in his seat. He settled back and sucked in a deep lungful of smoke, keeping one eye on the meter, which already registered more than two dollars. Then he heard a muffled bang, almost like a gunshot. Probably some hunter looking to bag a meal for the dinner table. Four more gunshots broke the silence of that hot August night, and set the mayhem in motion.

The Valentino Affair

Jack de Saulles, Yale football star and Broadway ladies man

ONE

The Flower of the Andes

February 5, 1911

The twenty-sixth running of the *Clásico El Derby*—the biggest event in the Chilean horseracing calendar—had drawn a crowd of more than ten thousand to the Valparaíso Sporting Club on this warm afternoon. The chunkily built, handsome New Yorker had no interest in win, place, or show, though. He had fixed his sights on a greater prize.

But first he had to find her—no easy task in this pulsing sea of Panama hats and white flannel suits. Everywhere Jack de Saulles looked he saw pockets of elegance and tidbits of gossip passing from mouth to mouth. It had been the same in London the previous year when the thirty-two-year-old former Yale football star had dipped his toe in the iciest society on the planet. First came the cursory glance, then the sly inquisition. After that, it was either acceptance or rejection. Jack had passed muster in London and didn't doubt that he could repeat the trick here in Valparaíso. While others fussed and argued over the thoroughbreds in the paddock, de Saulles preferred to run an appreciative eye over the two-legged beauties as they paraded in their finery. Some showed off the latest fashions from Paris, while others opted for traditional garb that dated from the conquistadors. This constant battle between old and new never ended in Chile. Outside the main entrance, gleaming carriages, both horse-drawn and mechanical, lined the leafy avenues that led to the Valparaíso Sporting Club.

The name itself was something of a misnomer: The club lay in the beach resort of Viña del Mar, about five miles north of Valparaíso. According to legend, Viña del Mar (Vineyard by the Sea) had been born out of a dream. In 1874 a young engineer named José Francisco Vergara had been working on the construction of a railroad between Chile's capital, Santiago, and the port of Valparaíso when reputedly he woke one day with a blinding revelation:

Why not build a separate city—on which he could stamp his own identity—just to the north of Valparaíso, close to those fabulous beaches? After four years of bureaucratic heel-dragging, the Chilean government finally gave the go-ahead, and work began on Vergara's vision. Within a few short years, Viña del Mar blossomed, earning the nickname of the Garden City because of its beautiful parks and boulevards. Serving as a bolt-hole for the rich, somewhere to escape the oppressive summer heat of Valparaíso, here gentle sea breezes, cooled by the Humboldt Current, kept temperatures bearable and tempers in check as racetrack bettors struggled to find the next winner on the card.

Even for someone used to competing in front of thousands of spectators, de Saulles found the sheer exuberance of these Latin racegoers overpowering. They cheered or jeered with equal enthusiasm bets won and lost, and every bar in the grandstand teemed with patrons either toasting a win or drowning their sorrows. But Jack, a different kind of connoisseur, reserved most of his attention for the rows of sultry señoritas. Many stole coquettish glances over their fluttering fans, and they liked what they saw. He wasn't tall—only a shade above medium height—but he glided through the crowded stands with the confident, muscular athleticism that had hallmarked his gridiron career a decade earlier. It also didn't hurt that he had a wicked smile.

He had fetched up in South America at the tail end of 1910 as a representative for the South American Concessions Syndicate (SACS). Freewheeling outfits like this characterized American capitalism at the beginning of the twentieth century, when a handful of like-minded entrepreneurs banded together and combed the globe in search of opportunities to increase their net worth and influence. The SACS had one aim: to promote the possibilities of a broad-gauge Trans-Andean railroad linking Chile to Argentina. Until this dream became reality, the only route between the markets of Asia and the east coast of America was around Cape Horn, one of the world's most treacherous seaways. (The Panama Canal wouldn't open for another four years.) When completed, the railroad would shave a month off the time required to ship goods from China to Washington and New York. Backers who got in early could expect a huge return on their investment, and de Saulles wanted as large a piece of the action as possible.

He was well qualified for the task at hand. Years spent grappling in the tough New York City real estate market had given him a solid background in structuring complicated land deals, and he spoke excellent Spanish—twin talents that had proved invaluable in opening doors among the notoriously conservative Chilean business community. Nor was he alone, either in his business endeavors or the racetrack. Alongside him stood Edward P. Coyne, an old friend from New York and former judge. Coyne was two decades older than Jack and brought a savvy legal brain to contract negotiations, but that told only part of the story. Around the Belmont and Aqueduct racetracks in New York, "hizzoner" had earned a reputation as one of the biggest plungers in the horseracing world, ready to wager thousands on whichever thoroughbred took his fancy. Coyne also took that gambling mind-set into his matrimonial undertakings. His most recent waltz down the aisle had soured in 1909 when his bride of just one year fled to Reno and filed for divorce on grounds of desertion . . . though of course friends winked and wondered if the twenty-seven-year age discrepancy between bride and groom also played its part. Coyne shrugged, mentally tore up his marriage certificate as though it were some worthless betting ticket, and looked around for the next big opportunity. He was gambling that the Andes venture would pay off like the trifecta of his dreams.

Thus far the SACS venture had proved lucrative, but Jack de Saulles still wasn't satisfied. In his portfolio he carried letters of introduction to all the great business families of Valparaíso, but one dynasty had yet to invite this ambitious investor into their home. He was banking on this afternoon to change that.

The Errázuriz family hailed originally from the Basque region of northern Spain. The first of their number to set foot on Chilean soil was Francisco Errázuriz in 1735. His glowing testimonials to family members in the Old World triggered a mass migration to Chile and the foothills of the Andes, the mountainous countryside similar to the Pyrenees they had left behind. In short order, the family amassed a vast fortune from mining silver, and in this fledgling nation great wealth automatically generated enormous political power, transforming them into top-drawer Chilean nobility.

By the time de Saulles visited in 1911, the Errázuriz family had provided their new nation with no fewer than four presidents, a clutch of lesser politicians and diplomats, two archbishops of Santiago, and countless industrialists.[1] The family's center of power lay in the Palacio Vergara, an intimidating Venetian Gothic–style edifice built on the ruins of a house destroyed in the 8.2-magnitude earthquake that struck Valparaíso on August 16, 1906, killing close to four thousand people. The Palacio, situated in the Quinta Vergara park, was the grandest house in the city, its elegant French furniture—mostly Louis XVI—juxtaposed against an impressive collection of modern European paintings.

Stewardship of this magnificence fell into the uncompromisingly capable hands of dynasty matriarch Señora Blanca Errázuriz-Vergara, daughter of the man who had founded Viña del Mar. In her youth, Blanca Vergara had been called the Star of Santiago in recognition of her breathtaking beauty, which combined classical bone structure with the unmistakable aristocratic air of her Spanish forebears.[2] Her marriage to Guillermo Errázuriz, a lawyer and member of parliament, had united two of Chile's most powerful and wealthy families, but theirs was not a long-lived union. In 1895, just ten years into the marriage, Guillermo died of tuberculosis, leaving his widow to rule the Errázuriz-Vergara dynasty in Viña del Mar. Such responsibility meant that her presence at the races today was not just likely but practically mandatory. She liked to keep a close eye on her fiefdom and its inhabitants. For his part, de Saulles certainly hoped so. Not that he particularly wanted to meet the dowager herself; no, he had set his sights on another family member.

He'd heard the stories—everyone had in Chile—that the señora had a daughter who, some said, had not only inherited her mother's fabled beauty but had surpassed it. Today at the races, Jack de Saulles intended on finding out if the rumors were true, relying on a friend, local vineyard owner Daniel Vial, to obtain an introduction. In between races Jack joined his cronies in the crowded clubhouse, but he had no time for the form card or the betting coups they had planned. His gaze raked the room. Eventually Vial gave a discreet nod toward a small group of people who had just swept into the clubhouse. De Saulles turned, and he beheld, in his words, "the loveliest woman in the world."[3]

Named after her mother, Blanca Errázuriz-Vergara might have stepped from the frame of a Goya masterpiece; she was slender, barely five feet tall, straight-backed, with an olive complexion and raven-black hair pulled tight against her head and tied in a thick plait that tumbled down onto her delicate shoulders. Her large, teak-brown eyes were simultaneously demure and demanding. At age sixteen she already carried herself with the haughty self-possession of an Andean noblewoman and, if the stories were to be believed, she had a line of suitors stretching from Viña del Mar all the way to Santiago, all of them begging for her hand in marriage. Her exquisite beauty entranced most; others lusted after a reported personal fortune of twenty-five million dollars, which made her one of the richest women in South America.

The object of all this adulation was born in Santiago on April 9, 1894, the youngest of five children. Her eldest brother, Hugo, had died in childhood after falling from a horse, and a sister, Manuela, had entered a local convent. (Dark rumors hinted at some kind of mental instability.) This left Blanca at home with her older sister, Amalia, and another brother, Guillermo, a year her senior. Blanca never knew her father, who died just eleven days after her first birthday, and so she grew up with no dominant male figure in her life. If she felt this lack, it didn't show. The quick smile and gracious hand on display at the Sporting Club concealed a streak of toughness that instantly set her apart from the other señoritas.

From an early age, Blanca knew the power of her personal magnetism and her place in the world. She owed much of her precocious self-confidence to her education: At age eleven, she enrolled in the exclusive Convent of the Sacred Heart in the Roehampton district of London (now the Woldingham School in Surrey).[4] Here, she revealed an extraordinary flair for languages, gaining fluency in English—which she spoke with a cut-glass Knightsbridge accent—and three other tongues. She also learned to play the piano to a high standard. More than anything else, though, London opened her eyes to a fast-changing world and broadened her outlook in a way unimaginable had she remained in the stuffy confines of her hometown. After three years of soaking up London's sophistication, she returned to Viña del Mar poised and elegant. Now, at the Sporting Club, every eye fixed on the young beauty they were already calling "The Flower of the Andes."[5]

De Saulles urged Vial to make the introduction. The two men elbowed their way through the throng. The meeting was rigidly straitlaced—in keeping with Chilean custom—and de Saulles did little more than present his credentials to Señora Errázuriz-Vergara. But in that short time he made quite an impact on her daughter. Even to a disinterested bystander, it was clear that the handsome American with the dazzling smile intrigued Blanca. She found his easy affability refreshing after the heavily starched formality that permeated Chilean etiquette. He laughed and joked, and soon enough Blanca was laughing along with him. No doubt about it, the meeting had gone well.

Just how well became fully apparent only the next day when Vial informed Jack that he had been invited to the Palacio Vergara. It was a high honor, indeed: Few Americans had been so graciously treated. When Jack arrived at the house, its opulence overwhelmed him, but it paled when compared to the gorgeous Blanca. De Saulles rose to the occasion and unleashed his legendary charm. He painted a vivid picture of the surveying

Blanca de Saulles, the "Flower of the Andes," one of the richest women in South America

trip that had taken him and his companions to the roof of South America, high in the Andes, dodging avalanches and fording treacherous rivers in search of the most favorable rail route to Argentina. The thrilling tale captivated her. Jack ended his saga by telling Blanca that he intended on staying in Chile for several months—to her obvious delight—and asking if he might call again.

Doing so required the permission of Señora Errázuriz-Vergara, who was cool at first and with good reason. After all, her daughter was a prize catch for any man, and she not unreasonably feared that Jack might be some ruthless fortune hunter out for a quick score. Plus, the señora wasn't about to see any daughter of hers married off to some penniless parvenu. Jack soothed her concerns with a smile and a spruced-up version of his family tree. To hear de Saulles describe it, he came from dyed-in-the-wool bluebloods. The reality was rather more prosaic.

His father, Major Arthur Brice de Saulles, born in Louisiana to Huguenot parents, had earned his rank while fighting for the Confederate army in the Civil War. Jack downplayed the fact that his father—rather than, say, dashingly commanding men on the battlefield—had served as an engineer under the hopelessly inept but hugely popular General Leonidas Polk. After the cessation of hostilities, the ambitious major kept his rank, switched his uniform for civilian garb, and resumed his engineering career. On August 19, 1869, he married wealthy New York socialite Catherine Heckscher. The Heckscher connection added considerable financial muscle to the major's social ambitions and gained him access to the coveted inner sanctum of northeastern society. It also secured him the lucrative post of superintendent of the New Jersey Zinc Company, handily owned by his father-in-law. In due course the major and his wife had four children, of whom John Gerard Longer de Saulles was third.

Jack was born in South Bethlehem, Pennsylvania, on May 25, 1878, and in his teens he followed in the footsteps of his brother, Charles, and attended Yale, where his exploits on the football field vaulted him into national prominence. In 1901 Jack was Yale's starting quarterback, and his performance against Princeton—where he "booted the hide of the ball until it sagged"[6]—became the stuff of varsity legend. He also featured on special teams, returning kickoffs and acting as place kicker, and he even managed to get himself knocked unconscious on one occasion, thanks to a rash tendency to launch "flying tackles"[7] on opponents almost twice his size. Such were his bravery and brilliance that in 1901 he was named an All-American.

After graduating the following year, he declined several offers to play professionally, instead taking on the role of head coach of the Virginia Cavaliers football team, where he compiled an impressive 8–1–1 record. But the restlessness that hallmarked his life soon grabbed hold, and he abandoned the gridiron in favor of a career in real estate. He went into business with former New York senator William H. Reynolds, putting together companies to build hotels and cottages on the boardwalk at Long Beach on Long Island. That Jack's cousin George McClellan happened to be mayor of New York at the time certainly helped grease the bureaucratic wheels. Another cousin, art collector Philip M. Lydig, married to the famed beauty Rita de Acosta, acted as a useful conduit to deep-pocketed clients.

Señora Errázuriz-Vergara absorbed all of this information approvingly. She could find no faults in Jack's pedigree, but another hurdle remained. At sixteen years old, Blanca was exactly half Jack's age. Even given Blanca's sophistication and the Chilean tradition of young brides, it was still a talking point. But de Saulles had a youthful vigor and, above all, immense charm, so before long he swept all her concerns about the age gulf entirely under the carpet. Later, when psychologists took turns dissecting every aspect of Blanca's baffling character, they speculated that, in Jack, Blanca was seeking the father figure that she never had.

Whatever her motivation, the couple became inseparable. An accomplished equestrienne, Blanca introduced Jack to the joys of horseback riding, and before long he was matching her, stride for stride, as they galloped along Reñaca Beach, treading mile after mile of shimmering golden sand. They took long, dreamy walks along the Avenida Peru, Viña del Mar's main shoreline boulevard, near which the mighty Pacific rollers crashed onto shore, sending plumes of spray into the brilliantly clear sky. In July 1911, as the southern hemisphere grew chilly, Blanca realized that she was in love. Jack, too, was besotted. Friends had never seen him so spellbound.

The following month Jack formally approached Señora Errázuriz-Vergara and asked for her daughter's hand in marriage. Blanquita, as he called her, was, in his words, "a trump."[8] The señora, however, still had misgivings. Friendship was all well and good, but marriage demanded closer scrutiny. She questioned Jack on his intentions. He declared his readiness to set up permanent home in Chile, where he would purchase a large estate, one guaranteed to keep Blanca in the manner to which she was accustomed, and he gave a solemn assurance that they would never return to America to live. Comforted on this point, Señora Errázuriz-Vergara broached an even thornier topic: religion. Blanca had been raised a staunch Catholic, while Jack de Saulles was Episcopalian. The marriage could not proceed, declared Señora Errázuriz-Vergara, unless the Vatican issued a special dispensation. That said, given the family's generous financial support of the Church—and that her cousin Rafael Errázuriz had been Chile's ambassador to the Vatican since 1907—she had no reason to believe that official permission would be withheld. Rome would soon forget a few ruffled feathers.

Pending a satisfactory papal response, the señora gave her blessing to the union and even offered the couple a house that she owned adjacent to the family estate. Such an offer came as a huge relief to Jack, whose ambitions always ran considerably deeper than his pocketbook. Although his mother was the niece of August Heckscher, the fabulously rich German-born industrialist, said uncle had announced publicly his determination to bequeath most of his fortune to charity. Hardly any of the Heckscher millions would filter down to the in-laws.[9] This marooned Jack financially; he was on his own, and since leaving Yale he had struggled to make ends meet. Nobody doubted his business acumen—the real estate deals on Long Beach having generated sizable profits—but de Saulles ran through money like air. Sure, hobnobbing with the Winthrops, Whitneys, and Vanderbilts did wonders for his social standing, but it made his bank account buckle. Now, though, the señora's generous gift of not just plush but *free* accommodation changed the game. After years of almost drowning in a sea of red ink, de Saulles had caught a financial lifeline.

He and Blanca made tentative plans to marry in Paris at the end of the year. Before that, though, Señora Errázuriz-Vergara told Jack that she intended on visiting New York, and could he smooth her entry into the right circles? New York, he warned, was a "rough and uncouth place," where a woman traveling alone was in "great danger."[10] Far better to go straight to Paris. So grim was Jack's description of day-to-day life in Gotham that, in October 1911, mother and daughter caught the steamer to Europe while Jack remained in Chile to tie up some loose ends.

As he watched the liner slip its moorings, Jack must have heaved a sigh of relief. The last thing he needed was a prospective mother-in-law asking awkward questions in New York. In Manhattan, the talk concerned less of Jack de Saulles's business ventures and more of his bedroom escapades. He was a notorious rake. His preferred hunting grounds were Broadway dressing rooms and round-the-clock nightclubs, where he could take his pick of the latest ingénues and chorus girls only too eager to throw themselves at the glamorous former football star with the ever-open wallet.

At times his sexual excesses threatened him with banishment from New York's notoriously brittle social scene. The first real doubts about his character emerged publicly on January 8, 1907, when the parents of heiress Marie Elsie Moore took the extraordinary step of issuing a statement that, contrary to published claims, their daughter was *not* engaged to Jack de Saulles. The original announcement, huffed millionaire machinery maker Mr. Charles A. Moore, had been a "practical joke."[11] Those familiar with de Saulles's reputation as a ladies' man gave a knowing wink. It sounded like "Handsome Jack" had been up to his tricks again, dangling the carrot of matrimony to some gullible gal in return for a quick tumble between the sheets.[12]

Then, bizarrely, it happened again just three years later: another phony engagement announcement—to New York socialite Miss Eleanor Granville Brown—followed closely by another embarrassing retraction. This time, the affronted father, wealthy banker Waldron T. Brown, announced his intention of getting hold of Jack and giving him "a dressing down."[13] Jack, on business in Albany when the story broke, loudly protested his innocence, proclaiming himself the victim of a setup. For once he got it right. When reporters began digging, they discovered that the fake announcement had been planted by a woman, one of Jack's castoffs, reportedly jealous of Miss Brown. It had been a close call, but Jack had dodged the bullet successfully. Still, the incident didn't reflect well on the ambitious realtor. One such episode might be considered careless, but two within three years added fuel to the view that Jack de Saulles was nothing more than a "light o' love."

In the meantime, blithely unaware of her future husband's past indiscretions, Blanca soaked up the sights in Paris and readied herself for the big day . . . if that day ever came, that is. Unexpectedly the Vatican was dragging its heels over the special dispensation, and Blanca was fuming. Convent-educated, maybe, but her allegiance to Rome was flexible at best, and she wouldn't tolerate papal interference in her future happiness. She was young, willful, and determined to marry the man she loved. But she had to overcome her equally iron-willed mother. Without papal approval, said the señora, no wedding would take place.

On November 4, Jack left Valparaíso aboard the SS *Orcoma,* bound for England. There he caught the boat-train to Paris, where bad news awaited him—still no word from Rome. Tensions between mother and daughter reached a fever pitch, catching Jack in the middle. Several nail-biting days passed before that all-important telegram arrived on December 13, 1911. It declared that the Vatican had issued the dispensation that Señora Errázuriz-Vergara craved, and the formal paperwork would follow by mail. But Rome had one condition: Any offspring of the marriage had to be raised in the Catholic faith. Jack made no quibble and wasted no time. That same day, he and Blanca appeared before the mayor of Paris and, in a civil ceremony, became husband and wife. A day later, on Thursday, December 14, the English Church on Avenue Hoche solemnized their union.

Despite the rush, the arrangements were sumptuous. The church hosted a riot of white lilies and palms that haloed Blanca as she stood at the altar, angelic in a magnificent creation of white liberty satin and rare old Spanish lace. The Chilean minister to France gave away the bride, and Jack's old sparring partner from the Andes, Edward P. Coyne, served as best man. On the other side of the aisle, the Chilean expat community in Paris had turned out in force for one of the social highlights of the year. Señora Errázuriz-Vergara nodded regally as she received the congratulations of everyone present, but the event surely held bittersweet memories for her. It was in Paris where she had married her darling Guillermo, and it was in Paris where her husband, emaciated and coughing blood into a handkerchief, finally succumbed to tuberculosis on that awful day in 1895. But life moves on, and Blanca looked radiant. Jack, too, seemed ecstatic. In a letter written shortly after the marriage to a friend in America he poured out his feelings: "Until I went to Chile, all it meant to me was a long pink strip on the map in my geography. Now it means the whole world and all there is in it."[14]

Originally the couple intended to honeymoon in America, but at the last moment they decided to remain in France for a few weeks, motoring south to visit Jack's older sister, Georgiana McClintock, who lived in Pau, close to the Pyrenees. From there they journeyed to England, and in Liverpool on January 1, 1912, they loaded their trunks onto the RMS *Baltic* and sailed for America.

They docked in New York six days later. The weather was frigid, with the mercury struggling to just twenty degrees. Thick snow flayed the quayside as Jack strode down the gangway, determined to show off his seventeen-year-old trophy wife. Four days later he presented her on Society Day at the Twelfth National Automobile Show at Madison Square Garden, where "prominent members of the Four Hundred"[15]—the top members of the social scene—were out in force. Blanca became an instant hit. So great was the crush to see Jack's new bride that he had to hold an impromptu reception at one of the booths. Among those who came to toast the "Chilean belle"[16] was twenty-nine-year-old Franklin Delano Roosevelt. Then it was back to another glittering party at the Plaza Hotel, just off Central Park, where they had taken rooms.

Jack's triumph received coverage across America. The *Chicago Daily Tribune* ran a long piece, "How a Young American Wooed and Won the Richest and Most Beautiful Girl in All South America."[17] It read like a Harlequin romance novel, but it got most of the facts right, even if it did conclude that Jack had gone "down to South America as a plain-business amateur, and carved out a richer prize than the handsomest little fiction hero who ever tramped the tall grass with revolver and saber."[18] Other papers indulged in similar euphoria. One splashed the headline Jack De Saulles' Capture of

Chile's Richest Beauty,[19] spicing up the tale with an account of how Jack had battled on the polo field with a mysterious character named Juan—none bothering to record his surname if in fact he ever existed—who was also pursuing Blanca. Apparently, Jack "played like a man possessed"[20] and won Blanca's heart. It was stirring stuff and almost certainly the product of Jack's prolific imagination. As a self-promoter, he was fearless and peerless. On his return to America, he told one reporter, without any trace of irony, how "scores of suitors" had pursued his wife, "so to gain her hand in marriage was the task of a hero."[21] Another heard how, on discovering that Blanca had gone to Paris, our hero had grasped the nettle: "There just wasn't anything for me to do but follow her. . . . I took the next steamer for France, just two weeks after she sailed. I found her in Paris, asked her mother's consent, got it, asked the daughter, found her willing, and then it was all right."[22] Again, this highly romanticized version played fast and loose with the facts because subsequent events made it plain that Jack proposed to Blanca long before she left Chile.

Jack's door at the Plaza always stood open to the press. When one journalist came knocking in search of the gilded couple and Blanca happened to be out shopping, Jack invited the man in anyway and insisted that he wait until she returned. "You've just got to stay and see her," he said. "She's a wonder."[23] In other encounters with the press, he expounded his views on Chile-American relations. "The last 18 months have seen a great improvement in the feelings of Chileans toward Americans"—mostly because—"we have a better class of Americans down there."[24] The rest of the interview staggered into a name-dropping extravaganza, with Jack claiming close personal contact with just about the entire Chilean politico-military machine.

Once he had temporarily exhausted his New York connections, Jack decided the time had come to introduce Blanca to her in-laws at their home in Pennsylvania. The meeting didn't go well. According to Blanca—and as with so much in this story we rely wholly on her word—Arthur and Catherine de Saulles disliked her from day one, bitterly resenting that their hotshot son had tied the knot with some Catholic foreigner barely out of school. At no time did they ever try to make her feel welcome. South Bethlehem, too, came as a visceral shock. A smoky, industrial town that owed its existence to the manufacture of zinc oxide, South Bethlehem lay light-years away from the golden sandy beaches and Mediterranean-type climate of Blanca's beloved Viña del Mar. It felt cramped, parochial, and dirty, and she hated it. It was also bitterly cold. Back home, Viña del Mar was basking in the height of summer, and, while Blanca always suffered when temperatures really sizzled, right now she would have taken Timbuktu over the bone-chilling rigors of a Pennsylvania steel town in midwinter.

To her immense relief, their stay in South Bethlehem was just a brief stopover before they sailed for Chile. It would be the homecoming she had dreamt of. She and Jack could look forward to a life of ease and elegance at the very pinnacle of South American society. As they sailed slowly southward and the weather warmed, Blanca put all thoughts of grimy South Bethlehem behind her. There was too much to anticipate. Indeed, by the time she reached Santiago, she realized that she was already pregnant. Jack was delighted. After years of carousing on the Great White Way, partying till dawn, and bedding an endless string of actresses and showgirls, he finally had captured the woman of his dreams. Ahead lay a golden future with a gorgeous wife, practically limitless wealth, and an heir. As Jack gazed out across the waters, he saw not a single cloud on his horizon.

But a tempest was brewing.

TWO

An American in Paris

When they arrived in Chile, the newlyweds decided, before moving permanently to Viña del Mar, to set up home temporarily in Santiago, staying at one of the many Errázuriz-Vergara residences dotted about the country. It would give Jack a chance to make himself known at the exclusive Union Club, where all the big players in Santiago gathered to trade gossip, cook up business deals, and cement alliances. Jack fit in perfectly. With the señora in Paris, he set about playing the role of a freshly minted grandee, and among his first tasks he applied to the administrator of the estates of his wife's late father for all securities and title deeds belonging to Blanca. Under Chilean law at the time, a bride's assets automatically became the property of her husband after marriage.[1] Jack was sounding her out. If he were to realize his dream of building a vast real estate empire, one to rival any in South America, he required an accounting of Blanca's financial worth. When the documents arrived on his desk, he sifted through them with a practiced eye. After a few minutes he grew puzzled. A few minutes more and confusion turned to disbelief then bemusement that gave way finally to boiling rage. He rushed from his desk and went looking for Blanca. When he found her, he waved the papers in her face. "That's hardly anything at all," he yelled. "It is practically nothing. It is absurd to call you an heiress."[2]

What Jack and every other potential suitor didn't know was that most of Blanca's assets were held in trust. Through a series of complicated legal maneuvers, her father had ring-fenced Errázuriz-Vergara millions to guard them against predatory fortune hunters by ensuring that his children gained access to the capital only upon their mother's death. As it stood, Blanca was worth approximately one hundred thousand dollars[3] in her own right—enough for the couple to live comfortably but nothing like the staggering twenty-five million dollars that would have catapulted Jack into the upper echelons of Chile's plutocrats.

Jack raged at Blanca that he'd been negotiating to buy their own estate in Chile and now the deal would collapse. If that happened, he'd be the laughingstock of the Union Club; his future in Chile would be ruined! He ordered Blanca to write to her mother in Paris and demand that she forward sufficient funds to complete the transaction. Then his tone grew more menacing. If the funds were not forthcoming, he told Blanca, he would return to America and take her with him. If that happened, he swore that Blanca's mother would never set eyes on her grandchild. The ferocity of Jack's onslaught left Blanca reeling. She grabbed a pen and paper and dashed off a letter to her mother, spelling out Jack's demands and threats. The reply came by cable. Señora Errázuriz-Vergara protested that, like Blanca, all of her wealth was locked up either in real estate or long-term securities, none of which could be liquidated easily. It was impossible for her, at such short notice, to find the cash that Jack needed to close the deal. However, as promised earlier, she was prepared to sign over one of her houses in Viña del Mar; perhaps he could use that as collateral to buy the estate?

The offer was generous—but not generous enough to placate Jack. He was like an enraged bull, convinced his mother-in-law was lying, deliberately withholding money so that she could keep the couple under her financial thumb. His response was astonishing: He booked passage for himself and Blanca on a steamer to Europe, determined to tackle the señora face to face. Ahead of Blanca—pregnant, remember—lay an arduous forty-five-day voyage across the tempestuous South Atlantic in winter. Years later, Blanca credited Jack's frenzied insistence on this madcap venture with opening the fault lines in their marriage. Nothing had prepared her for this turn of events. In a few short months, she had gone from the giddy delirium of a glittering society wedding in Paris to cowering in front of a violent and vengeful gold digger. Her dismay would have been doubled had she known that, in order to fund the European bailout mission, Jack had plundered her inheritance, going behind her back to sell six thousand dollars worth of her securities without telling her. Only later would she discover that her husband was a serial embezzler, emptying her accounts of every penny he could grab.

The showdown between Jack and his mother-in-law took place in Paris in mid-July. While Blanca listened, quaking, in an adjoining hotel room, Jack implored the señora to finance the farm purchase. But his entreaties proved no more successful in person than they had by mail. Señora Errázuriz-Vergara stood firm, contemptuous of his grasping avarice, adamant that she didn't have that kind of spare cash just lying around. He flatly accused her of lying.

She told him to get out. After more abuse and arm waving, Jack stormed out of the hotel—alone—and at the Gare du Nord booked passage on the boat-train to London. Blanca remained behind, sobbing in her mother's arms. We don't know what passed between mother and daughter, but we safely can assume that the custodian of the Errázuriz-Vergara fortune spelled out some pretty tough ground rules over Jack's future access to the family's money. The señora had no intention of allowing this Yanqui marauder to squander the wealth of generations.

A week in London—always one of his favorite places—cooled Jack's temper but did nothing to allay his vengeful nature. He returned to Paris and told Blanca that they were leaving immediately. They crossed the channel to England and, on July 28, 1912, boarded the SS *Amerika* at Southampton. Eight days later they docked at New York. Jack de Saulles would never see his mother-in-law again.

By now, he didn't just need to rebuild his marriage, he also needed to throw a veil of secrecy over his humiliation in Paris, which meant acting as normally as possible. Through his network of real estate contacts, he found a rental cottage in the village of Larchmont in Westchester County, just eighteen miles north of Midtown Manhattan. Still, the cottage's remote location unsettled an edgy husband concerned about his wife's pregnancy.

One day while they were in the city, Jack took Blanca into a pawnshop and purchased a black-handled .32 Smith & Wesson revolver. When the gun arrived at their home a few days later—the pawnshop owner delaying shipment because Jack initially didn't have a license—Jack gave it to Blanca with instructions to keep it by her at all times. Blanca was no stranger to firearms, though; she and her siblings had regularly fired weapons on the family's estate in Viña del Mar, and, while she suspected that Jack was overreacting, she did promise to keep the gun within easy reach. Then she got on with the business of trying to make her marriage work.

Despite the ghastly scene in Paris and the insults to her mother's name and reputation, Blanca held traditional views about wedlock. It was her duty, as she saw it, to support her husband in every venture, even if that meant ostracizing her own family. As she prepared for the birth of her child, solitude might not have been the preferred option, but Blanca always knew how to hide her feelings, and she seems to have coped well with the awkward existence that Jack forced upon her. Not that she saw much of him during this period.

Once again, Jack had undergone another of his capricious career shifts. Now politics overtook his life, which meant temporarily abandoning his business interests and throwing himself, body and soul, into the presidential campaign of then–New Jersey governor Woodrow Wilson, a progressive Democrat stumping on a commitment "to place man above the dollar."[4] For a copper-bottomed capitalist like Jack de Saulles, Wilson's was an alien philosophy indeed, but financial pragmatism has a knack of ironing out ideological differences, and Jack always did keep his eye on the big picture. Even this far ahead of the election, Wilson was already a heavy favorite to romp home.

On August 30, 1912, de Saulles called a press conference in the Hotel Imperial, at the corner of Broadway and 32nd Street. He had been handpicked, he told the assembled journalists, to form the Woodrow Wilson College Men's League. There was nothing new in the concept: Presidential candidates had a long tradition of hitching their campaigns to some affiliated college league, but nothing on this scale had ever been attempted before. It was a kind of political pyramid selling. The intent was to recruit as many graduates from every major university as possible to Wilson's cause and for them to spread the message through meetings and discussion groups. Jack's superstar football status made him the standout pick when William F. McCombs, chairman of the Democratic National Committee, went scouting for a suitable candidate to oversee the recruiting drive.

But other motives were at work. Complaints had plagued the campaign that Wilson, a Princeton man, was overloading his staff with cronies from his alma mater. McCombs reckoned that Jack's Yale background would help stanch this criticism. So Jack got the job and soon proved himself a top-flight organizer and communicator. At the Imperial, he gave the assembled journalists a tour of campaign headquarters. He waved an arm, saying that the league had taken over half of the hotel's second floor. Already the place was humming with dozens of stenographers and typists working nonstop to mail out campaign literature.

Jack always gave the press good value, nor did he intend to waste this opportunity for self-aggrandizement. He sheepishly blamed his belated arrival at Wilson's campaign headquarters on a string of setbacks that would have taxed the most intrepid explorer. Deep snowdrifts in the Andes, he said, had blocked all transcontinental railroad tracks, forcing him to travel around Cape Horn, by way of Portugal, to America. He boasted that he had traveled fifteen thousand miles to throw his support behind the man whom he believed would guarantee America's future.

Singularly absent from this frothy narrative was any mention of the real reason underlying this transatlantic marathon. Nor did any journalist query him as to why anyone, in such a rush to reach New York, would dally in Europe. Most were too busy scribbling down the formidable string of gridiron analogies that Jack fired at them: "We are already in the field with our uniforms on and are lined up for a Wilson touchdown," he said, ending by predicting that, "Our flying wedge will sweep the country from Maine to California."[5]

As the press conference drew to a close, Jack no doubt sighed in relief that no one had mentioned that tricky incident from a few weeks prior. Just four days after disembarking from the SS *Amerika,* he had been served with papers alleging nonpayment of a nine-thousand-dollar debt—hardly the homecoming that he desired. The plaintiff was the celebrated architect John Russell Pope.[6] The suit claimed that in November 1909 Pope had been retained by de Saulles to draw plans for a $1.5 million amusement pier and theater at Long Beach. The pier was intended to stretch fifteen hundred feet out into the Atlantic and to accommodate twenty-five thousand people. Facilities on offer would include a convention hall capable of seating five thousand, a recreation park with a promenade, and landing stages for yachts and steamboats. Pope drew the plans and made color pictures on a large scale, only to be yanked suddenly from the project. De Saulles offered no explanation and then salted the wound by refusing to pay Pope for work done. Understandably miffed, Pope claimed compensation under the rules of the American Institute of Architects, which held de Saulles liable to pay three fifths of 1 percent of the total cost for drawing plans and 15 percent for superintending construction. Because all mention of this lawsuit speedily vanished from the papers, we can only assume that it was settled out of court, but it did highlight, once again, Jack's recklessness. First that ruckus over those embarrassing phantom engagements to two society belles, now another tarnish spot against his name.

Blanca likely didn't hear anything of it because Jack always kept a lid on his business deals, and, on the few occasions when he was at home, talk centered mainly on his ever-widening circle of contacts within the Social Register—which delighted Blanca. After a rocky start, she was sure that the marriage was now on a much more stable footing.

After each brief visit to Larchmont, Jack kissed Blanca good-bye and returned to his rooms at the Yale Club in Manhattan. With the presidential campaign building to a climax, he was working around the clock. In a brave move—given his shaky track record in financial matters—the organizers named de Saulles league treasurer. But there was no doubting his effectiveness. Membership of the Woodrow Wilson College Men's League eventually topped seventy-five thousand, much of that number due to Jack's untiring efforts. A world-class PR man, he squeezed even the most seemingly insignificant snippet of news into the papers. For instance, on September 11, 1912, de Saulles proudly announced to the press that the campaign had received a cable from Punta Arenas, Chile—the "southernmost town in the world,"[7]—authorizing the transfer of eighty pesos (approximately one hundred dollars) to the Wilson fund. The cable came from Enrique Balmaceda, one of Jack's classmates at Yale and the son of José Manuel Balmaceda, president of Chile from 1886 to 1891.[8] In terms of financial impact, it represented little more than a drop in the ocean, but the symbolism loomed large. It reinforced the view that Jack, through his marriage and his business dealings, had his finger on the South American political pulse, surely putting his name at the top of the list of contenders when it came time to dole out coveted ministerial jobs to South America.

In the run-up to election day, the bookmakers placed Wilson as a strong favorite over his rivals, the incumbent William Taft and former president Theodore Roosevelt, who—having lost the Republican nomination to Taft, his successor—was running under the auspices of the Bull Moose Party. Not that there was much betting. By splitting the Republican vote, Roosevelt all but handed the election to Wilson, and the press was reporting that the odds on Wilson were so cramped that the only wagers being laid were whether Roosevelt would pip Taft for second place.

Glowing news reports ensured a buoyant mood at the Hotel Astor on the night of September 28 when Jack attended a dinner to honor William F. McCombs. Outside, in Times Square, hundreds of supporters bellowed their appreciation as the evening's featured speaker, the Democratic nominee himself, arrived. Inside, though, a strangely subdued mood prevailed. The dinner had been organized to celebrate McCombs's recovery from a bout of ill health, but the celebrations were looking a tad premature, word coming at the last moment that the guest of honor had been confined to bed in one of the hotel rooms. Downstairs, in the grand ballroom, the thousand guests raised toast after toast to impending victory, but the biggest cheer of all came when thirty-six-year-old McCombs, looking frail indeed, made a belated appearance. "Here's to the grand young man of America,"[9] shouted one of the guests. Women in the gallery applauded, while men rose from their tables, waving napkins above their heads and giving the Princeton, Yale, and Harvard yells. The demonstration of affection lasted fully ten minutes. Eventually McCombs waved them to silence. "I said I would come if I had to come on a shutter,"[10] he laughed weakly, leaning against the table for support. Further cheers drowned out the rest of what he had to say. In anticipation of a resounding victory, a Democratic Parade Committee was formed, and high on the list of participating committee members was the name of John L. de Saulles.

Before that, though, there was another parade to organize. On election eve, Margaret Wilson, the candidate's daughter, reviewed a parade of the Wilson College Men's League. At 8:30 p.m. a red flare lit up the night sky, and then a squadron of mounted police led the parade as it marched up Fifth Avenue. An estimated seventy thousand spectators jammed the side-walks to see city commissioner and Princeton football great William "Big Bill" Edwards lead the pageant. Alongside him was Jack de Saulles. Many in the crowd recognized the former Yale quarterback from his college days, and cheers met him every step of the way. It took forty-five minutes for the six-thousand-strong parade to pass the Hotel Imperial, where Miss Wilson stood brandishing an American flag that she waved enthusiastically every time a float caught her eye.

The next day—November 5—delivered the expected landslide. With the Republican vote hopelessly split, Wilson steamrolled into the White House with a whopping 435 electoral votes, almost four times more than Roosevelt and absolutely swamping Taft, who could muster only a dismal 8 electoral votes, the worst performance in history to date by any incumbent president seeking reelection.

De Saulles celebrated victory with even greater relish than most of his Democrat companions. He knew and expected that those long arduous months of loyal service would reward him in some way. Already his name was being mentioned in diplomatic terms. On December 3, the *Washington Times* confidently predicted that following Wilson's inauguration Jack would be named the minister to Chile. But that lay in the future. Just now, Jack had more pressing matters at hand. Blanca had entered the final month of her pregnancy. She had expected to give birth at the family home in Larchmont, but Jack dropped a last-minute bombshell: He wanted the child born at his parents' house in South Bethlehem. No matter how much Blanca pleaded, nothing would budge him from this directive.

Blanca was appalled. From their first meeting she had abhorred being around her in-laws—especially Catherine de Saulles, whom she cordially loathed. What made her ordeal doubly onerous was that she was obliged to deal with the cantankerous Mrs. de Saulles on her own. True to form, Jack dumped Blanca on his parents and then departed for New York as fast as possible. What should have been one of the happiest times of Blanca's life plummeted into a nightmare. She was still just seventeen years old, on her own in a foreign land, and she saw her husband only on weekends, when he paid fleeting visits and then dashed off as quickly as possible. Jack did make it home for the holidays, however, and he was there on December 25 when Blanca gave birth to a healthy boy.

A boy born on Christmas Day in (South) Bethlehem—for a devout Catholic the occasion couldn't have been more auspicious, and Blanca prayed that the birth of her son would cement the family back together. For his part, while Jack might have been a careless and even callous husband, everyone agreed that he was utterly devoted to his son.

On February 14, 1913, Jack de Saulles kept at least one promise to Señora Errázuriz-Vergara when his son, John Longer de Saulles Jr., was baptized at the Holy Infancy Church in South Bethlehem. The Reverend Father Chambers of New York conducted the Catholic service. Pride of place in the packed congregation went to the boy's godfather, Charles M. Schwab, owner of Bethlehem Steel, the second-largest steel maker in the world, and a longtime friend of the de Saulles family. The steel magnate was feeling especially ebullient as he congratulated the new parents in the church that Friday. He recently had secured the operating rights to the El Tofo mine on the Bay of Cruz Grande in Chile, estimated to contain forty *million* tons of 67 percent pure iron. Mining engineers gaped at the quality as they extracted ore samples that Schwab called "the richest in the world."[11] If the Washington rumors proved true, and Jack did receive the ministerial posting to Chile, he and Schwab would be doing a great deal of talking over the next couple of years. For the time being, though, as soon as the service ended, Jack hightailed it back to Manhattan, leaving Blanca in the icy hands of her hated in-laws.

A little more than two weeks later, on March 4, 1913, Woodrow Wilson was sworn in as the twenty-eighth president of the United States. Standing at the president's shoulder in the Washington sunshine, de Saulles added his cheers to the swelling acclaim. Blanca was present, too, accompanied by a new addition to the family circle, a nurse from Philadelphia named Ethel

Jack de Saulles Jr., the innocent cause of a terrible tragedy

Whitesides. Later that evening, Ethel looked after little Jack Jr. while his parents made the rounds of the post-inauguration parties. It was a time to see and be seen, and Jack was determined to wring every last drop of kudos from his campaign efforts.

The following night, he and Blanca hosted a dinner at the newly refurbished Shoreham Hotel on 15th Street in honor of Navy Secretary Josephus Daniels. It was a lavish affair. Three large arrangements of spring flowers decorated the main table, and the women wore corsage bouquets. In between the toasts and the celebrations, Jack renewed his acquaintanceship with the president's daughter, Margaret Wilson, and schmoozed with Henry du Pont among others, all the while advertising his credentials for that diplomatic posting to Chile.

A few weeks later Jack and Blanca returned to the nation's capital to attend yet another society dinner, this one thrown by lawyer Perry Belmont, whose brother, August Belmont Jr., had built the eponymous racetrack on Long Island in 1905.[12] The guest of honor on this occasion was the German ambassador, Count Johann von Bernstorff, and his wife. Jack was meeting all the right people, and, as the post-election season in Washington drew to a close, he and Blanca returned to New York in confident moods.

Upon their arrival, it was Blanca's turn to shine. That Easter she attended a fund-raiser at the Waldorf Astoria in aid of the Loomis Sanitarium, a home for consumptives in the Catskills. The intention was to raise enough money to provide free beds for children with tuberculosis. Blanca didn't just attend, though; she posed in various *tableaux vivants* that gave her the chance to flaunt her already celebrated beauty.

But her time in the limelight was fleeting. Jack was growing impatient. Citing work pressures, he banished Blanca and the baby to another miserable spell at his parents' house while he caroused with his drinking buddies at the Yale Club. His constant absence from South Bethlehem continued to cause problems. Throughout the ensuing weeks, the antipathy between Blanca and Mrs. de Saulles—hitherto thinly camouflaged by social niceties—exploded into the open, the older woman constantly demanding to know when Blanca intended on leaving. "Ask your son," Blanca snapped back.

During this dark period, Blanca's only beacon of light was the close friendship that developed between her and Ethel Whitesides. Ethel acted as far more than just a nursemaid to Jack Jr.; she became Blanca's closest confidant and ally in America, an ever-present shoulder on which to lean. Over the years she gained an unrivaled insight into Blanca's troubled mind and marriage. For the moment, though, her main role was that of peacemaker, acting as a bulwark between a bitterly resentful mother-in-law and a despondent teenage mother who felt abandoned and distraught.

Meanwhile, hundreds of miles away in New York, Jack couldn't have been more relaxed and happy as he sat back, confidently awaiting the diplomatic summons from Washington. But he waited . . . and waited.

THREE

The Wayward Husband

PRESS PREDICTIONS THAT JACK WAS A SHOO-IN FOR THE POST OF MINISTER to Chile were falling wide of the mark. He had returned to New York, confidently anticipating an early summons from Washington only to endure an ominous silence. He grew anxious. Something wasn't right. Were his past exploits catching up with him? Had someone resurrected those phantom engagements and questioned whether Jack de Saulles was the kind of solid citizen suitable for representing America on the international stage? Whatever the reason, as April rolled into May and still no word from the White House, it was an increasingly frustrated and fractious Jack de Saulles who visited South Bethlehem that spring.

He rarely showed up midweek, preferring to breeze in on a Sunday, play for a few hours with Jack Jr., then scuttle back to New York that same night. Clearly the first bloom of matrimony had dulled. It's easy enough to blame Jack's neglect of Blanca on political frustration or work pressures, but other forces were at work. After barely sixteen months of wedlock, the couple's sex life had shriveled to nothing. In any marriage, only the two participants can ever know the true dynamic of their relationship, and years later Blanca swore that Jack had lied through his teeth when accusing her of having "refused to live with me as my wife,"[1] but the facts tell a different story.

In letters and in admissions to other people, Blanca acknowledged deep underlying problems in the marriage and that her own distaste for physical intimacy might have helped drive her husband away. One of the few friends she had made since moving to America was the wife of Jack's cousin and business partner, G. Maurice Heckscher. During one heart-to-heart with Louise Heckscher, Blanca confessed that, had she known what the physical side of married life entailed, she never would have walked down the aisle. It's also possible that Blanca's abhorrence of sex stemmed from a fear of a second pregnancy. Subsequent medical problems suggest that the birth of

Jack Jr. had proved difficult physically. But the real damage was emotional. Something inside Blanca snapped; she still loved her husband deeply, but henceforth she would do everything in her power to keep him at arm's length.

For a red-blooded alpha male like Jack de Saulles this was intolerable. When it came to a woman's marital responsibilities, he was an unreconstructed Victorian, and he began grouching to family members and friends alike that Blanca was neglecting her conjugal duties. Word soon spread that "Broadway Jack" was back. Secretly, Blanca was relieved, telling Louise that her husband could run around with other women all he liked—so long as he left her alone.

In the aftermath of this breakdown, Jack's visits to South Bethlehem became ever more sporadic. Blanca grew used to plans being made for a lengthy stay only for Jack to change them at the last minute to yet another of those galling lightning visits. Sometimes he didn't even bother to show up at all. On one particularly poignant occasion, Blanca dashed to the railroad station in excited anticipation of Jack's arrival only to find that he had missed the specified train. Stemming her disappointment, she waited for the next train . . . and the next . . . and the one after that. Each new arriving train first raised her hopes then dashed them as her wayward husband failed to show. After several torturous hours spent pacing the windswept platform, Blanca returned to her in-laws, red-eyed with disappointment. Ethel tried to console her but could do nothing. She watched helplessly as Blanca went to Jack Jr.'s room, knelt by the baby's cot, placed both arms around the infant, and said, "Oh, Toodles, Daddy doesn't love us anymore."[2]

It certainly looked that way, but Jack was a pragmatist. His lackluster interest in his wife always magically sparked back to life when he thought her well-connected presence might benefit his career. This was especially true when he visited Washington in pursuit of that maddeningly elusive diplomatic post. On one such mission, in May 1913, he summoned Blanca to join him at the Powhatan Hotel on Pennsylvania Avenue, just a couple of blocks west of the White House. Ethel went, too, and witnessed firsthand the gulf that had opened between Blanca and her husband, a gulf that was widening with each day.

In the hotel suite, Ethel was helping Blanca unpack when Jack dropped a photograph. Before he could retrieve it, Blanca snatched it from the floor. It was a professionally taken portrait of a very attractive young woman. On it was inscribed, "To Jack, with love."[3] Blanca's blood ran cold; she recognized the woman as a well-known actress.[4] She wheeled around and thrust the photograph into her husband's face. "What business has a married man with another woman's picture?"[5]

Jack batted away her concerns. "There's nothing wrong with it," he laughed, slipping the photo back into his pocket. "She's a nice girl."[6]

Red with embarrassment, Ethel lowered her gaze. It was terrible watching two people tear each other part. Jack's emollient excuses temporarily defused the overheated situation, but Blanca remained wary. Since arriving in America, she had heard whispers about her husband's former fondness for the good-time girls of Broadway. Now she had hard evidence that he had returned to his old ways. As noted, while she allowed herself to tolerate Jack's dalliances, she didn't want his affairs flaunted in her face. Such social crassness was entirely unacceptable.

After this incident, Jack returned to New York and Blanca reluctantly caught the train back to South Bethlehem. This time she had to battle the stony-faced Mrs. de Saulles alone, without Ethel to comfort her. The nursemaid had secured a new position in Philadelphia, her hometown, and one Anna Mooney, a thirty-four-year-old from Ireland, took her place. At first Blanca despaired of Boobie—as Jack Jr. called her—ever making the grade; after Ethel's smooth efficiency, Anna seemed gauche and ill at ease. It was a thoroughly miserable time for Blanca, made worse by Jack's erratic behavior. When, in the middle of June, he once again failed to make an appointment, Blanca unburdened herself in a letter to him:

> *Darling Precious Dada: I feel so sad tonight, as I had been looking forward with so much eagerness to your coming. It is ages since you left, and I am wondering whether you have forgotten your little wife who awaits you anxiously, and your darling baby boy. I had ordered the runabout for this evening, thinking we would have a delightfully quiet and old fashioned drive during which we could tell each other all the many things we have to say. But however much I was longing to see you, it is much better that you save yourself this unpleasant trip which in the end would only allow us a couple of hours together.*
>
> *I do hope that you are well—I am so afraid that you don't take the proper amount of rest. You must not worry about Toodles or me. We are both doing remarkably well. He has taken to the bottle like a duck to water, and I am not having any trouble as we had anticipated. If we are having a hard pull, we have still a great many things to be thankful for. It really is wonderful how well Toodles is doing and how little cause*

for anxiety he has given us. . . . I, thank God, have not felt any pain nor feeling of uncomfort.

Don't disappoint me again, darling, and please come Tuesday without fail. It's so lonesome without you and quite discouraging at times.

May God bless you and grant you success.

All the love in the world from Babyboy and me

Devotedly,
DADA GIRL[7]

In his reply Jack blamed his prolonged absence on the fact that that he was still "pulling wires"[8] to get the ministerial post in Chile, and he promised to hurry back to South Bethlehem as soon as possible.

The following month saw his pledge redeemed and the couple reunited. But even then Blanca was like a stranger to her husband. Jack spent most of his time playing with his son, whom he adored, or in deep discussion with his parents. Blanca's resentment at being sidelined began to fester. Eventually her frustration bubbled over one day when she caught Jack whispering to his mother in the living room. She demanded to know what they were discussing. Jack spun around. "Go to your room!"[9] he barked, dismissing her like some naughty infant. Blanca was too dumbfounded to stay and argue. Never in her life had anyone addressed her so rudely. She stamped off to her room, furious. That Jack departed immediately for New York, without offering any word of explanation, only compounded her humiliation.

A couple of days later, Blanca again put pen to paper, fearing that Jack was having regrets about their getting married. Her letter bitterly mixed indignation and sarcasm.

Darling Dar:

I have had a great big heartache ever since you told me to "Go to your room," and I had made up my mind that I would not write to you until you wrote to me or else spoke one sweet word through the 'phone, but I have relented and instead am going to tell you how harsh and unkind you were.

I did not think that ever in your lifetime, even if you lived to be 100 years, would you have ordered me out of that room, much less gone away without saying "good-bye" or where you were going to stay. That after a thousand and one professions of love! Well, I suppose everyone's ideals are shattered, and yours probably also, although I have tried not to shatter yours even when things did seem so hard.

I hope you are having a good time in New York. It must be such fun to play bachelor again. In fact, it must seem quite natural, and the last two years surely are but a horrid nightmare. Then so inopportunely the wife's letter comes. Why don't you race with Maurice and enjoy yourself! You will only get nervous and bored in Bethlehem and lose your appetite.

Devotedly, Blanquita.[10]

Shortly after writing this, Blanca fell ill and took to her bed. Ever since the birth of Jack Jr., her health had been precarious. "I feel as weak as a cat who has been drowned 8¾ times, and has but one quarter life left,"[11] she wrote to Ethel.

Blanca needed some kind of tonic, anything to lift her spirits, and just over a week later it duly arrived. On Friday, August 1, Blanca received a phone call from Washington insider Lester Jones, an official at the Bureau of Fisheries, who told her that the president's private secretary,[12] Joseph Tumulty, wished to meet Jack "either Tuesday, Wednesday, or Thursday"[13] of the following week to discuss his future plans. A wire from Tumulty to this effect reached South Bethlehem later that same day. Overjoyed at the prospect of returning to Chile, Blanca immediately phoned Jack at the Yale Club—but he wasn't there. Several more fruitless calls failed to establish his whereabouts, leaving Blanca no alternative but to send the wire by mail, with a covering letter explaining this exciting development.

She also told Jack that she was feeling "so much better . . . [and] looking forward with great pleasure to your return."[14] She urged him to catch the Black Diamond Express—the Lehigh Valley Railroad's flagship passenger service—and stay for the weekend, after which they could return to New York together on Monday. From there Jack could travel to Washington while she remained in Manhattan for a few days. On the back of the letter, evidently refering to his absence when she called the club, she wrote "Where were you!!!"[15]

In those supposedly slower times, the mail, which came and went several times a day, moved with astonishing haste. Jack received the letter that same day. In the evening he phoned Blanca with a suggestion: Instead of his traveling to South Bethlehem, why didn't she join him in New York for the weekend? Blanca's euphoria shattered, however, when her physician, Dr. Butler, advised that it would be "foolish"[16] to undertake any kind of journey in her debilitated state.

Feeling more trapped than ever in South Bethlehem, Blanca poured out her feelings in a letter to Ethel. It began on an upbeat note with news that "Toodles has cut a tooth today! The darlingest, weeniest, sharpest, whitest little tooth you ever saw. . . . You have no idea how excited I got when I saw it."[17] But her tone darkened as she described the day-to-day existence in South Bethlehem. "This last week has been purgatory in the worst form. If I were a man I should say 'hell' a million times over."[18] She went on to rail bitterly against her mother-in-law: "Mrs. De Saulles has almost got me frantic. I have to use the utmost strength of mind not to pull her hair; really I've been so patient and put up with so much that now my patience has turned into hate. Isn't that perfectly frightful. She is worse and worse from day to day."[19] Then came a lengthy harangue about how Mrs. de Saulles seemed intent on driving her from the house—"as if it were a pleasure for me to stay in a place which is exactly opposite in every way to the home I was brought up in."[20]

It was an ever-present thorn in Blanca's side, the perceived gap in social status between her family and that of her husband. In Blanca's mind, she was descended from Chilean aristocracy, practically making her an Andean princess. By contrast, her husband came from mere commercial stock. The de Saulles's family house in South Bethlehem emphasized this gulf; comfortable enough, maybe, but hardly the kind of glittering mansion that Blanca was used to. She amplified her resentment with yet another blast against her hated mother-in-law: "She ought to be thankful that her son has married a woman who has stood everything without saying a word, just for his sake, and for their sakes has never mentioned the immeasurable distance which separates them from her!"[21] The letter ended with a terrible cry from the heart: "Oh, how much I want to be happy!"[22]

In early August, Jack announced, to Blanca's enormous relief, that he had taken a bungalow at Deal Beach on the New Jersey shore, about sixty miles south of Manhattan. The new arrangement not only got Blanca out of his mother's hair, but he could travel home to see her and Jack Jr. much more frequently. Further good news—as far as Blanca was concerned—was that Anna Mooney needed an operation. Blanca contacted Ethel, pleading for her to return to help her get out of "this disgusting town."[23] But Blanca's hopes for a reunion with her favorite nursemaid died quickly. Work commitments in Philadelphia prevented Ethel from coming to Blanca's aid, leaving her to organize the move without any assistance from a maid.

The move to Deal Beach coincided with a heat wave that suffocated the northeast for days and left hundreds dead in New York City alone. Even after the worst of the heat had subsided, it was still blisteringly hot, and, one day while out playing golf, Blanca collapsed. A doctor diagnosed a mild attack of sunstroke. When Jack came to visit, he cruelly rationed his sympathies. Put some ice bags on your head, he snapped: "You're all right, the trouble is you're hipped on yourself."[24] Her health—never robust during this period—now declined sharply. Two weeks later, she suffered a postnatal hemorrhage and was rushed to the Sloane Hospital for Women in Manhattan, where she had an unspecified operation.

Her return to Deal Beach did little to aid her convalescence. Jack was changeable as the weather, one day phoning and promising to visit, the next either canceling or not bothering to show at all. On those rare occasions when Jack did make an appearance, his regular drinking buddy, Marshall Ward, usually accompanied him. Blanca despised the foppish thirty-four-year-old stockbroker, convinced that he was influencing a husband who needed precious little encouragement to neglect his marital responsibilities. According to Blanca, whenever the two men arrived at Deal Beach, they were usually so exhausted by the exertions of the week that they spent most of their time "sleeping and resting up."[25]

The pressure on Blanca was building from all sides. A string of vitriolic letters from her mother made it plain as a pikestaff that the señora thoroughly despised her son-in-law and found herself at a loss to understand how Blanca had failed to spot him for the grasping fortune hunter that he was. Considering just how complimentary Señora Errázuriz-Vergara had been when first introduced to Jack—his charm flooring her as it did everyone—this chunk of hindsight-driven condemnation stuck in Blanca's craw. But she resolved to keep her problems under wraps as much as possible and to do everything possible to help her husband secure that elusive post of minister to Chile.

Jack blamed the delay on a lack of finances, convinced that his lobbying campaign needed a fresh injection of capital—or so he told Blanca. He came up with a possible solution: Because he was temporarily strapped for cash, why didn't she offload a portion of her South American property portfolio to free up some money? Blanca, desperate to return to Chile at any price, agreed without a pause. The transactions netted twenty-five thousand dollars. From this sum, Blanca drew two checks, both payable to Jack, the first for fifteen thousand dollars, the second for five thousand dollars. Jack vowed to put the money to work.

But all remained quiet on the Washington front . . . partly due to a new development: The ever-mercurial Jack de Saulles was dividing his political loyalties. Out of the blue, on September 25, he offered his services to the campaign of John Purroy Mitchel, who was standing as the Fusion candidate in the upcoming New York City mayoral race. This development sent mixed messages to Washington. On the one hand, Mitchel was promising to rid New York politics of the graft and corruption that had blighted the city for generations—ideals close to President Wilson's heart—but such a stance threatened to sound the death knell for the Democratic candidate, Edward E. McCall. Privately, Wilson wanted to smash the Tammany political machine of course, which had become a national embarrassment to the Democrat party, but publicly he had to throw his support behind McCall. De Saulles wasn't making the president's task any easier.

For someone with Jack's eye on a diplomatic future, it was a curious move. But for a ruthless opportunist, it was par for the course. Jack had sensed which way the political wind was blowing, and he was hoisting his sail into Mitchel's reforming gale. After all, de Saulles existing business interests and therefore his financial prospects lay in New York. In October, he served on a committee to discuss how best to ensure that intimidation didn't come into play at the polls—no mean task given Tammany's fondness for cracking heads on election day—and he put himself about as a jack-of-all-trades.

It paid off. On November 4, Mitchel swept into office with a landslide victory. This elevation left vacant Mitchel's old job as collector of the Port of New York, and one of Jack's closest friends, Dudley Field Malone, filled the position.[26] On November 24, Jack—never far away from the centers of power—was present at Malone's swearing-in ceremony.

Just two weeks earlier, Jack had taken an apartment at 18 East 60th Street. For the first time since arriving in America, Blanca could not only live with her husband—a perversely novel prospect—but she could expect him home every evening. Except of course it didn't work out that way. He was always out hustling some business deal or other, and she rarely saw him before midnight. Most nights she fretted at home alone. For Blanca—raised in a milieu of elaborate parties, intimate soirees, and nonstop banter—such social isolation was purgatory. Theater visits with Jack were also out of the question—"it would bore me to death"[27]—and he treated her dinner parties with equal contempt. Invariably he would promise to attend only to phone Blanca at the last minute, claiming that something had come up and he couldn't make it, leaving the embarrassed hostess to fabricate some story to explain her husband's absence.

But he was never too busy for sports. At Yale, besides becoming a gridiron superstar, Jack also had shone on the baseball diamond, and on December 13 he drummed up plenty of press interest to witness the opening of what became known as the "Indoor-Outdoor Baseball Season."[28] It was a bizarre attempt by the gentlemen's clubs of New York to play baseball year-round, even in snow, if necessary. Jack captained a team from the Union Club, New York's oldest private social club, dating from 1835. The deeply conservative institution had a membership list plucked from the loftiest reaches of the Social Register. Former members included President Ulysses Grant and Civil War general William Tecumseh Sherman. In Jack's time, he had rubbed shoulders with the likes of John Jacob Astor IV, the multimillionaire who had perished in the *Titanic* disaster the previous year.

To launch the season properly, Jack called in a few favors from old friends, most notably railroad magnate William Vanderbilt, who suggested that they use one of his vacant lots on Fifth Avenue for the opening game. Jack observed dryly that the league's temporary home venue was "worth more than the Polo Grounds and Shibe Park[29] put together."[30] Looking resplendent in white flannel trousers and matching sweater, Jack played third base and led his side against the Twelfth Regiment officers, who bizarrely turned out in khaki uniforms and long puttees that unwound as they ran the bases or chased ground balls. The Union Club team won 25–6.

Watching from one of the bird's-eye maple bleachers, Blanca might have marveled at Jack's athletic prowess, but her heart felt heavy. Her fleeting moments of despair had plunged into full-scale depression—and other problems were developing. The red ink on her bank account was mounting in alarming fashion as she continued to write more checks for an ungrateful husband who insisted on remaining out till all hours. She spent long tormented nights in the apartment on 60th Street with just Jack Jr. for company. As 1913 drew to a close and Blanca steeled herself for what promised to be a thoroughly miserable Christmas, she must have wondered how her situation could possibly get any worse.

No such gloom lingered aboard the SS *Cleveland,* a seventeen-thousand-tonner out of Genoa, as it steamed slowly into New York harbor on the morning of December 22. Here, the mood was one of overwhelming optimism. Not even a biting easterly wind could dent the spirits of the hundreds of mainly Italian immigrants draped over the rails. Among those gazing in wonderment at the soaring Manhattan skyline stood a stylishly dressed young man, just eighteen years old, five feet nine inches tall, with brilliantined brown hair swept back flat against his head in the modern style. His olive skin and exquisitely chiseled features gave him a brooding sensuality, but it was his deep-set almond-shaped eyes that others—especially women—noticed. They were utterly hypnotic. In a few short years, the smoldering intensity of that stare would make him one of the most famous men alive, the world's great Latin lover, idolized and fantasized across the globe, the hero of a million erotic dreams. For now, though, he was just another nervous immigrant with all the hopes and fears that international relocation brings. His name was Rodolfo Guglielmi.

FOUR

The Man from Italy

His full name was Rodolfo Pietro Filiberto Raffaele Guglielmi, and he was born on May 6, 1895, in the ancient town of Castellaneta in southern Italy. His father, Giovanni, was a single-minded veterinarian who had devoted his life to eradicating malaria in animals, while his mother, Gabriella—a sweet-natured woman, refined and blessed with a gift for languages that Rodolfo would inherit—had been born in France. In a poor town mostly populated by peasants, the Guglielmis were considered to be solidly middle class. By prevailing standards, theirs was not a large family with just three children. Rodolfo, the second son, had a younger sister. (Another older sister had died in infancy.) He was a scrawny kid who right from an early age struggled to fill out his growing frame. At school his runty appearance made him an easy target for the bullies and he performed poorly in sports of any type. And he was similarly handicapped in the classroom, where his crippling myopia turned the blackboard into a hazy blur. These twin afflictions made his life at school a time of utter misery. But no matter how mean the other kids and teachers might be, there was one ally on whom he could always depend.

Gabriella had been almost forty years old when she bore Rodolfo into the world, and from the day of his birth she spoiled him endlessly. Nothing was too good, and no expectation was too great for her favorite son. It was Gabriella who filled the boy's head with stories of a lineage that hinted at aristocratic blood, fueling the imaginative and fertile tendency for autobiographical embellishment that would remain with him throughout life. She worshiped Rodolfo and he worshiped her.

It was an entirely different story with his father. Giovanni Guglielmi was an old-school patriarch, a brutal disciplinarian, quick with a strap or stick, determined to beat some manliness into his feeble son. When Rodolfo was nine years old, the family moved to the coastal city of Taranto. One year later the lad's domestic torture came to an end when his father died, ironically from the very disease he had slaved so hard to eradicate. But if the physical chains were broken, the emotional terror was still intact, and for the rest of his life Rodolfo would fight to measure up to the standards set by the father whom he feared and loved in equal measure. It was an uphill struggle. The disappointments kept on coming: At age fifteen he applied to join the military. It had been his ambition for years, spurred on by the thought that nothing would have made his father more proud. He sailed through the written exam only to be thwarted by his physical shortcomings—his chest was an inch too small—and poor vision. Rodolfo was crushed.

More to please his mother than anything else, he enrolled in an agricultural college, though he lacked any ambition in this area. And it showed. After obtaining his graduation certificate, he made no attempt to find a job in landscaping or farming and instead began hanging out with a rough crowd, frequenting dance halls and chasing girls. The latter two diversions went hand in hand as Rodolfo discovered that his slender body shape was ideally suited to the latest flamboyant dances, and with his lissome grace on the dance floor and brooding manner, he became an instant magnet for women of all ages and from all walks of life. Few were the kind that Rodolfo would have wanted to take home to meet Gabriella, who became adept at turning a blind eye to her son's misdeeds.

Other family members weren't so tolerant. His straitlaced uncles and aunts, appalled and humiliated by a lifestyle that consisted of sleeping all day and partying all night, urged Gabriella to renounce the black sheep who was bringing so much shame on the family name. Even Gabriella began to despair of her favorite son, a despair that turned to outright alarm when, at age seventeen, Rodolfo suddenly announced that he was up and moving to Paris. Wearily, she gave him her blessing.

The City of Light was everything that Rodolfo expected: vibrant, exciting, how he wanted his life to be. Nighttime found him in the demimonde, either the bars of Montmartre or the smoky cafes and bistros half-hidden down a Latin Quarter side street, sipping Pernod with some adoring *fille* or else soaking up the heated philosophical debates that frequently lasted into the dawn. The relaxed Left Bank liberalism was several light-years removed from the stuffy Catholic confines of Taranto, and, for a young man eager to drink his fill of life's pleasures, it was heaven on earth.

It was also hugely expensive. In a matter of months, the wild young man frittered away the nest egg provided by his ever-generous mother—he had never made any serious attempt to find employment—and he was reduced to wiring home for more money. Ever sweet, ever obliging, Gabriella came through once more. Rodolfo, his pockets once again bulging with francs, now decided on one huge flourish: He headed for the gaming tables at Monte Carlo. The plan was to win a fortune at roulette or chemin de fer, enough to set him up for life. The reality was a sudden, jolting lesson in fecklessness. He lost every sou. With his tail planted firmly between his legs, Rodolfo Guglielmi slunk back to Taranto.

His homecoming was predictably grim. Members of his extended family unleashed a storm of biblical contempt upon this prodigal son, cursing him for not being more like his older, more responsible brother, Alberto, who held down a steady job in local government. Why, they growled at Gabriella, don't you take a firmer grip on this wastrel? To her credit, she did try. But every attempt was doomed to failure. Just one of those flashing smiles from her son was enough to melt any anger beating in Gabriella's breast. Deep down, she knew that Rodolfo was not destined for the conventional life. And when he began to talk of the riches rumored to exist in faraway America, she bowed to the inevitable, even promising to sponsor his journey—though with the proviso that this time, once he landed on American soil, there would be no more handouts; he would stand or fall on his own. Other members of the Guglielmi family lit candles of celebration. Putting an ocean between them and this embarrassing spendthrift was the answer to all their prayers.

On December 9, 1913, Rodolfo hefted his luggage up the gangway of the SS *Cleveland* as it lay docked in Genoa harbor. In his pocket were a second-class ticket and a banker's draft for a hefty sum. As the ship's whistle moaned its mournful good-bye to his homeland, Rodolfo's first move on board was typical—he sold the draft at a discount and traded up to a first-class cabin.[1] This gave him the opportunity to rub shoulders with the kinds of socially prominent passengers whom he hoped might ease his passage in America. Thanks to his mother, he had already added French to his native Italian and the first-class salon provided the right setting to hone his faltering English. The voyage also gave him an opportunity to show off his dancing skills. In Paris he had been quick to pick up the latest dance sensations, especially the sultry and provocative Apache with its air of masculine domination, and he used this now to great effect during the organized dance sessions on board the ship. Lithe and sinuous, he looked magnificent in his tuxedo—even if at this stage his puppy fat was corraled by a corset—and his exotic Latin air ensured a ready supply of dance partners. He was a prodigious networker:

His calling cards—gaudy affairs printed on expensive paper and bearing a heraldic crest that hinted at a lineage soaked in old European nobility—were scattered around the salon like confetti.

After twelve champagne-filled nights spent dancing into the early hours, Guglielmi got his first glimpse of the promised land as the *Cleveland* nosed into New York harbor. The fastest-growing city on earth, with its swaggering architecture, took his breath away, and Rodolfo fell in love at first sight. The next day he passed through the Great Hall at Ellis Island and out into America. There was nobody waiting for him at the "kissing post,"[2] and it was a similar story as he went searching for the Manhattan ferry; he was entirely on his own.[3]

The city was everything he had imagined it to be and more: fast-paced, overcrowded, and, above all, exciting. He watched openmouthed as flashy automobiles rolled impressively past. Although the teeming streets of Lower Manhattan were still filled with the sight and often overpowering smells of horse-drawn carriages, Detroit was already reshaping the American landscape, and, for a car nut such as Rodolfo, it was like wandering through the world's greatest auto showroom. He vowed that one day it would be him sitting behind the wheel of some gleaming roadster.

For now, though, he had to fathom the subway system. After several false starts, he eventually made his way to Giolito's on West 49th Street, a hotel that catered mostly to Italians fresh off the boat. He had been given the address by a fellow passenger on the ship, and after renting a suite—half measures were not in his nature—he celebrated at Rector's, a nearby restaurant famed for its lobster and other succulent dishes. Rodolfo chomped his way through the expensive menu, and then, flushed with adrenaline, he cruised out to take in the sights.

At first he found himself caught up in the joyous festive spirit, the sidewalks full of happy, smiling faces, wide-eyed children pressing their noses against brightly lit store windows, but slowly his sense of well-being began to fade, and the next day, Christmas Eve, found him overwhelmed by a sense of utter isolation. He was 4,500 miles from home, and only now did the enormity of what he had undertaken really hit home. He missed his family and, above all, he missed his beloved mother, the rock who had always been there to bail him out whenever times got tough. Never had he felt so alone. By his own admission, that night he threw himself on the bed and "cried like an infant."[4]

Just a few blocks north, Blanca de Saulles was also alone and thoroughly miserable that Christmas. Over the holidays, Jack had been harder to pin down than Harry Houdini. The early part of 1914 brought no improvement. Most evenings Jack contrived to absent himself from the apartment, either leaving his young wife alone or else obliging her to attend the theater in the company of some friend, usually some sympathizer from the Chilean expat community. But all that changed on March 10, 1914.

That was the day when, after fifteen months of behind-the-scenes maneuvering, Jack was finally nominated for that prestigious diplomatic post. But it wasn't Chile, as he'd been angling after and the press had so confidently predicted. No, he had been nominated for the post of minister to Uruguay.[5] This must have stung. Chile was one the South American "A-B-C" countries as they were known in Washington, Argentina and Brazil being the others. These were the major South American players on the international stage. Uruguay, by contrast, was a political minnow, but any disappointment that Jack felt was well camouflaged at his confirmatory press briefing. "President Wilson selected me for this post because he knows that I am in hearty sympathy with his policy as to South American republics, which, as I understand it, is to establish a common understanding with them all."[6] Newspaper editors dug into their morgues and exhumed Jack's daredevil credentials, rehashing the tale of his pursuit of Blanca, spicing up the saga with ever more outlandish deeds of derring-do. One breathless account had our hero dueling to win "the hand of the señorita," adding with a swagger: "he did not get the worst of it in any of these duels."[7]

Although Blanca would have preferred that Jack land the plum posting of Chile, she realized that Uruguay wasn't a bad second choice for a man in his mid-thirties just getting his foot on the diplomatic ladder. And there were other considerations in play. Uruguay, like its South American neighbors, was a Catholic stronghold, a place where unmarried women were still chaperoned; as such, it would be unlikely to offer Jack the kind of temptations that had been so freely available on the Great White Way.

After a year of political foot dragging, the confirmation process now moved on apace. And it became apparent that any skeletons lurking in Jack's closet had been thoroughly exorcised when, on March 24, the Senate Foreign Relations Committee reported favorably on the nomination of John de Saulles as envoy extraordinary and minister plenipotentiary to Uruguay. Shortly thereafter he was sworn into office. All he needed now was the date of his posting.

Until that happy day arrived, Jack suggested that Blanca take a vacation in Europe. The break would be good for her health, he said. Blanca didn't need to be asked twice and immediately booked passage on a steamer bound for Liverpool. Jack decided to cash in on Blanca's euphoria. While she was packing, he tutted that his new position would entail higher living costs; a minister for the US government would be expected to maintain certain standards and to entertain all the right people, even before leaving to take up the appointment. And because most of his money was tied up, he wondered if Blanca could cover his temporary financial shortfall. Of course, she said, and left two blank checks to fund any emergencies.

Then she and Jack Jr. headed for the port. Also traveling with them was Anne Mooney, now fully recovered from her throat operation. Once Blanca had resigned herself to the fact that Ethel would not be returning, her relations with Boobie had improved markedly, with the nurse proving herself a more than capable replacement. After a week at sea they docked in Liverpool, and from there Blanca caught the train to London. She spent the first few days with an aunt who was married to the chief of the Chilean Naval Commission at London, Admiral Joaquim Munoz Hurtado, a well-connected figure who proved invaluable in gaining Blanca entrance to the rigidly formal London social scene.

In his wife's absence, Jack traveled to Washington and his regular haunt, the Shoreham Hotel. Checking in alongside him was his old buddy from the Democrat trenches, Dudley Field Malone. The two men began making the rounds of the Washington power circles and the after-hours parties.

Once Rodolfo Guglielmi shook off his initial bout of homesickness, he fared well in New York. Rather than settling in the densely populated Italian neighborhoods of Lower Manhattan and Brooklyn, he took rooms in Midtown's bustling theater district. He could afford it. Unlike most immigrants, he was flush with money and in no rush to find work. As a consequence, his appetite for extravagance ran amok.

He became a regular at exclusive restaurants and danced till dawn in the trendiest nightclubs, where his slick footwork, tuxedoed chic, and lavish spending drew all manner of admiring glances from the female customers. It was during this period that Guglielmi had his first, if unconfirmed, parts in the movies. Some sources claim that in the spring of 1914, the handsome

Rodolfo Guglielmi sporting a bookish, studious look

young Italian showcased his dancing talents as an uncredited extra in *The Battle of the Sexes,* directed by D. W. Griffith and starring Lillian Gish, quickly following this up with another bit part in *My Official Wife,* a melodrama set in Russia. Because both films are now lost, these claims cannot be verified, but what is certain is that, within a few months of his arrival in New York, Rodolfo fell victim to that old familiar bugbear: a lack of cash.

Suddenly all those previously open doors were slammed in his face. Charm and a debonair appearance might be all well and good, but anyone who couldn't stand his round on the nightclub circuit risked being branded as just another gigolo on the make. His fall from grace was swift and dramatic. And as he struggled frantically for some means of paying the rent, he discovered, like millions before and since, that when hardship comes knocking the sidewalks of New York are often paved with more heartaches than gold. His innate haughtiness prompted him to turn up his nose at what he considered to be menial jobs, until, drawing on his agricultural background, he landed a job as landscape gardener at the Jericho, Long Island, estate of millionaire financier Cornelius Bliss Jr. Rodolfo's resentment was palpable. He hated getting his hands dirty, and his abhorrence of manual labor set his boss's teeth on edge. He further antagonized Bliss by taking a fellow worker's motorcycle without permission and smashing it into a telegraph pole. (Traffic accidents would be a recurring problem for the myopic Rodolfo, whose love of speed far exceeded his ability to see where he was going.) But it took the arrival of Bliss's wife from Europe to bring matters to a head. She decided that she would prefer to overlook a golf course rather than some Italianate grotto, and Rodolfo was sent packing.

Bliss did write Guglielmi a letter of introduction to the Central Park commissioner in the hope that he might secure a position as a landscape gardener, only for Rodolfo to learn that such positions were restricted to American citizens. He was out of work and broke. Financial belt tightening reduced him to a two-dollars-a-week skylight room in a boardinghouse on Times Square. "A cubby-hole in which brooms and mops were kept," he recalled. "There was an iron sink. I wiped my hands on newspapers." He added ruefully: "It was too luxurious for me. I couldn't afford to keep it."[8] This foreshadowed the bleakest time of his life.

He tramped the streets of New York, penniless, often hungry. He took work where he could find it: busing tables in restaurants—at one point working at Rector's, where, just twelve months beforehand, he had celebrated his arrival in the United States with lobster and champagne—washing cars, sweeping sidewalks, even picking up garbage. An empty belly is a great motivator, though, and he speedily acquired an encyclopedic knowledge of those bars that served free food with a drink. His favorite hangout was the H & H Automat on Fifth Avenue at 45th Street—later joking that the initials stood for the "Hungry and Homeless"[9]—a diner that served cheap meals. He showered at the nearest fire hydrant, and some nights found him sleeping rough on benches in Central Park. His only consolation during this forlorn period was that his mother couldn't witness his downfall; it would have broken her heart. To maintain the facade of success, he stole stationery from ritzy hotels and used it for the highly fictionalized accounts of his life in New York City that he sent back to Italy.

Guglielmi had just about reached rock bottom when a chance encounter changed his life. He was washing cars when he and a passerby fell into conversation. At some point the subject of dancing arose, and the stranger suggested that Rodolfo try his luck at Maxim's, a fancy restaurant on 38th Street that offered European cuisine, live music, and a supply of handsome young men willing to teach unaccompanied ladies the latest dances. Rodolfo's ears pricked up. American society was gripped by dance fever. Everyone, it seemed, wanted to learn the Maxixe, the Cakewalk, and, above all, the Argentinean tango. The tango, with its grinding embrace and heavy overtones of sexual promise, was tailor-made for someone with Rodolfo's Latin appeal. Figuring he had nothing to lose, he followed the man's advice and went along to Maxim's, spoke to a piano player, auditioned briefly, and got hired on the spot. As part of the arrangement, he had the use of an upper-floor room with a Victrola, where he could give private lessons for the more reticent clientele or those requiring a higher degree of discretion.

Downstairs, in the club proper, he hired out as a "taxi dancer," squiring elderly dowagers around the floor at ten cents a pop during the *thé dansants*—tea dances—that were currently all the rage. The pay was nothing special, but the tips and the perks were great. He also got to rub shoulders with the likes of Clifton Webb and George Raft, two professional hoofers who would later go on to find fame in Hollywood. From them he learned the tricks of the trade: how to flatter, how to turn clumsy customers into graceful swans, and how to look classy. Scanning his fellow taxi dancers at Maxim's, Rodolfo noticed that the chief exponents of effortless snootiness was a band of lower caste European nobles who had fallen on hard times and were out to revive their fortunes by trading on their royal lineage. Any hint of aristocratic blood—no matter how tenuous or even imaginary—definitely shifted one up the terpsichorean pecking order; reason enough for the veterinarian's son from Castellaneta to start calling himself "marchese." It worked.

In no time at all, Rodolfo was pocketing seventy dollars a week at a time when most workers in America would struggle to earn that in a month. For the young émigré, life in America was good, very good indeed. And he was starting to make some useful show business contacts as well. Chief among these was a petite blonde named Mae Murray, a Ziegfeld showgirl with ambitions to break into movies. Six years older than Rodolfo, Mae—"The Girl with the Bee-Stung Lips,"[10]—became a kind of mother figure to the young man, taking him under her wing, helping to smooth the few rough edges that remained on his social graces. Mae's influence on Rodolfo would profoundly change his life, and not always for the better.

Across the Atlantic, Blanca was bubbling with excitement. She adored London, with its fashionable shopping arcades, glitzy hotels, and seductive social whirl. This was her natural environment, the world she had been born to, where she felt at home, and she fitted in perfectly. She took rooms at the Cadogan, the posh Knightsbridge hotel where Oscar Wilde was infamously arrested in 1895 on charges of homosexuality.[11] From there she sampled all that London had to offer. She even undertook an airplane flight—considered frightfully daring for a woman in 1914—but her main diversion was shopping. Each day she toured the emporiums of Bond Street and Jermyn Street, buying lavishly in readiness for the upcoming move to Uruguay. And when she had exhausted the Mayfair salons, she hopped across the Channel to continue her shopping spree on the boulevards of Paris.

But the undoubted highlight of her extended vacation came on the evening of June 4, when she was escorted into Buckingham Palace, where King George V and Queen Mary were holding court. It was a glittering occasion, with practically the entire overseas diplomatic corps in attendance. Blanca had been invited as a guest of the Chilean minister to London, Señor Don Augustin Edwards. As she was presented to the king and queen, Blanca curtsied low and then drew back as proper etiquette required. In a room glittering with glamour, her radiant beauty gave rise to much comment and many admiring glances. It was probably the most memorable night of her life. But her joy was short-lived. When she returned to the hotel, she received a cablegram from Jack. It read: "I have resigned Uruguayan post."[12]

The news hit Washington like a thunderbolt. Jack explained his shock announcement in a letter to the Secretary of State, William Jennings Bryan:

> *I am deeply sorry that an unexpected turn in my personal affairs prevents me from fulfilling the ambition of a lifetime, to serve my country as one of its diplomatic representatives in Latin America. I the more regret it because I would have felt deeply sensible to the honor of serving under you as my chief in carrying forth your policies toward the development of more friendly relations between the South American republics and ourselves. The only consolation I feel in the circumstances is the thought of the honor that you and the President did me in selecting me for the post at Montevideo.*[13]

Such a volte-face was unprecedented. Never before in the history of the US diplomatic service had anyone earned the right to be called the minister to a foreign country without having ever left American soil. Jack's pathological unpredictability had won out again. In conversations with friends, he disclosed the real reason for his decision: money. At an oddly late juncture, it had dawned on him that diplomatic life was fine and dandy if one had a sizable independent income or inherited wealth. For lesser mortals, it could prove a precarious venture. At the eleventh hour, Jack had crunched the numbers and decided to pull the plug on his diplomatic dream. In doing so, he had crossed the Rubicon; all his dreams of exerting influence in the political sphere dissolved instantly and forever. He had delivered an astonishing personal snub not just to Secretary of State Bryan but to President Wilson as well.

Blanca was astounded. A hasty exchange of cables did little to ease her distress. In the end, Jack attempted to assuage her disappointment by saying that he had rented a house in Huntington, on Long Island, for her return. This move backfired badly. Earlier he had assured her that a new apartment at 22 East 78th Street would be their family home. She wrote back: "Your last cable saying about the cottage in Huntington has absolutely taken my breath away. I can hardly understand. Why rent a house now, Dinky, what else are you going to do with a house? You first buy one, then you rent one. Dinky, you must be house crazy."[14] She was sounding a rare note of disapproval. Despite later protestations to the contrary, on paper, at least, Blanca could not stay mad at Jack for long.

Later, in the same letter, she wrote: "Dinky, London is too delightful. You must get named Minister just as soon as you've made enough money to live comfortably, or, in other words, luxuriously. It's nicer to be a Minister here, because there's the court and all that makes it very interesting and amusing."[15] This extraordinary suggestion, tossed off so casually, speaks volumes about Blanca's naivety. She had failed utterly to grasp the enormity of Jack's capitulation. After humiliating the White House so profoundly, it would take far more than a fat bank account to breathe life into Jack's diplomatic career; such treachery would require a revival of Lazarus-like proportions. Blanca closed the letter with an update on the ongoing feud between herself and the señora. "I've got another beastly letter from my mother, so that I've given up trying to bridge the gulf. She is out of her mind."[16]

Blanca was in no hurry to return to New York; in London she dined and danced with nobility and high-ranking politicians, and generally conducted herself in a manner befitting a Chilean aristocrat. This was life in the Gilded Age, and few saw any prospect of it ever ending. So it was hardly surprising that, caught up in the giddy whirl of parties, receptions, and endless cocktails, Blanca, like most around her, paid scant heed when, on June 28, a pistol-wielding Serbian nationalist named Gavrilo Princip assassinated the heir to the Austro-Hungarian throne, Archduke Franz Ferdinand, and his wife on the broiling streets of Sarajevo. Just another tiresome incident in the Balkans; nothing to worry about, and certainly nothing to interrupt the social round. But behind the scenes, in the corridors of European power, old alliances were coming under strain.

Meanwhile, a storm of a quite different kind was brewing on the other side of the Atlantic. Blanca had now been dallying in Europe for three months, and Jack's patience was wearing thin. On July 7 he cabled, demanding that she return immediately. Her response was a mix of bafflement and despair: "Dearest Dink:—You send me such an extraordinary cable. I could not believe it came from you. I got it on the 7th and you tell me to sail on the 11th. Dinky, how could you imagine I would be ready in time?"[17] She itemized a litany of reasons to explain her delay: Her linen wouldn't be ready until the end of the month; Mrs. Mooney was still in Ireland; the baby's special milk needed to be ordered so that it would last through the weeklong voyage; she needed to buy a trunk for her clothes. Oh, she had "a billion million things to do."[18]

Jack cabled a compromise: What about the eighteenth? Blanca wired back her agreement, but then had second thoughts. That date still gave her only one week to make all the arrangements; she needed more time. After more hemming and hawing, Blanca finally booked passage on the SS *Olympic,* which sailed from Southampton on July 29.

She left a continent teetering on the brink of disaster. The political dynamic was changing almost hourly. In a bewilderingly fast chain of events following the assassinations in Sarajevo, Austria-Hungary declared war on Serbia. Russia, tied by treaty to Serbia, mobilized its forces. Four days later, Germany, straining at the leash for a chance to flex its military muscle and allied by treaty to Austria-Hungary, declared war on Russia and France. On August 4, when German troops overran neutral Belgium, treaty obligations forced the final European heavyweight, Britain, into the fray. The Great War was under way.

One day after Britain's declaration of war, the *Olympic* docked in New York. Even if the "lamps were going out all over Europe,"[19] life in Manhattan remained blissfully unaffected.[20] Jack met Blanca at the port, throwing his arms around her with delight and fussing wildly over Jack Jr., who had grown considerably in the three intervening months and was now an accomplished walker. As they drove to the apartment on East 78th Street, Jack casually mentioned that he had used her two blank checks to complete the purchase at a cost of twelve thousand dollars. Blanca thought the apartment very smart indeed and was still cooing with pleasure when Jack dashed her rapture with the announcement that she wouldn't be staying there. He needed the apartment for business, he explained, and wanted Blanca to take the rented bungalow in Huntington. Blanca needed every ounce of her iron self-control to fight back her disappointment. She said nothing and retreated to Huntington.

At about this time a strange incident occurred. It involved Rodolfo's confidante Mae Murray, who also happened to be on very cozy terms with de Saulles—so close that many assumed she was yet another of Jack's secret lovers. The notoriously unreliable Mae—her memoirs were penned with an eye on sales and self-promotion rather than accuracy—later wrote of attending an extravagant party at Jack's new apartment. When she arrived Jack proudly placed her at the head of the table, a spot normally reserved for the host's wife. When Mae queried this, Jack laughed. "Mrs. de Saulles is not here. She was not invited. She's out on Long Island where she belongs."[21] Mae glossed over the awkwardness and concentrated instead on the guest list—"every celebrity on Broadway sat around that table"[22]—and the sumptuous food; pheasant in wild rice served on a silver tray was washed down with vintage burgundy and champagne.

With each toast Jack's leering admiration for Mae grew more pronounced. Eventually he staggered up and asked her to dance. While they were grinding against each other on the dance floor, Mae's beau at the time (and later husband), Jay O'Brien, burst in, uninvited, and a shouting match ensued, one that ended with O'Brien flattening Jack and then yanking the tablecloth, spilling the flowers, wine, and food everywhere. When Jack regained his feet, several waiters had to restrain the enraged host. According to Mae, Jack broke free, threw her across his shoulder, and bundled her out of the apartment and into a car. A madcap ride through Central Park ensued, and later, when he had sobered up, he apologized and dropped her off where she was living. At this point, Mae's already unlikely tale becomes truly surreal. When she entered her apartment, who should be waiting there but none other than Blanca de Saulles.

Apparently, Blanca had heard the gossip about Jack's craving for Mae and had decided to investigate. How this squares with Blanca's stated indifference to Jack's affairs was never explained. When Blanca accused Mae of trying to steal her husband, Mae protested her innocence. Nothing, she cried, could be further from the truth. At that point Blanca allegedly began to sob, and Mae threw a comforting arm about her. What you need is a diversion, Mae said, something to take your mind off your problems. Have you thought of attending any of the afternoon tea dances? When Blanca shook her head, Mae promised to accompany her. And, said Mae, you simply must meet this absolutely divine young man from Italy; his name's Rodolfo.

FIVE

When Blanca Met the Signor

The intervening months had been a dizzy blur for the young immigrant. It was all happening so fast. He had been spotted by a professional dancer named Bonnie Glass, who was on the lookout for someone to replace her partner, supersuave Clifton Webb, who had recently departed for Broadway. Bonnie ran an experienced eye over Rodolfo, liked what she saw, and offered him a job. Although it meant a cut in pay—Bonnie was offering just fifty dollars a week—Rodolfo realized this was a smart career move, and in short order, Bonnie and "Signor Rodolfo" were wowing audiences all over Manhattan. They headlined swish eateries such as Delmonico's, the Boulevard Cafe, even Rector's, where Rodolfo had once bused tables, before graduating to a string of Broadway vaudevilles. Then they took their exotic routines to Bonnie's own club, the Montmartre, in the basement of the old Boulevard Cafe. When that nightspot folded, Bonnie opened up another, the Chez Fysher, at 121 West 45th Street, which quickly became a favored hangout for the Manhattan party crowd, including Mae Murray.

Making good on her promise, Mae took Blanca along to the Chez Fysher. This was a time of enormous upheaval in the societal status of women; the skirts were getting shorter, so was the bobbed hair, and as the attitudes loosened up, the sight of two attractive women entering a nightclub unaccompanied hardly registered on the social seismograph. The dance craze in New York was then at its peak, with star performers like Bonnie drawing big crowds and earning phenomenal salaries. But Blanca, like most of the female socialites sipping champagne at the tables, scarcely noticed the leading lady; she couldn't take her eyes off Bonnie's gorgeous dance partner.

Clad in an elegant tuxedo and collar, Rodolfo Guglielmi exuded an animalistic male dominance as he swept Bonnie around the floor. The long, lingering dips of the tango gave him plenty of time to survey the audience, and he found his gaze being repeatedly drawn to the ravishing brunette alongside

Mae Murray. She embodied everything that he adored in a woman: obvious refinement, mysterious eyes, dark hair, and an alabaster, almost translucent complexion that gave her the Madonna-like beauty so reminiscent of his mother. In between performances, Mae called Rodolfo over and introduced him to Blanca. One tip Rodolfo had picked up from his taxi-dancing buddies was the importance of a good first impression. Courtliness was the secret. His deep bow and brushing of lips against Blanca's extended hand were designed to impress and did. The couple hit it off immediately.

When Rodolfo invited Blanca to dance, his delight reached another dimension. She wasn't just beautiful, she danced superbly as well. By night's end Rodolfo was smitten. "I adored her," he said later. But he feared that he could never bridge the social divide between them. "She seemed so far above me that I never dreamed she would look at a mere tango dancer."[1]

He was right to be skeptical. Although Blanca was obviously attracted to him—he was, after all, devastatingly handsome and much closer to her age-wise than her husband—she was still a married woman and acutely aware of the social gulf that divided a Chilean aristocrat from some immigrant, even one as seductive as Rodolfo. For this reason, despite the sparks that flared between them, she resolved to keep this glorious stranger at arm's length while she went back to the business of making her marriage work.

Before her banishment to Huntington, which she hated, Blanca was given a guided tour of the real estate operation that Jack had established with his cousin, Maurice Heckscher. They had taken a plush suite of offices at 734 Fifth Avenue. Blanca nodded appreciatively. It might not have been a ministerial legation in Montevideo, but it was impressive all the same, even if recent global events meant that Jack was already eyeing business opportunities elsewhere.

Someone always makes money out of human conflict, and Jack reasoned that the European war had the potential to yield a rich financial harvest. It was merely a question of finding a niche and finding it fast. The announcement of a British Expeditionary Force to be deployed in France provided the opening he sought. Despite the increasing mechanization of the military in the early twentieth century, when it came to transportation, the armed forces of Europe still relied overwhelmingly on horses. Already the British government had raided factories and coal mines as well as farms for animals that could be press-ganged into service. Once that supply ran dry, Jack figured, official eyes would be forced to look elsewhere, and there was only one viable option: the rolling plains of North America. The vast prairies could provide a practically limitless source of weather-toughened horses and mules with the potential to generate hundreds of thousands of dollars in profit for the contractor.[2]

But securing the contract to supply these horses wouldn't come easy. Jack needed a transatlantic associate, someone with political clout able to open doors and negotiate the labyrinthine corridors of power in Whitehall. William Angus Drogo Montagu, 9th Duke of Manchester, was just such a man. Montagu was an old-school peer of the realm, with a fabulous ability to squander money. In a few short years, he managed to exhaust a vast family fortune that had taken three centuries to accumulate. He was the quintessential aristocratic wastrel, fat and feckless, dissolute beyond belief, and an enthusiastic adulterer.

Montagu had fetched up in New York after having been hounded from his home country by an army of creditors, and in 1900 he followed the time-honored British aristocratic tradition of marrying a wealthy American to prop up his flagging bank balance. His bride was Helena Zimmerman, daughter of a railroad president and a major stockholder in Standard Oil. Monogamy, however, wasn't to the duke's taste. He had an eye for the ladies, and they had an eye for his title. His sexual indiscretions, frequent and flagrant, made him a regular fixture in the gossip columns.

Jack, too, fell under his spell, especially when the "Happy-Go-Lucky Duke"[3] secured a mutually lucrative contract to transport horses to Britain. Outside of working hours, the two men became bosom buddies, much to the delight of New York's sensationalist yellow press. Blanca warned Jack against this newfound friendship, but he was incorrigible, utterly deaf to her entreaties. In the duke he had found an "inseparable companion,"[4] and the two men practically lived in each other's pockets. One day while Blanca and Jack were dining at the Long Island home of his uncle, August Heckscher, a messenger arrived with news that the duke needed to see Jack urgently to discuss business matters. To Blanca's annoyance, Jack made his excuses and left. Later that day the Heckschers tried to raise Blanca's spirits with a yacht ride across Long Island Sound. At one point they hoved alongside the duke's schooner—hired but not paid for—moored in the bay. There, frolicking on the quarterdeck, were Jack and the duke, practically submerged beneath a swarm of Broadway beauties. Blanca's humiliation was total. When she later confronted Jack about this incident, he just brushed her off like an annoying fly. And then he left for Canada, to buy more horses. After this, Blanca saw him no more that summer.

The gossip began to mount. A stark indicator of Jack's fading reputation came in early fall when his mother, of all people, contacted Blanca and urged her to persuade her husband to put some distance between himself and the duke. This puzzled Blanca. Ordinarily her mother-in-law would barely give her the time of day; now she was trying to enlist her assistance. She asked why. Mrs. de Saulles stalled for a moment then asked if she had seen the September 24 issue of *Town Topics*. Blanca paled. Despite her brief time in America, she knew all about New York's raciest scandal mag.

Town Topics had begun life as a highbrow, low-circulation journal that covered music and the arts, until it was bought by Colonel William d'Alton Mann. Thereafter it switched focus to the sexual peccadilloes of upper-crust society members. As a result, circulation soared. "New York," Mann once famously declared, "is inhabited by jackasses, libertines and parvenus."[5] He might well have included himself on the list of culprits because Mann was a journalistic highwayman who set about emptying the pockets of his subject matter. It worked like this: His editorial staff crafted carefully worded articles that slavered over the latest hot gossip or scandal without actually mentioning any of the guilty parties by name. However, any reader eager to discover these identities—and most were—had only to turn the page, where a second, this time quite innocuous article just so happened to mention all the names that were missing overleaf. The reading public quickly caught on. And they lapped it up. Provided, of course, that the article actually appeared in print, because many of the magazine's juiciest stories never saw the light of day, thanks to the ever-inventive Mr. Mann. Whenever a particularly scandalous piece was in the pipeline, Mann's reporters would contact the unfortunate subject and inform them of impending publication. Such a call generally turned spines to jelly, but it was made clear to the quaking victim that any hint of embarrassment could be avoided if they agreed to purchase a chunk of overpriced advertising in that particular issue, thus ensuring that the offending article would be spiked. Hundreds succumbed to this blackmail until *Town Topics* went, unlamented, to its grave in 1937.

Blanca rushed out immediately and bought the latest issue. She thumbed through it until reaching the magazine's most eagerly read column, "Saunterings." To her horror it contained a lurid account of a shindig thrown by the Duke of Manchester[6] at a venue overlooking Long Island Sound, which was described as "some party."[7] The article referred to a "horde of weird males and females,"[8] one of whom "did the Lady Godiva stunt by a sans clothing plunge into the ocean,"[9] a recklessness that nearly cost the woman her life, as other guests had to dive in to save her. She was pulled from the water "much subdued in spirit."[10] Among those partygoers named in the article was the duke's business partner, Jack de Saulles, whom it called that "white light luminary,"[11] a clear reference to Jack's hell-raiser reputation on Broadway.

When Jack returned from his horse-buying trip to Canada, Blanca tore into him for his stupidity. He professed his innocence; it was just sensationalist reporting of ordinary high jinks, he said. To help cool Blanca's temper, he threw in a sweetener—allowing her to move into the apartment on 78th Street. This had the desired effect. She always had preferred big-city bustle to dreary rural life on Long Island; but any hopes that Blanca entertained about settling down with her husband were quashed when Jack announced that he was off again, this time to Britain to finalize a deal with the Canadian government. And to prove his charm was still intact, he wheedled another thousand dollars out of Blanca to finance the trip and promised that he would be gone only for a couple of weeks.

Although Europe was at war, the high seas were still relatively safe for passenger ships, especially those on the high-profile North Atlantic run. For now, at least, the trip posed few dangers for Americans. Before leaving, Jack told Blanca that he intended to decorate the new apartment with furniture from a business acquaintance named George Young. The furniture would be in lieu of a debt that Young owed Jack. Within days of Jack's departure, Young did come to the apartment. He didn't bring any furniture, however; instead he brought a promissory note for money that Jack owed him, and, twisting the knife into what was now an ugly open wound, he showed Blanca a cable from Jack in England, in which he had instructed Young to collect the debt from his wife. Blanca bit back her frustration and settled the obligation.

These were lonely days for her. She needed company, and she found it in Jack's sister, Caroline Degener. Despite a ten-year gap in their ages, the two women had always hit it off, and in October they joined the society rush for the hottest ticket in town: the murder trial of Florence Carman.

Few events agitate upper-class ennui more than a juicy scandal—especially if it involves one of their own. Mrs. Carman was the wife of Dr. Edwin Carman, a well-to-do physician of Freeport, Long Island, and if the Nassau County District Attorney's Office was to be believed, on the evening of June 30, 1914, at about 8:30 p.m., she smashed the window of her husband's surgery and fired a single shot that ended the life of thirty-six-year-old Lulu D. Bailey. Mrs. Bailey, the wife of a prosperous hat manufacturer, had been closeted with the doctor for some considerable time before being shot. According to Dr. Carman, he was treating her for malaria, though why Mrs. Bailey would travel five miles to see a gynecologist, whom she had never before consulted, about some tropical disease was puzzling to say the least. Especially when an autopsy revealed that Mrs. Bailey was in the early stages of pregnancy.

Much the most damaging evidence came from the Carmans' African-American maid, Celia Coleman. She told the police that immediately after the shooting Florence Carman appeared in the kitchen and said, "I shot him—see,"[12] drawing a gun from beneath her shawl and flaunting it. Further investigation led state prosecutors to believe that the intended victim had been Dr. Carman and that Mrs. Bailey had been shot by mistake. Florence, they theorized, had suspected her husband of exceeding his professional interest in many of the women who visited his surgery, a premise borne out by the discovery of a Dictograph[13] that she had hidden in her husband's surgery. Mrs. Carman professed her total innocence of the crime.

Largely thanks to Celia Coleman's evidence, Mrs. Carman was hauled off to the Mineola jail to await her trial. It began on October 19 and swiftly became a highlight of the social season. The spectators in the packed public gallery—mostly female—brought well-stocked picnic hampers to ensure that they wouldn't lose their seats during recesses, and some even knitted to while away the more tedious interludes. The defense gave Celia Coleman a savage time on the stand, but she withstood everything they threw at her, remaining firm in her insistence that the defendant had confessed to the shooting within minutes of its occurrence.

Among those listening to Celia's testimony that day was Blanca de Saulles. She had driven Caroline Degener to the trial, and the two women had soaked up every titillating detail. Like most in the fashionably dressed public gallery, Blanca was repulsed by the notion that anyone could accept the word of a black maid over that of a wealthy white gentlewoman, and it was confidently predicted that the statuesque Mrs. Carman would be acquitted. But it didn't work out that way. The jury deadlocked, and Florence was freed on twenty-five thousand dollars bail to await a second trial.

Blanca found the trial a welcome diversion at a time of unusual stress. For the first time in her life, she had money worries. Jack had already frittered away large chunks of her hundred-thousand-dollar dowry, and, as Blanca dug deeper into the accounts, she discovered further cause for alarm: The apartment had cost not twelve thousand dollars, as Jack had claimed, but rather seventy-five hundred dollars. The balance had disappeared into his pockets.

While Blanca smarted, Jack played the goat in London. His intended two-week stay in England began to stretch out. When conscience finally got the better of him, he cabled Blanca and suggested she join him. Her protest that she was strapped for cash was countered by his insistence that she come anyway. Blanca found the fare and set sail for England alone, leaving Jack Jr. in the care of Anne Mooney. When Blanca reached London at the end of November, she took a cab to the Berkeley, Jack's hotel in Knightsbridge. If she was expecting a blissful reunion, she was gravely disappointed. Jack almost burst a blood vessel, furious that she had interrupted him at the hotel. The Berkeley, he snapped, was his business address, the headquarters for the company he had founded to handle the shipping of horses to England, and he was determined not to mix business and domestic life. Besides, he added petulantly, the Berkeley was full and didn't have any spare rooms. He ordered Blanca to stay with her aunt, Mrs. Munoz Hurtado.

Blanca meekly did as she was told. But her humiliation became the talk of the Chilean expat crowd in London, and further embarrassment lay in store. For seven consecutive days Blanca dutifully reported to the Berkeley and asked to see her husband. After a brief audience he invariably shooed her out the door and told her to go shopping. Then one day, when she went to the Berkeley, a strange face greeted her at the check-in desk. When Blanca asked for Jack, the clerk asked who she was.

"I am his wife," she replied.

"Which one?"[14] he smirked.

Like most of the alleged incidents between Blanca and Jack, we have only Blanca's word that this occurred, but Jack does seem to have been remarkably difficult to track down on this trip. The couple did manage to coordinate schedules one lunchtime when Jack entertained the private secretary to the American ambassador, Harold Fowler.[15] Over dessert, Jack invited Fowler to dinner that night at the Carlton Hotel on the corner of Pall Mall and Haymarket. Fowler agreed. However, that evening, just minutes before the appointed time, Jack phoned Blanca to say he had been delayed and would be arriving late at the Carlton. Blanca kept the dinner date with Fowler and then had to make a string of apologies as Jack pulled another of his notorious no-shows. After dessert, Blanca ran into the lobby and got Jack on the phone. He was up to his eyes in work, he explained, and suggested that she accompany their guest to the theater, after which he would meet them back at the Carlton. Blanca did as requested. But when she and Fowler returned to the Carlton, they still found no sign of her missing husband.

Blanca excused herself and took a cab to the Berkeley, determined to confront her uncaring husband. He wasn't there. Midnight came and went. Still no sign of him. Exasperated beyond belief, she made her way back to her aunt's house. The next day Jack was as effusive as ever with his apologies; he had been busy, he said, and spent the night with his old friend Judge Coyne. When Blanca chided him for his selfishness, Jack scoffed that she was "silly to take it that way,"[16] blithely ignoring the fact that he had expected his wife to entertain a complete stranger for several hours.

More heartache dogged Blanca during her London stay. On the one occasion when she did manage to see Jack alone for an extended period of time in his hotel room, he was leafing through some mail when he happened to drop a card. Blanca picked it up and froze. It came from a woman, and the address was Maida Vale. She expressed surprise that he knew anyone living in such a "fast section of London."[17] He replied that she was "a very charming woman and had donated an automobile to the Ambulance Corps."[18] After more questions, according to Blanca, Jack declared himself "crazy about her."[19]

"Have you ever kissed her?"

"Yes"[20] came the offhand reply.

Blanca took off at once for Paris for some hard-core retail therapy.

Nowadays her decision might seem bizarre, reckless even, in light of the bloodshed occurring in Flanders, just sixty miles north of the French capital. But throughout the war Paris remained oddly immune to the horrors of the Western Front, and the city was never occupied by German troops.[21] When, on September 12, the German army did make a major push toward Paris, they were thwarted at the Battle of the Marne—at a cost of 263,000 Allied casualties. Keeping the Champs Élysées safe for the dedicated shopper was an expensive business.

Blanca found life in the capital pretty much unaffected. She renewed old acquaintanceships, dined out in bistros and restaurants, attended parties, and bought racks of clothes. Despite later protestations of relative penury throughout her married life, her wardrobe never suffered. After a couple of hectic weeks in Paris, she returned to London and the news that Jack now intended traveling to Paris on business. She brightened up. She would go with him. Far too dangerous, he insisted, no place for a woman, better off returning to America. Blanca protested that Paris's enchanting boulevards hadn't seemed that perilous a couple of days earlier, but Jack put his foot down. He insisted that she return to America. Glumly, Blanca made arrangements to leave. She traveled with a heavy heart to Liverpool where, on December 16, she boarded the RMS *Lusitania.*

To her chagrin, she had been assigned a tiny interior cabin, all the way forward, always one of the uncomfortable spots on any ship in high seas. When she complained to the purser, he explained that the ship was packed to the gunwales with passengers fleeing Europe and that no other single cabins were available. Blanca thought quickly. Earlier, while waiting on the platform at London's Euston Station to catch the boat train to Liverpool, she had bumped into her son's godfather, Charles M. Schwab. Schwab had been in London to cancel a fifteen–million-dollar contract to build submarines for Britain and France, as such a deal was thought to violate American neutrality.[22] Blanca asked the purser for Schwab's cabin number. When she found him, she begged him to help her find a larger cabin. Schwab told her not to worry and secured her superior accommodation—though it was still forward and tucked away beneath the bridge.

The voyage was dreadful. Mountainous seas made it a nightmare for passengers and crew alike. In a letter to Jack, Blanca described how "the boat pitched and tossed about so that, lying in bed, one moment I stood on my head and the next on my feet."[23] Even an old hand like Schwab didn't emerge unscathed. By his reckoning this was his fifty-second transatlantic voyage and the first time that he'd been seasick.

On December 23, the *Lusitania* finally found sanctuary in New York harbor. It was bitterly cold when the ship docked and Blanca shivered miserably on the quayside as she waited for her case of jewelry and silver to be extracted from the hold. By coincidence, her dinner guest from London, Harold Fowler, had also been on board and, like most men who met Blanca, he was instantly bewitched. He introduced her to a customs official named Downey, who was almost overcome. "Although we all know who Mrs. De Saulles is," he gushed, "we have not all the honor of knowing her,"[24] and he allowed her to pass through without a second glance at her luggage. Blanca treated Downey to a dazzling smile and topped it off by inviting the awestruck customs official to visit the family home. "Of course, he was in the seventh heaven of delight," she wrote Jack. "You know better than anyone what saying that means to people of that class. It was all very amusing and very useful."[25]

New York had pulled out all the stops to welcome Christmas. The streets blinked with twinkling lights, and Blanca was ecstatic upon reaching the apartment on 78th Street. "When I got home to Toodles boy my heart almost burst with joy," she wrote to Jack. "He threw his arms around my neck and hugged and kissed me, and it thrilled me so that it almost made me cry."[26] The next day a heavy snowfall draped the city in white. Blanca and her little boy sat by the window and reveled in the spectacle. Finally, she thought, a turning point had been reached in her marriage; she had a husband, she had a healthy child, and now, at long last, she had the home that she craved. At long last, Blanca's life seemed to be set fair.

SIX

Enter Ms. Sawyer

Shortly after Blanca's return to New York, her husband's business partner, Maurice Heckscher, acting on Jack's instructions, deposited fifteen hundred dollars in her bank account. After several false starts, Jack's business dealings were finally paying off. In one spectacular coup, he and the Duke of Manchester had cleared fifty thousand dollars on a single horse-dealing contract with the Canadian government. Whether Blanca knew of this windfall remains unclear as she always claimed that her husband kept her in the dark about his financial transactions.

Blanca's domestic situation appeared to be on the upswing, especially when, in February 1915, she received a telegram from Jack begging her to join him in London. She gave notice to her servants and started packing at once. Then came a second cable announcing a change in plans: Jack told her to remain in New York. Blanca choked back her disappointment and began the chore of hiring new servants. She was just starting to keep house again when another cable arrived from Jack: "Have taken apartments at Paris. Come at once."[1] Understandably wary, Blanca hedged. But March brought another cable beckoning Blanca to join him. Just a few days later, he canceled again. Blanca was twisting in the wind.

In late April she received still another summons to Paris, and this time she had progressed to the stage of having her trunks packed and sent to the steamer . . . only to suffer yet another last-minute rebuff: "Don't come; I think I am coming back."[2] Blanca just had time to contact the shipping line and arrange for her baggage to be removed before the ship sailed. It was a fortunate cancellation. The liner was the *Lusitania,* which, on May 7, just five days after leaving New York, was sunk by a German U-boat off the coast of Ireland with the loss of 1,198 lives, including 128 Americans. In conversations with friends, Blanca would dramatize her near brush with death by declaring that she was "sorry she was not on it."[3]

However, the immigration records at Ellis Island tell a different story. By the time the *Lusitania* sailed on its doomed last voyage, Jack was already back in New York, safe and well and living at 78th Street. He had returned on April 24, "after serving three months with the Red Cross in France,"[4] as he told the press. Again, Jack was the only authority for this claim, and given his prodigious talent for autobiographical embellishment, it should perhaps be taken with a hefty pinch of salt. Interestingly, though, there are witnesses who claimed that it was Jack—mired in depression over his turbulent marriage—who made the notorious remark about wishing to have gone down on the stricken *Lusitania.* Like so many incidents in this complicated saga of "he said, she said," it all depends on which version one believes.

Barely noticed in all the press clamor about the *Lusitania* was the revelation that, on May 8, a second jury had acquitted Florence Carman of shooting her husband's lover. The jury, apparently, took to heart the defense counsel's novel closing argument that Celia Coleman and two other black witnesses should be "tied in a bag . . . and thrown into the river."[5] Such vicious bigotry was part and parcel of acceptable courtroom strategy at this time, and it was commonly agreed that Mrs. Carman's team of high-priced lawyers had pulled off a legal miracle.

The prosecution retired to lick its wounds, disappointed but hardly surprised. In early twentieth-century America, trying to gain a murder conviction against any female defendant was tough enough; trying to put a white, middle-class woman in the electric chair was frankly impossible. Mostly this was due to the so-called "unwritten law," a murky legal concept that every attorney knew existed yet few would admit to having adopted. In essence, it granted women, especially wives, the emotional license to kill any errant male with little fear of retribution. The reasoning worked along the lines of: "The bastard had it coming." Since the turn of the century only four women had been executed in the United States; two were black, and all were dirt poor. Women might not have had the vote yet, but in capital cases across America female defendants enjoyed a judicial leniency that their male counterparts could only dream about.

Florence Carman left court rejoicing, her liberty restored and her marriage intact.[6] The acquittal racked up another triumph for the unwritten law, and although Blanca was not in court to see the outcome, she doubtless read the newspaper accounts and agreed with the verdict. Little did she realize how, not so far off in the future, her interest in the Carman case would come back to haunt her.

That same day, half a world away, the Italian government gathered in the aftermath of the *Lusitania* outrage to discuss that nation's position regarding hostilities. Like the United States, Italy had remained neutral, but growing alarm about German military ambitions had sparked a public backlash against political fence-sitting, with mobs taking to the streets of Rome and demanding that Italy join the Allies. On May 23, the cabinet buckled, and Italy declared war on the Central Powers. This had two immediate consequences: All young men were banned from leaving the country, and any Italian male citizen under the age of forty was eligible for the draft—even if he lived abroad. Failure to return to Italy would be regarded as desertion, the penalty for which was a jail term or even death. In light of such drastic penalties, many Italian emigrants did indeed return to their homeland.

Rodolfo Guglielmi found himself trapped in a quandary. He loved living in America and was desperate not to jeopardize his immigration status, but he also felt a patriotic duty to his homeland. And, of course, always at the back of his mind was the specter of a disapproving father taunting his worthless son. Driven to prove himself, Rodolfo duly presented himself to the draft board in New York City, only to be rejected because of his poor vision. He might have been spared the horror of Europe's killing fields, but as a letter to his mother, dated September 20, 1915, and written from Washington, DC, makes clear, the young man's conscience was clearly troubling him. In it, he tells of meeting "a gentleman . . . who has a great influence in politics" who had promised to help him obtain US citizenship, "so this saves me in an honorable way to be obliged to return for the war." The identity of this "gentleman" remains a mystery, and as several years would pass before the young Italian did attempt to obtain US citizenship, we can only assume that nothing came of this promised assistance. Later in the same letter, he mentions being offered a chance to "make a lot of money" in San Francisco, along with talk of trying to get into the movies. It was already clear that Rodolfo Guglielmi knew where his future lay.

In the fall of 1915, Blanca had a new problem to contend with. Jack had always been a heavy drinker, but now his alcohol consumption was getting out of hand. It played havoc with the couple's already skimpy social life. On those rare occasions when Blanca invited friends for dinner, Jack brandished his contempt either by fleeing early to hit some nightclub or, if he was really loaded, by stumbling off to bed, leaving his embarrassed guests still sitting at the table. Deep in her heart Blanca feared that the marriage had come to an end. In August she sat down with Jack and poured out her feelings. She told him that his behavior was "driving her crazy." He allegedly replied that he "couldn't help it, that he wasn't made to settle down."[7] In that case, Blanca said, she wanted to return to Chile. Jack just shrugged and said, "You get a divorce and take the boy."[8]

The finality of this response jolted Blanca. Although by no means a staunch Catholic, she still harbored a deep-rooted revulsion for divorce, due in large part to the fact that divorce was not even recognized in her homeland.[9] If she returned to Chile bearing the stigma of a divorced woman, she ran the risk of being permanently shunned by the deeply conservative upper class. Before taking such an irrevocable step, she needed to clear her mind, and that meant having a complete break from Jack, from New York, from everything. In October she booked passage to Chile. Before leaving she signed, at her husband's request, a deed transferring ownership of 22 East 78th Street to Jack's business secretary, Stephen S. Tuthill.

As Blanca sailed out of New York harbor, watching the skyline slip beneath the horizon, her overriding emotion was "a wonderful feeling of relief."[10] Perhaps now she could get on with her life. After all, she was still only twenty-one years old; she had her son by her side, and she had Anna Mooney to help her.

A few weeks later Blanca arrived in Chile to a joyful family welcome. It was the first time that Señora Errázuriz-Vergara had seen her three-year-old grandson, and she couldn't have been more ecstatic. As much as possible Blanca kept details of her domestic life under wraps, downplaying her troubles with Jack, working hard to close the marriage-related rift that had opened between her and the señora. After a frosty start, mother and daughter reconciled. At this point, Blanca had no reason to think that she would ever return permanently to the United States; she was back in the family fold, once again enjoying the untroubled luxury of her youth. Nor did she have any qualms about raising Jack Jr. in Chile. When it came time for the boy to be educated, he would learn from the very best private tutors, and then, if family tradition was any guideline, it would be off to Europe and one of the top universities, either Oxford or perhaps the Sorbonne. With her life back on track, Blanca relaxed. She also demonstrated that the daredevil streak that had prompted the airplane ride in England was still intact.

It resurfaced one day in December when a friend named Felipe Cortez arrived at Palacio Vergara by car and Blanca pestered him to take her for a drive. He tried to dissuade her. The bodywork on the Ford was hanging off, he protested, and besides there weren't even any seats for the passengers. Blanca pooh-poohed his concerns and perched herself on the running board. Cortez roared off. They had hardly gone any distance when someone darted in front of them. Cortez yanked the steering wheel, sending the car into a skid and throwing Blanca from the car. She was fortunate. All she sustained was a small cut on her chin that required three stitches, and "she never even whimpered,"[11] recalled Anna Mooney, who described her mistress as "very plucky."[12] That same night Blanca attended a concert and joked about the small bandage that covered her wound.

Her calendar was full. Later that season, in January 1916, she and Jack Jr. spent time at the fashionable summer resort of Osorno, some 620 miles south of Valparaíso. Next on the agenda was a planned trip to China. And it was while Blanca was back in Viña del Mar, finalizing arrangements for this Orient adventure, that she received a surprise letter from her husband. He had undergone a change of heart, filled with remorse over how heartlessly he had treated Blanca. He begged her to return to New York "for the boy's sake."[13] After much soul-searching, Blanca agreed.

On April 13, 1916, Blanca's six-thousand-mile voyage—the opening of the Panama Canal in August 1914 had sliced three uncomfortable weeks off the sea passage—ended when the *Almirante* docked in New York. Jack was waiting on the quayside for her—blind drunk. In that instant she knew nothing had changed.

From there, the heartaches just kept multiplying. Jack installed Blanca and Jack Jr. in a rented apartment on East 60th Street then went to stay at his brother's place, three blocks away. Even when Blanca pointed out that Charles de Saulles wasn't actually living there, Jack still refused to allow her to move in with him. Blanca bit her tongue and applied herself to the task of salvaging her marriage. Her efforts seemed to rub off on Jack. The next few days saw a distinct improvement in his demeanor and his drinking, leading Blanca to wonder if she had judged him too harshly.

One Sunday Jack arrived at Blanca's apartment and asked if he could take Jack Jr. for the day. Blanca agreed, and father and son departed. A short while later a messenger arrived bearing a huge bouquet of flowers with a note: "To our one and only sweetheart, from Big and Little Jack."[14] Blanca melted with delight at this token of Jack's renewed love for her. Later that day, when Jack Jr. returned, he was bubbling with excitement at the day's events. He burbled that they had visited the Central Park Zoo, where he had seen the lions and made them roar. The youngster continued in this vein for some time until blurting out how he and "Miss Jo" had laughed at the lions.

Blanca's antennae began to twitch. "Who is Miss Jo?"

"Oh, Miss Jo is a lady who was with us. Daddy called her Jo and told me to call her Miss Jo and not to tell you anything about her."[15]

It was a dagger to the heart. When Blanca confronted her husband, he admitted that "Miss Jo" was a nationally known cabaret dancer named Joan Sawyer.

Joan Sawyer always was coy about her antecedents. Some claim that her real name was Bessie Morrison Sawyer and she was born in El Paso in 1887. Others put her birthplace as Cincinnati some seven years earlier and said she took her stage name from an ex-husband, Alvah Sawyer, whom she had married in 1902. Whatever the truth about Joan's background, by 1914 she had become one of the top "exhibition dancers" in New York City, cashing in on the dance craze sweeping the nation. She specialized in bringing a ladylike decorum to styles of dance that might otherwise have been considered racy.

Audiences swooned over her dreamy dark looks and the exotic outfits she wore in musicals staged at the Persian Garden, a nightclub atop the Winter Gardens on Broadway. Joan didn't just star in the revues, she also managed the Persian Garden—becoming one of the first women to run a New York nightclub—and in a move that outraged many patrons, she insisted on employing black musicians in her orchestra. Nonconformity was hardwired into her genes. She was also an ardent suffragist who used her high profile to advance the cause of women both at the ballot box and in the workplace. Besides starring regularly at her own club, Joan also tripped her talents just a few blocks farther along Broadway at another nightspot called the Jardin de Danse. Among the many dancers she bumped into at this venue was a much heralded newcomer named Rodolfo Guglielmi.

He was still playing second fiddle to Bonnie Glass, but Joan—no mean judge of dance flesh—saw instantly that Rodolfo's languid elegance was stealing the show and carrying the act. So when Bonnie suddenly announced her retirement to marry artist Ben Ali Haggin, Joan didn't hesitate. She jumped right in and grabbed Rodolfo before anyone else could get their hands on him.

The sultry Joan Sawyer and one of her dance partners

At this time the Argentinean tango was all the rage, and the elegant Miss Sawyer—a far superior dancer to Bonnie Glass—reasoned that a sensual Latin partner was all she needed to catapult her to the pinnacle of Broadway dance acts. And so it proved. Rodolfo's fiery exoticism offered a perfect counterpoint to Joan's demure gentility, and the couple became an immediate hit. Excited nightclubbers reckoned they might even rival Vernon and Irene Castle, the current king and queen of exhibition dancing, who were raking in thousands of dollars from shows and lessons. Unlike the Castles, though, the partnership between Joan and Rodolfo was purely professional. Joan's romantic interests lay outside of work—as Blanca de Saulles was finding out.

Jack protested that he and the alluring Miss Sawyer were acquaintances, nothing more. To prove his fidelity, one night after a dinner party he'd thrown for the Heckschers, he begged Blanca to spend the night with him at the West 57th Street apartment. She agreed on one condition: Jack had to swear that he had never "entertained" another woman at this apartment. Jack put his hand on his heart and summoned all the deities. Blanca believed him and headed for the bedroom. That same night, at about midnight, the telephone rang. Jack hurried to the phone and attempted to keep the conversation muted, but even from some distance away Blanca could hear a woman's voice. She also heard her husband say, "No, I can't tonight—not tonight."[16]

Blanca stewed in anger. When Jack put the phone down, she again challenged him, demanding to know the true nature of his relationship with Joan Sawyer. His response was brutal. "Do you think you are the only woman who has ever been in love with me?"[17] Blanca felt as if she had been punched in the face. And the final ignominy was not long in coming. One night, as she and Jack entered the Arrowhead Inn, a chic tavern in Washington Heights, a drunk female customer yelled out, "Who is that with Jack de Saulles?"[18] causing gales of laughter around the tables. Blanca realized that she had become the laughingstock of Manhattan. Something had to give.

If Jack knew of his wife's distress, it didn't show. He was too busy adding to his already extensive real estate portfolio. In May 1916 he acquired yet another home, this time in the "millionaire colony"[19] of Westbury on Long Island.

This was where the fabulously rich—the Morgans, the Belmonts, and the Whitneys—built their summer homes, vast porticoed mansions that stared down imperiously from inclines built to catch the breeze and offer fabulous views. Jack's house was more modest. Called The Box because of its square shape, it stood on eight heavily wooded acres and formed part of the sprawling Ladenburg estate. It also lay handily close to the Meadow Brook Country Club, home to the famous hounds and the oldest polo club in America, thus allowing Jack to indulge two of his great passions.

Blanca rarely visited. She preferred the hurly-burly of city life, where she could gossip with friends and, more important, where she could keep her ear close to the ground. It paid off. Close friend John Milholland—brother of Inez Boissevain, poster girl of the suffragist movement—took Blanca aside and whispered that Jack indeed had been sleeping with Joan Sawyer at the apartment all through the preceding winter. It was common knowledge, he said. Blanca's expression hardened. She had the confirmation she had always dreaded but long suspected. Jack's egregious lie formed the final act of betrayal. It was divorce now, and damn the consequences.

As discreetly as possible, Blanca set out to gather evidence of her husband's adultery. First she tackled his valet, Julius Hadamek. The diminutive Austrian, displaying the best instincts of his calling, refused to say a word, much to Blanca's annoyance. Unpicking the seams of this marriage, she realized, would require a much broader approach and probably a lot more money. A friend suggested she contact the Diamond Detective Agency, a discreet Fifth Avenue firm that specialized in obtaining divorce evidence for high-society couples. The detectives began to ask around, and soon their questions led them to Joan Sawyer's dancing partner, Rodolfo Guglielmi.

In all likelihood it was Blanca herself who steered the detective agency in Rodolfo's direction. Since their first meeting she and the young dancer had met often, usually in some after-hours cabaret when he was winding down from his nightly performance. Blanca needed to be ultracareful. If news of these secret assignations filtered back to her husband's lover, it could be disastrous. For now, though, she was ready to run that risk in order to draw Rodolfo into her web. She began slowly, emphasizing their similarities. There was the kinship of a shared language—Guglielmi was able to speak Spanish—both were in their early twenties, and both were aliens in a foreign country. Rodolfo sat hypnotized, scarcely believing his good fortune. Blanca fulfilled all of his girl-woman fantasies: She was young, beautiful, and already the mother of a boy. For a young man raised in the Catholic faith, with deeply traditional views of womanhood, she was perfection in human form. As for Blanca, she had acquired far more than a sympathetic ear for her outpourings of domestic abuse and duplicity; she had enlisted an invaluable ally in the battle to rid herself of an unwanted husband. Because, as Blanca suspected, her adoring admirer had the inside track on Jack de Saulles's highly colorful private life.

The two men first crossed paths in January 1916 when Rodolfo was still partnering Bonnie Glass. Jack's reputation as a hell-raiser was already the talk of Broadway, and, when Rodolfo graduated to the role of Joan Sawyer's dance partner, he quickly discovered that she and de Saulles were hitting the sack together, and had been for some time. Rodolfo had even attended wild parties at Jack's apartment, giving him a chance to witness the riotous relationship firsthand. Now Blanca had come to him for help. And when she fixed Rodolfo with that yearning expression, he was helpless. Common sense and self-preservation were cast to the wind. Without regard for his own future, he agreed to provide the evidence that would draw a line under Blanca's marriage.

Many have wondered if Blanca and Rodolfo became lovers at this time. No concrete evidence suggests that they did, and the balance of probabilities supports this view. Blanca was a hard-nosed negotiator and sharp as a tack. She knew she was playing a dangerous game. If she gave herself to the sensual Italian, not only was she risking a countersuit of adultery, but she would have had to contend with the possibility that, having once bedded her, Guglielmi would disappear without delivering the goods she so desperately needed. So, it is far more likely that Blanca dangled the carrot of postdivorce intimacy before her gullible admirer, promising that, once the divorce was signed and sealed, she would be his and his alone.

Rodolfo swallowed the bait. In a lengthy interview with the detective agency, he passed along every grubby detail of the affair between Jack and Joan. Once the agency's dossier was complete, they put Blanca in touch with the law firm of Prince & Nathan, longtime specialists in the sexual antics of the affluent and the influential. On July 5, Blanca delivered advance notice of her intentions by taking her belongings from The Box and moving a few miles north to the village of Roslyn, where she had rented a cottage called Crossways. Two weeks later, on advice of counsel, she left Crossways and went into hiding. On July 27, with their client safely out of sight, Prince & Nathan filed suit for divorce, claiming that Jack had committed adultery with two women.

News of the split caused a sensation. Papers as far away as California carried the story. South American Beauty Demands Her Freedom[20] cried the *Los Angeles Times.* Back in New York, hordes of journalists laid siege to Jack's apartment. His only comment was: "It is a most unfortunate affair,"[21] but he warned his estranged wife that he would "fight her in every court in the country."[22]

In the meantime: Where was Blanca? Reporters wanted to know. One possible answer to that tantalizing question was provided by dinner guests at the Majestic Hotel on West 72nd Street, who alternated glances at press photos of Mrs. de Saulles with sly peeks at the beautiful woman eating alone in the dining room. A call to the press did the rest. In short order reporters beseiged the front desk. The check-in clerk confirmed that a "Mrs. John Smythe" had checked in on July 20, that she did indeed bear a striking resemblance to the elusive Mrs. de Saulles, and that, yes, it was true that "Mrs. Smythe" had removed her wedding ring. Within days of Blanca taking up residence at the Majestic, she was joined by her sister. That Amalia had journeyed from Chile to be with Blanca suggests that Blanca's decision to go into hiding had been no spur-of-the-moment decision, but rather a carefully planned exercise.

But others were also making plans. And what neither sister realized was that more than just inquisitive diners were monitoring their every movement at the Majestic. Jack had made good on his threat to torpedo Blanca's suit by hiring a private detective, Harry V. Dougherty, to investigate persistent rumors that his estranged wife had been sleeping with some young Italian stud. Dougherty stationed a band of operatives at the Majestic, keeping Blanca's room under round-the-clock surveillance. At the same time another team was staking out Guglielmi's residence on West 57th Street, just two blocks from where de Saulles lived. Both teams came up empty-handed. If Blanca was conducting an affair with Rodolfo, both parties were displaying remarkable levels of discretion.

The divorce suit was fast-tracked. And the provisional hearing, held before Referee Phoenix Ingraham, was packed with explosive evidence, much of it provided by Rodolfo Guglielmi. He testified that he and another woman had once attended a dinner party at Joan Sawyer's apartment at which Jack was also a guest. The hostess and Jack had seemed on the coziest of terms. "He called her Joan, and she called him Jack and dear. He called her sweetheart."[23] Rodolfo told the court that he and Joan had first worked together in March 1916 at Keith's Theatre in Washington, DC, and on this same visit they had danced before President Wilson. Afterward, instead of spending the night in Washington, the performers returned to New York by train. At Penn Station, Rodolfo and Joan caught a cab to Times Square, where Rodolfo alighted, telling the driver to take Joan to de Saulles's apartment, where he would pick her up the following day at 8:45 a.m. The next morning, on schedule, Rodolfo arrived to collect Joan. As she got into the car, Rodolfo saw Jack in pajamas at his apartment window. "He waved at Miss Sawyer, and she waved at him as we rode off."[24]

Another time, said Rodolfo, he and Joan worked together for a week in Providence, Rhode Island, dancing at the Albee Theatre. "I saw Mr. de Saulles in Providence at the Hotel Narragansett, closing night. . . . After a party in her honor, [Joan Sawyer] and Mr. de Saulles retired to her room upstairs. Her room had one large bed."[25] The next day they all returned on the same train to New York. "Mr. de Saulles and Miss Sawyer shared a drawing room on the train. I had an upper berth in the same car, opposite their drawing room."[26] From his vantage point he was able to spot a douche in Joan Sawyer's traveling bag.

"How did you come to be looking through her dressing case on the train?"[27] asked Jack's lawyer, Lyttleton Fox.

"She just opened it in front of me."[28]

When Fox pressed Rodolfo on whether he thought he was doing an ill turn to his dancing partner, he bizarrely replied, "No, I don't think so."[29]

"Are your relations friendly with Miss Sawyer?"

"They were friendly the last time I saw her; I don't know now. I volunteered to testify here."

"For what reason?"

"I have a special reason, but if you don't mind I won't go over the matter"[30] was Rodolfo's mysterious response.

Even more mysteriously, Fox didn't press him on the point. This string of puzzling answers, however, does reveal the childlike naivety that would hallmark Guglielmi's lifelong dealings with the opposite sex. In the months prior to the divorce hearing, he had been earning $240 a week dancing with Joan Sawyer ($4,100 in today's dollars); for an immigrant barely two years off the boat it was a fortune, yet he was prepared to sacrifice it all to save a perceived damsel in distress. Playing the knight in shining armor might have done wonders for his self-esteem, but it made him an easy target for the strong-willed women to whom he was irresistibly drawn. He may have seen beleaguered damsels, but all they saw was some credulous dupe who could be manipulated like modeling clay.

Rodolfo wasn't the only witness, though. The famously discreet Julius Hadamek, testifying under subpoena, admitted through gritted teeth that he had seen Miss Sawyer at his employer's apartment many times during April, May, and June of 1916 "and that she remained there overnight, sleeping in defendant's bedroom, which contained but one bed"[31] and in which he later found hairpins. Annie Curtis, Miss Sawyer's cook, told of seeing her employer and Jack kissing passionately on several occasions.

Blanca's own appearance on the stand was brief, merely to confirm that she had not condoned any of the acts of which she was complaining. Otherwise, she gave no direct evidence against her husband. Important though the testimony of Hadamek and Curtis had been, it was Rodolfo who provided the knockout blows that allowed Supreme Court Justice John M. Tierney to make a provisional award on August 14, pending further testimony, of three hundred dollars monthly alimony to Blanca. He also ordered that Jack pay Blanca's legal fees of one thousand dollars.

Earlier that month Blanca had taken refuge with the Igleharts, some friends who also lived on Long Island. While there, her dependable sister Amalia and her brother, Guillermo, came to lend moral support. They reportedly found her laid up with "nervous prostration"[32] and begged her to return with them to Chile.

"No," said Blanca defiantly. "I won't leave the boy."[33]

The reality was rather different.

On August 26, right in the middle of divorce negotiations, Blanca, accompanied by her brother and sister, boarded the SS *St. Paul*, bound for Liverpool. The plan, after a stopover in London, called for traveling to Scotland, where Guillermo had a shooting box for the season. This was a bizarre decision for two reasons. First, the hostilities in Europe showed no signs of abating,[34] and while the *St. Paul*, unlike the *Lusitania*, flew the American flag, there was still a very present danger of German U-boat activity in the North Atlantic. The second curiosity was purely domestic. For some reason, Blanca chose to leave Jack Jr. at Crossways in the care of Anna Mooney, even though, just recently, antagonism had been mounting between Blanca and the nursemaid.

According to Blanca, Mooney's attitude had undergone a recent and profound change. She seemed far more proprietary in her attitude toward

Jack Jr., almost as if "the child belonged to her."[35] Blanca suspected that Jack somehow had orchestrated this change to sabotage Blanca's relationship with the boy. Just before leaving for Europe, Blanca poured out her heart in a string of letters to her former servant Ethel O'Neill (née Whitesides), complaining about "the perfectly horrible nightmare I have been going through."[36] Then she set sail.

While Blanca was soaking up the Highland hospitality in Scotland, Jack's sense of injustice began to fester. Despite a frustrating lack of hard evidence, gut instinct told him that Blanca and Rodolfo had been a hell of a lot more than just dancing partners, and the thought of some greasy gigolo—a former taxi dancer, no less—sharing a bed with his wife proved more than this Yale blueblood could stomach. As jealousy gnawed away at his innards, he began to scheme.

SEVEN

"Revenge Should Have No Bounds"

On the morning of September 5, 1916, at about half past seven, a task force of NYPD officers swooped in on an apartment at 909 Seventh Avenue, just up the street from Carnegie Hall. The raid, led by Assistant District Attorney James E. Smith, was supposedly part of an investigation into two vice squad detectives, William Enright and David Foley, who were suspected of offering protection to brothels in return for a weekly kickback.

Such accusations were commonplace in the early twentieth century. This was the era of the so-called "millionaire cops," when a string of crooked NYPD officers banked fortunes from shaking down the very criminals they were supposed to catch. The most egregious of these was Lieutenant Charles Becker. For years the bluff and hearty Becker lorded over Manhattan's red-light Tenderloin District—an area that consisted of portions of Chelsea, the Flatiron District, Hell's Kitchen, and the Theater District—raking in thousands of dollars a month in bribes. But his sleazy reign finally hit the buffers in 1912 when he was convicted of ordering the murder of Herman Rosenthal, a small-time bookmaker who was threatening to blow the whistle on Becker's corrupt empire.

Becker was undoubtedly crooked, but whether he arranged the shooting death of Rosenthal remains open to doubt. At the time, mounting unease over the conviction sparked numerous calls for a reprieve, but newly elected New York governor Charles Whitman—the very prosecutor who had put Becker on death row—was in no mood to see his own work undermined, and he declined to exercise clemency. Becker died in the electric chair at Sing Sing on July 30, 1915.

On this morning, however, when the officers—plus a gang of handpicked reporters—burst into the Seventh Avenue apartment, instead of the expected string of hookers and their red-faced clients the only people present were a fifty-year-old gray-haired lady named Georgia Thym and a young male companion who looked scared out of his wits. Assistant DA Smith stepped into the room and beamed, "Hello, Rodolfo."

"Rodolfo hasn't been here since last May,"[1] the young man mumbled.

Smith gave him a disbelieving look and told him to try again.

Utterly crestfallen, Guglielmi caved in and admitted his identity. He and Thym were arrested and hauled off to the district attorney's office on suspicion of running a brothel that paid protection money to the police.

The next day's newspapers gloated over Guglielmi's humiliation, denigrating him as "a bogus count or marquis."[2] According to District Attorney Edward Swann, Guglielmi made statements "which, if true, are of immense importance in this investigation."[3] He described the young man as "a handsome fellow, about twenty years, [who] wears corsets and a wrist watch. He was often seen dancing in well-known hotels and tango parlors with Joan Sawyer and Bonnie Glass."[4] The reference to the corset was a clumsy slur on Rodolfo's sexuality; so too was the comment about the wristwatch. In 1916 the chunky pocket hunter was the preferred choice for "real" men while the more slender wristwatch was still viewed with suspicion in some quarters.

Surrounded by pressmen, Swann held up visiting cards found in the prisoner's possession. These proclaimed him to be the "Marchese Guglielmo Roma," an affectation, said Swann, adopted by Guglielmi "to please the ladies."[5] The district attorney said he was investigating reports of widespread blackmail involving rich people "on the fringes of New York society."[6] He claimed that 909 Seventh Avenue had hosted "many vicious parties,"[7] at which prominent members of society had been inveigled into compromising situations with young women and then blackmailed. It had been a sophisticated operation, said Swann; three adjoining houses opposite Carnegie Hall were used as brothels. In the event of a police raid on any one of them, the occupants could flee upstairs and escape across the roof to avoid being traced. The way Swann told it, he had single-handedly wrapped up an entire white slavery ring. When pressed, however, he reluctantly conceded that the raid failed to provide the conclusive proof that he was seeking of New York's "gilded vice."[8]

While Rodolfo was in custody at the DA's office, he asked to make a phone call. In the presence of surprised investigators, he rang no less a personage than the Deputy Police Commissioner Frank A. Lord, saying, "I'm in trouble, Frank. I wish you would come down here and help me."[9] Lord hung up immediately, according to Swann.

Journalistic ears pricked up. How come some foreign nightclub dancer knew the deputy commish? And why had Lord been so quick to hang up?

Smelling a good story, reporters soon tracked down Lord to the Prince George, an elegant hotel on East 28th Street. The deputy commissioner was cagey. After much spluttering he grudgingly admitted knowing Rodolfo but couldn't recall where they had first met. Philadelphia, Rodolfo told the police; he and Joan Sawyer had dined with Lord in the domino room of the Café L'Aiglon when Lord had taken an extended vacation from his duties. Lord flatly denied this. "I would find it quite difficult to remain away from New York for three weeks, as this fellow charges."[10] His only recollection of Rodolfo had been as Miss Sawyer's dancing partner, and he professed astonishment that this semistranger had called him to ask for assistance. "I told him I was unable to help him."[11]

An already peculiar case now took another puzzling twist. Although neither Rodolfo nor Mrs. Thym was charged with running a brothel or any other vice offense or blackmail, they were held as "material witnesses"[12] in the ongoing investigation against Enright and Foley. Judge Otto Rosalsky set bail in the jaw-dropping sum of ten thousand dollars. As neither prisoner had a prayer of raising this kind of money, it meant a trip to the gloomy Tombs prison. Rodolfo was frantic. If convicted of any crime that came under the catchall phrase of "moral turpitude," he ran the risk of losing his immigration status and being deported. His dream of a life in America would come crashing down. After two anxious days behind bars, his bail was lowered to the more reasonable, though still high, sum of fifteen hundred dollars, and he was set free. How he was able to secure such a sum has sparked wild speculation. Some have claimed, without a jot of proof, that Blanca was the anonymous benefactor; other, equally unsubstantiated claims point to Mae Murray.[13]

Quite why the Seventh Avenue apartment should be raided on such flimsy evidence initially perplexed reporters, but whispers suggested that the operation had been engineered by none other than Jack de Saulles. The official police version stated that they had been tipped off by "a well-to-do businessman who said he had been victimized."[14] This could well be de Saulles. But it does not begin to explain the most puzzling aspect of this incident: What was Rodolfo doing at the apartment at half past seven in the morning? If the apartment did double as a cathouse and he'd gone to procure the services of a prostitute, then he was out of luck. And if that was the case, why spend the night? Unless, of course, he really did have some dubious dealings with the enigmatic Georgia Thym? Stranger still: If Jack's was the hidden hand behind this operation, how did he know that Rodolfo would be present when police raided the place?

Much the likeliest scenario is that Jack had Rodolfo shadowed—probably by one of Dougherty's hirelings—and then all it took was a phone call to a police contact to exact his revenge. This would also explain why Assistant DA Smith, who had never before set eyes on Rodolfo, was able to address the terrified young man by name when he entered the apartment. De Saulles might have come up short in gathering evidence to prove that Blanca had slept with Rodolfo, but he was determined to make the phony marchese pay a terrible price for crossing him.

It worked. Rodolfo's reputation was ruined. He had been arrested at an alleged brothel, spent time in jail, and now had a permanent police record. Overnight, he became a showbiz untouchable, a pariah. He had already been dumped by Joan Sawyer—understandably miffed at having her sex life paraded in public, courtesy of her perfidious dance partner—and, although all charges against Rodolfo were dropped quietly in mid-September, the perception endured that he was somehow mixed up in white slavery and blackmail. It was a stain on his character that would never fade. And there were wider ramifications. All this talk of vice and white slavery tolled the death knell for those afternoon tea dances where Rodolfo had performed and squired wealthy female patrons. It was guilt by association. Within a year *thé dansants* and the exhibition dance craze had twirled into show business history.

Rodolfo was in a daze, stupefied as his world collapsed around him. Not just dancing but films, too. Like millions of others he had caught the motion pictures bug. Stars of the fledgling industry like Charlie Chaplin were earning fabulous salaries—as much as ten thousand dollars a week—and Rodolfo desperately wanted to join the party. All summer long, he'd hung around the Fifth Avenue studio of the Famous Players-Lasky Motion Picture Company, which later became Paramount, scrabbling for any kind of casual work.

And his persistence had paid off. He landed a bit part in *The Quest of Life,* starring the dance team of Maurice and Florence Walton. Although an uncredited extra, Rodolfo is plainly identifiable, and most film historians count this his first confirmed appearance. Unfortunately for Rodolfo the movie came out barely two weeks after his arrest. The timing couldn't have been worse. More isolated than ever, he had reached rock bottom. With Blanca enjoying the Scottish shooting season and with dancing opportunities all dried up, he could only hunker down and await her return to America.

That happy day came on November 4, when the SS *Baltic* docked at New York. Also aboard were Amalia, Guillermo, his twenty-three-year-old wife, Maria, and their infant daughter, Maria. When Anna Mooney walked down the gangway, she left Blanca's employ forever and went to work for Jack instead. He knew how fond his son was of Boobie, and Blanca always suspected that he had deliberately hired Mooney to drive a deeper wedge between her and Jack Jr.

Blanca's legal team gave her an update on the divorce proceedings. As she studied the papers, she recalled that the family home on East 78th Street had been bought with her money, and that Jack said he later sold the property for $5,500. But documentation revealed that Jack had disposed of the property through his secretary, Stephen S. Tuthill, for $14,500. Blanca demanded the balance of $9,000. Yet her lawyers oddly dissuaded her from pursuing this perfectly justified claim on grounds that it might "disturb"[15] the divorce negotiations. Nor could such a strange directive be blamed on poor advice because Blanca's legal team had brought in Max D. Steuer, nicknamed "The Magician," to plead her case before the judge.

Steuer was arguably the top civil attorney on the East Coast, and he didn't come cheap. On one occasion a client came to Steuer with a problem and didn't quibble at Steuer's demand for a ten-thousand-dollar retainer. When the animated client launched into details of the case, Steuer cut him off sharply, reminding him about the fee. Undeterred, the client insisted that the funds would be forthcoming, but Steuer was adamant, snapping, "I can't even think about the case until I've had the money!"[16]

Nowadays little remembered, Steuer was a legal titan of the early twentieth century. A story—possibly apocryphal—goes that when Chase National Bank found itself threatened with a serious lawsuit, one that threatened the company's very existence, an anxious board of directors gathered together and the chairman said, "Gentlemen, we must have the best lawyer in the world. I am going to pass out twelve cards, and I want each director to think of the man he believes to be the world's best lawyer and write that lawyer's name on the back of the card."[17] When the cards were collected and given to the chairman, he spread them out on the table in front of him: On every one of the cards was written "Max Steuer."

After two secret hearings, neither of which Jack attended, the divorce decree was issued. The court found that de Saulles had misconducted himself with "a woman not his wife."[18] The decree also made references to adultery with another woman (Mae Murray's was the most oft-whispered name on the grapevine). The decree, double the usual length, with five pages devoted to the custody issue, ordered that Jack Jr. remain in America until the end of the war. Until then, Jack would have custody of the boy for five months and Blanca seven, on an alternating monthly basis.

After the cessation of hostilities, Blanca would have the boy from October to May, during which time she could take him abroad, provided that she returned him to the United States by June 1. When the boy reached the age of eight, Jack would assume entire control over his son's education, and Blanca's custody rights would be restricted to July through September, except for three-hour periods during the rest of the year, arranged in such a way as to not interfere with his schooling. Tacked onto the end of the decree came a paragraph stating that if Blanca remarried her three-hundred-dollar monthly alimony would be cut in half.

The published terms of the decree stunned the legal community. At the time, the guilty party in a divorce action usually surrendered most if not all custody rights, and yet here the courts had bent over backward to accommodate a proven adulterer. So why did such a tough negotiator as Max Steuer agree to a 7–5 split on custody? Despite Blanca's subsequent claims of penury, funds weren't an issue when it came to the child's upbringing, so it is evident that some other factor informed Steuer's atypical concession. One possible reason—and the only theory that makes sense—is that the opposing legal team dug up something shadowy in Blanca's background.

For while no one doubted that Jack was the arch villain in the breakup, some wondered if Blanca's antecedents weren't quite as lily-white as painted in the press. The rumors refused to die down. Later, Blanca's lawyers would twice be forced to deny publicly that her name had been "mentioned in connection with a cabaret dancer in a counter suit that was alleged to have been threatened by De Saulles."[19] As we have seen, Jack was convinced that Blanca and Rodolfo had slept together, and quite possibly there was a meeting between the two that hinted at some kind of intimacy. Rather than allow any suspicion of scandal to sully her name—especially because she was the more innocent party—Blanca followed Steuer's advice and yielded to the other side's demands. The decree was issued on December 23.[20]

And so, as 1916 drew to a close, the once glittering marriage of Jack and Blanca de Saulles officially reached its shabby conclusion. Jack went back to renovating The Box—spending thousands in the process—while Blanca picked up the broken pieces of her life in Manhattan.

To help her through this difficult period, she hired a new servant. Blanca had met Jean Mallock in London, where she served as nursemaid to the Chilean minister to Britain. The thirty-seven-year-old Scottish woman had jumped at the opportunity when Blanca offered her the job of looking after Jack Jr. in New York. On December 18, Miss Mallock cleared immigration at Ellis Island and reported immediately to the Hotel Gotham on Fifth Avenue, where her new mistress was staying while renovations were being carried out at Crossways. Mallock joined a household weighed down with depression. Blanca's ordeal at the hands of the American justice system had left her feeling embittered and trapped, condemned by world events to live in a land for which she had no empathy and to which she had few ties apart from her son.

Although the full details of the divorce suit remain tantalizingly elusive—the files are not due to be unsealed until 2017—we know that in her eyes she was victimized by prejudice, more sinned against than sinning. For years the bedroom escapades of her husband, a drunken libertine, had titillated millions of newspaper readers, and yet he had emerged almost unscathed from the divorce. How much of this, Blanca wondered, was due to her nationality? Would the courts have treated her so harshly had she been American? She doubted it. Steuer had warned her that in divorce cases, American courts traditionally favored homegrown plaintiffs, especially where children were involved. But Blanca had ignored that warning and swanned off to Scotland during a critical phase of the divorce settlement. It had cost her dearly.

Guglielmi was puzzled. He knew Blanca had returned and was living on Long Island, yet every attempt to make contact with her resulted in disappointment. Letters went unanswered, telephone calls, too. Gradually and grudgingly, the realization dawned on him that his idealized Madonna-like inamorata wanted nothing to do with him. Having served his purpose, he was now thrown to the wolves.

It was a bitter pill to swallow, and the hurt was double-edged. Not only had he been duped by the woman he loved—and who he thought loved him—but three years after coming to America he was once again penniless. He had had a few uncredited parts in minor films that paid five dollars a day—but nothing to replace the kind of money he had lost since being fired by Joan Sawyer. As he exchanged hard-luck stories with other extras on the film set, however, one subject kept cropping up in their conversations: Los Angeles.

With reliable sunshine that allowed for longer shooting days, the City of Angels was just beginning to overtake New York as the movie-making capital of America. Guglielmi mused over whether to join the exodus.

Although contemporary popular taste dictated that romantic leads were generally blond, square-jawed, All-American types, Rodolfo suspected that his brooding, saturnine looks would be perfect for those directors looking to cast "heavies" in their movies. But he had no contacts on the West Coast. What few roots he had lay here in New York, so he stayed put, resolving to tough it out, find work as a dancer, and maybe win back the hand of the most beautiful woman he had ever seen.

Blanca, on the other hand, didn't spare a thought for the savior who had changed her life so radically. Since returning to the refurbished Crossways, her mind had been consumed by the custody issue, which now escalated into full-scale domestic warfare. The boy was being batted to and fro like a shuttlecock and picking up some pretty undesirable personality traits along the way. For instance, Blanca noticed that whenever the lad returned to her custody he was recalcitrant and fractious, newfound idiosyncrasies that she blamed on Anna Mooney. Once, when the boy came home from staying with his father, he allegedly told his mother: "Boobie said that she loved me more than you [do]."[21] Another time, he threw himself on the floor, kicking and screaming, for no apparent reason. After calming down, he announced: "Boobie told me that I must be a bad boy when I'm with you."[22]

Just about the only consolation for Blanca during this painful period was that her name finally had disappeared from the newspapers. Good old "Broadway Jack," on the other hand, was still bagging headlines, and, if the gossip columns were to be believed, it wouldn't be long before Blanca had a new Mrs. de Saulles to contend with.

Ruth Shepley was a twenty-five-year-old blonde actress, who, in early 1917, was playing the part of Grace Tyler in the stage comedy *The Boomerang*. The show had been a hit on Broadway eighteen months earlier and was now touring the country on an extended run. On March 14, Miss Shepley—"a vision to behold"[23]—was besieged at Powers' Theater in Chicago by local reporters following up on a hot story on the wires. A New York tabloid had fired off a cable to one Chicago newspaper: "Please ask Ruth Shepley if she will marry Jack De Saulles in the fall?" When queried, Ruth was at first evasive, then decided to laugh it off. "It is a unique proposal," she said. "I have never been proposed to in that manner before. May I have that telegram? I shall keep it to my dying day."[24]

If news of this development filtered through to Blanca it must have made her shudder. Her worst fears were coming true. Jack Jr. was already mentioning his father's latest paramour. Apparently, after returning from a visit to The

Box, Jack Jr. said that his father told him he was going to have "two mothers," the second being Ruth Shepley. "Daddy says she will love me as much as you do."[25] Blanca felt more marginalized than ever.

While Blanca's situation roiled, events on the world stage had taken a pivotal turn. In January 1917, British Naval Intelligence intercepted a coded telegram sent by the German foreign secretary, Arthur Zimmerman, to his country's ambassador in Mexico, Heinrich von Eckardt. When the code breakers in the Admiralty's Room 40 decrypted the message, they could scarcely believe their eyes. In it, Zimmerman revealed Germany's intention to wage unrestricted submarine war on any ship from any country starting on February 1.

As such action would undoubtedly result in drawing neutral America into the conflict, Zimmerman proposed an alliance with Mexico against the United States. To sweeten the deal, the German foreign secretary promised to cede New Mexico, Texas, and Arizona back to Mexico in the event of a successful invasion. The "Zimmerman Telegram," as it became known, caused diplomatic outrage, especially when, as forecast, German U-boats began laying waste to shipping in the North Atlantic regardless of what flag they were flying. On April 6, after seven American ships had been sent to the bottom, Congress finally declared war on Germany.

Five days later, Jack was sworn in as a special deputy mechanic at the port of New York by his old friend Dudley Malone. At age thirty-eight, Jack was too old for the draft—initially restricted to men between ages nineteen and twenty-five—and he was delegated to inspect several German and Austrian ships that had been interned in New York harbor. His duties were far from onerous. They left him plenty of time to oversee the construction of his own polo field at The Box—an obsession with him—and also to exhibit his string of polo ponies. On April 19 his gray mare, Vinilla, won second prize at the Brooklyn Horse Show. Seven days later she went one better at the New York Spring Horse Show, an annual event held at Durland's Academy on the Grand Circle in Central Park.

To judge from the favorable press coverage, Jack had sailed through the divorce action with his name and reputation if not fully intact, then largely unsullied. At the same time, his real estate business was thriving on news that he and Heckscher had leased twenty thousand square feet of space in the new sixteen-story Heckscher Building at 244 Madison Avenue to the

National Aniline and Chemical Company. The hefty commissions that Jack earned on these deals were plowed back into improving the polo facilities at The Box and building a child's playground, complete with merry-go-round and swings, for when Jack Jr. came to visit.

The harsh New York winter of 1916–17 saw Rodolfo Guglielmi at his lowest ebb. Job opportunities had dried to a trickle, he was flat broke, and Blanca, by her continuing silence, had banished all hopes of reconciliation. Once again he began to eye the West Coast. His chance to make the big break came in April 1917 when he auditioned for a musical comedy called *The Masked Model.* The producer, John Cort, thought the young man showed promise and offered him a place in the chorus. Rodolfo jumped at the chance.

The weekly paycheck of seventy-five dollars might have represented a fraction of what he had once earned with Joan Sawyer, but it was a fortune compared to the pittance he had been scraping by on for the past six months. On April 28, the show finished its run at the Duquesne Theater in Pittsburgh, and then, boasting "The Snappiest Chorus in Many Moons,"[26] it headed west with stopovers at Iowa City, Omaha, and Denver en route to San Francisco. After a three-night run in Salt Lake City, which ended on May 18, for some reason Rodolfo disappeared from the cast.

Accounts vary as to why this happened. Some claim that the show folded—unlikely since the musical opened at the Mason Opera House in Los Angeles on June 18. Others suggest that Rodolfo was fired in a dispute over pay. Whatever the reason, the spring of 1917 found the young Italian in California. By June 1 he was living at 7364 Sunset Boulevard, Hollywood, the address shown on the American draft exemption card that excused him from war service on grounds of being an alien. An alien, maybe, but he couldn't have felt more at home. He was enjoying a Mediterranean climate—the air was filled with the scent of orange blossoms and olive groves stretched for miles—and at long last he was ready to apply himself to his greatest ambition: breaking into motion pictures.

Two and a half thousand miles away, on Long Island, Blanca's resentment was turning septic. She felt she had been hoodwinked in the divorce negotiations that had been so heavily skewed in favor of her unfaithful ex-husband. In particular, she detested the onerous travel restrictions that the courts had imposed on Jack Jr., and she filed an application with the County Clerk's Office to have these restrictions rescinded. Her affidavit stated that she was "possessed of great wealth," and she offered to charter a steamship, if necessary, to provide the boy with safe conduct. "It is an extremely painful situation in which to be placed," she said. "I must either give up my child and let him remain here, or give up my mother and friends in Chile. I have but few friends here, and my mother is aged and anxious to see my son. If my application is denied I am certain it will impair my health."[27] It was a well-reasoned argument, and yet, in a mysterious turn of events, the application was withdrawn the same day it was submitted.

Press reports hinted that the change of heart had resulted from rumors that the couple was discussing a reconciliation, with friends close to both parties saying that only pride was keeping them apart and that "if anyone ever brings them together it will be Baby De Saulles."[28] Nothing could have been further from the truth. Blanca's bitterness over the custody issue was playing havoc with her mental state. An air of unreality now took hold of her, driven by a fear that Jack, having won in court already, now was winning the battle for the heart of their son. Conveniently shoved into some dark recess at the back of her mind was the fact that twice she had chosen to abandon Jack Jr. for extended periods of time while she traveled overseas. The wrench hadn't troubled her then. But the divorce changed all that. In the parlance of her homeland, gaining permanent custody of her son now became a *punto de honor* (point of honor).

But there were diversions. On June 30, Jack wrote a letter to Blanca in which he complained about Nurse Mallock's influence on their son. He accused her of being anti-American and of having frequently criticized Chile in the presence of other servants. She was, he said, "solely in favor of England and its flag."[29] Six days later Blanca heeded Jack's advice and fired the nurse. Judging from Miss Mallock's furious reaction—and sharp-tongued antipathy toward both Jack and Blanca—there was more to her dismissal than meets the eye.

In her stead, Blanca hired a young woman from France named Suzanne Monteau to look after Jack Jr. It proved to be an inspired choice. In the tumultuous times that lay ahead, Suzanne would prove to be a loyal servant to Blanca, which was just as well because she and Jack were wrangling harder than ever over custody. In June, while Blanca perspired in Manhattan waiting for Crossways to be made ready for her occupation, she received another letter from Jack. As The Box was well provided with pets and pleasures for the boy, he wrote, it would be a shame to keep him in town during the steamy month of July, and he offered Blanca the use of The Box for that month while she had the child. Blanca turned him down flat. Jack made a counter-offer: How about if he kept the boy until she was settled in at Crossways? That was more agreeable to Blanca, and Jack Jr. went to stay with his father. He remained there through all of June. On July 3, Blanca moved back into Crossways, and that same day Jack Jr. was returned to her custody.

By the opulent standards of its neighbors, Crossways was a low-key, English-style bungalow painted white, set on three acres, and surrounded by a profusion of trees, dwarf evergreens, and flowering plants and fountains. A high redbrick wall with two sturdy oak gates encircled the whole estate. Owned by Walter Watson, the property had an ill-starred history. Locals called it "The House of Trouble"[30] because of its checkered past. It had once been home to society belle Mary Jane Tatum, the wife of a wealthy cotton broker, and a lady whose boudoir indiscretions in 1915 entertained millions of newspaper readers. Before that at Crossways, on January 13, 1914, a Japanese butler, Sukezi Namina, had shot and killed a married woman named Tessa Simmons, who spurned his attentions, before turning the gun on himself.

Shortly after moving back into Crossways, Blanca received a letter from Jack in which he said that since Jack Jr. had been so happy at The Box, with his favorite pony, pet dog, and, of course, the playground, it seemed churlish to remove him from this environment. If Blanca wished their son to avail himself of these facilities, he [Jack Sr.] would vacate The Box so that Blanca and their son might enjoy it without him being there. Blanca gave this proposal some consideration. While she had no objection to her son enjoying the superior amenities on offer at The Box, she resisted breaking the terms of the original court agreement, fearful of a possible disadvantageous outcome. Accordingly, she declined. Jack countered with a compromise. What if Jack Jr. came over each day for a couple hours and returned that same evening? Blanca began to bend. But before giving her final consent, she wanted clarification. Under the court stipulation, she was scheduled to have custody for all of July, and she felt that Jack owed her three days' custody to make up for the time she had lost at the beginning of the month. Jack protested that those three days had been for the boy's benefit, to get him out of sweltering Manhattan for a few days at the height of summer, but Blanca refused to see it that way. She had lost three precious days with her son, and she wanted them back.

Finally, in exasperation, Jack agreed in writing that Blanca could retain custody for three extra days at the beginning of August to make up for any perceived shortfall in July. Blanca phoned Jack to give her agreement to this understanding.

Following this, each afternoon throughout July, at three o'clock, an automobile would arrive to pick up Jack Jr. and take him to The Box. There, the youngster twirled on the merry-go-round or played on the swing, surrounded by his favorite pets, before returning to his mother that same day at 6:00 p.m. It seemed a generous enough arrangement, one that had the boy's best interests at heart, but as the days passed Blanca's paranoia grabbed hold. She feared that the delights on offer at The Box were seducing Jack Jr. away from her. Worse still, she feared that Jack was using this opportunity to poison her son's mind against her. Stoking her foul mood was a merciless heat wave that pushed the mercury into the nineties. She had always hated hot weather, and as the thermometer soared so did her temper.

On August 3 it finally boiled over.

EIGHT

"It Had to Be Done"

August 3, 1917

The day started much like any other. At eight o'clock one of the three maids woke Jack Jr., dressed him, and took him downstairs, where another servant had prepared his breakfast. After this the youngster went outside to play in the blazing sunshine. Slightly less than an hour later, Blanca rose and took a cold shower to combat the heat. After breakfast, she went into the garden to check on her son. A short while later a maid ran out to say that Mr. de Saulles was on the phone. Blanca took the call. Jack asked for a favor: His father and sister were coming over that evening and would love to see Jack Jr.; could he send a car over that afternoon to pick him up? According to Blanca, he gave his solemn promise that, after the brief visit, Jack Jr. would return that same evening. After some hesitation, Blanca agreed to the arrangement.

But over the course of the day, she had second thoughts. Under the terms of the court settlement, Jack was entitled to custody from August 1, but, because Blanca hadn't taken custody of their son until July 6, by her reckoning she had the right to keep him three more days, until August 6. Blanca thought she had been robbed, and the more she brooded on this perceived theft, the more peevish she became.

Later that morning she used the phone again, this time to call the local police station. Constable Leonard Thorne dealt with Blanca's agitated claim that someone had attempted to break into her garage the previous day. She demanded that he come to investigate right away. Deciding that the day-old incident didn't sound that urgent—nothing had been taken—Thorne excused himself on the grounds that he was tied up for the rest of the day, but he did promise to call on Blanca the following morning. This setback, coupled with the enervating heat, did nothing to lighten Blanca's darkening mood.

Jack de Saulles had no such worries, either about his domestic situation or the weather. Late morning found him on Sixth Avenue in broiling Midtown Manhattan for a lunch date at Sherry's restaurant, one of the Four Hundred's favorite watering holes. This was where, in 1905, insurance-magnate James Hazen Hyde had outraged New Yorkers by splurging a reported two hundred thousand dollars on turning the restaurant's ballroom into a rose petal–strewn facsimile of the court of Louis XIV at Versailles. Even the waiters wore powdered wigs. Public indignation was mitigated somewhat when Hyde protested that his little shindig had cost a mere one hundred thousand dollars.

Overwhelmingly opulent, with its vast chandeliers and dining tables practically the size of football fields, Sherry's might have been custom-built for an unabashed social climber like de Saulles. He was a regular patron, and joining him today were his father, Major de Saulles, newly arrived that morning from South Bethlehem for a two-week visit, business associate and drinking pal Marshall Ward, and longtime friend Dudley Field Malone. The men had no shortage of lunchtime banter. Much of it centered on Malone's knack for ruffling political feathers. Just recently the Collector of the Port of New York had hit the headlines by threatening to resign his post in protest after sixteen female suffragists, arrested for demonstrating outside the White House, were sentenced to sixty days in the workhouse. Thanks largely to Malone's noisy protests, the women were pardoned and freed after two days.

Following a long, good-humored lunch, Jack bade farewell to Malone and then, with his father and Ward, motored back across the Queensboro Bridge and onto the newly constructed Long Island Motor Parkway. Thirty minutes' easy driving brought them to The Box. Jack's first point of business was to dispatch a maid by automobile to pick up his son, as per the telephone arrangements made earlier that day.

Over at Crossways, Blanca had asked Suzanne to ready Jack Jr. for the trip. At three o'clock on the dot, the roadster pulled into the driveway. Without thinking, a maid sprang from the car and rang the bell. Seconds later the door flew open. Blanca stood in the doorway, her face like thunder. "What do you mean by coming to the front door?"[1] she snapped. Before the poor woman could splutter an apology, she was sent packing, ears ringing with a demand that some other servant—one with better manners—should come to collect Jack Jr.

About half an hour later, a suitably contrite manservant arrived and presented himself at the rear entrance. Blanca, still glaring daggers at the newcomer, shepherded Jack Jr. personally out to the car, kissing him good-bye and saying that she would see him soon. Once back indoors, she ordered dinner for seven o'clock and told her butler, Noe Tagliabue, to lay a place at the table for Jack Jr.

As the afternoon wore on, Jack Jr. cavorted happily on the rides and played cowboys with his pet pony. His father, either willfully or subconsciously, turned a blind eye to the clock and encouraged the lad to keep playing, unwilling to halt the youngster's fun. At 5:00 p.m. Caroline arrived, expressly to see her elderly father. After greeting Jack and her nephew, she joined Marshall Ward, who had been invited to stay for dinner with the family, in the lounge for a pre-prandial cocktail. Shortly afterward, Jack and his son entered through the French windows that led from the garden to the living room. Upstairs, Julius Hadamek had temporarily relinquished his duties for Jack and was acting as valet for Major de Saulles, helping him dress for dinner.

Six o'clock, six-thirty, and Blanca's mood was growing darker by the minute with still no sign of her son. In an atmosphere of frozen silence, the servants dutifully laid the dinner table. At 7:00 p.m., when the first course was served, Blanca didn't touch a bite. Instead, she sat very still, staring blankly. Suddenly she leapt from the table, snatched up the phone, and called her ex-husband.

Hadamek answered.

"Where is Jack?"[2] Blanca shouted.

Hadamek explained that the boy had already been put to bed. Blanca exploded. She demanded that he bring the boy back to her house immediately. Hadamek said that, unless instructed by his master, he was powerless to intervene. Hovering at Hadamek's elbow, Jack heard his incandescent ex-wife ask if he was in.

"Tell her I'm out—that I've gone to the club and will be back in an hour,"[3] he whispered.

"The master is out, madam," said Hadamek. "He has gone to the Meadow Brook Club. He will be back in one hour."[4]

According to Hadamek, Blanca then said, "Very well, then do not say that I rang him up. I will be right over to get little Jack."[5]

She slammed down the phone and immediately called Mr. and Mrs. D. Stewart Iglehart, who lived at East Williston, a village between Crossways and The Box. They were old friends. Aida Iglehart had been born in Chile, and her polo-playing husband worked as an executive with W. R. Grace & Co, a multinational with extensive South American interests. Blanca begged Iglehart to accompany her to The Box to reclaim Jack Jr., but he understandably resisted, saying that he would "rather not take any part in the matter."[6] He did offer to send his car over to pick up Blanca and bring her back to their place so that she might have dinner with them.

"No," said Blanca. "I want to get Jack and put him to bed early after dinner."[7]

Iglehart further tried to defuse the situation by saying that he felt sure Jack Jr. would be all right and that Blanca was worrying unnecessarily. But Blanca was past mollification. She ended the call and shouted for Suzanne to get dressed. While Suzanne did so, Blanca placed another call.

At 7:15 p.m. she spoke to Raymond Hamilton, who ran a taxi service from Hamilton's Garage in nearby Roslyn. He promised to send a cab immediately. Fifteen minutes later the cab still hadn't arrived. Blanca called again, this time much angrier. Hamilton, anxious not to upset a high-value customer, did his best to appease Blanca, assuring her that the cab was on its way and would be with her soon.

Another half an hour passed, and still no cab. By now Blanca had become apoplectic. Just before eight o'clock, Hamilton took a third call. He wasn't sure if the irate lady on the other end of the line was Blanca, but the caller was plenty steamed. In between the loud complaints, he offered his apologies, explaining that there had been some kind of mix-up and that another driver, James J. Donner, had been dispatched and would be there in a couple of minutes.

Reassured, Blanca and Suzanne readied themselves to leave. Blanca told Tagliabue that she would be gone only a matter of minutes, that she would eat later, and that he await her return to the dining room. While Suzanne fastened the leash on Senator, Blanca's white English bulldog, her mistress gathered some last-minute items for the journey, and then the two women let themselves out the front door. They had just reached the front gate when James J. Donner skidded his automobile to a halt. He tried to apologize for the delay, but Blanca brushed him aside and climbed quickly into the vehicle, telling him to drive to The Box as soon as possible.

Her fury took on an icy chill as the car barreled across Hempstead Plain. When they reached The Box, she and Suzanne left Senator with Donner, then made their way across the lawn. Parked directly in front of the house was Jack's automobile. As she'd suspected, he hadn't gone to the club at all. He was still at home.

What happened in the next few minutes depends on which version of events one believes. According to one of the servants, who happened to be outside the house at the time, Blanca and her maid crept up to the living room and peered through the window. Blanca would later insist that she had done nothing so underhanded. No, she and Suzanne had marched up the front steps and glanced through the window as they did so. Only then did she see her little boy, in his pajamas, still up and playing with his grandfather in the living room. Blanca glowered. Hadamek had lied to her not once but *twice,* albeit on his employer's instructions. Also in the front room were Jack, Caroline Degener, and Marshall Ward, sipping drinks and listening to the Victrola. Whether the inhabitants of the house knew that Blanca was outside is not known, but for some reason Caroline chose that precise moment to whisk Jack Jr. out of the living room and toward the broad Colonial staircase.

Blanca rang the bell. Hadamek answered. Behind him, Caroline and little Jack had reached the fourth step on the stairs when Blanca entered the front door. Blanca didn't spare them a single glance. Instead, she snapped at Hadamek, "Where is Mr. de Saulles?"[8] Hadamek replied that her ex-husband was in the living room.

"What is the meaning of it that you keep Jack here?"[9] Blanca demanded of Hadamek. The lean and swarthy valet shifted uncomfortably as Blanca tore into him. "It is my time to have him."[10]

At that moment—much to Hadamek's relief—the phone rang in the hallway. He excused himself and backed away to answer the call. Only then did Blanca acknowledge her ex-sister-in-law, who stood protectively beside Jack Jr. on the stairs. "Good evening, Blanca," said Caroline, coming down the stairs, leaving Jack Jr. behind her. "This is an unexpected call."[11]

"Good evening, Caroline. I wish to see Jack."[12]

Caroline reiterated that Jack was in the living room, then watched as Blanca swung right and marched into the front room. Suzanne, a pace or two behind, stopped just short of the doorway. Caroline didn't follow Blanca into the living room but remained in the hall alongside Suzanne, ears pricked for the bust-up she felt sure was about to ensue. Behind her on the stairs, her little nephew dutifully remained where she had left him.

In the spacious living room, Jack had draped himself across a sofa that overlooked the wide French windows. Some way to his right sat his father on a couch. In front of them both, Marshall Ward was perched on a small stool in the center of the room. As a thunderous-looking Blanca, hands plunged deep into the pockets of her white silk sweater, stalked into the room, Ward rose and inched his way toward the mantelpiece. He would have squeezed past Blanca if he could, but she was blocking the doorway. Jack rose from the couch and approached, hand extended, until he stood about three feet from his ex-wife.

"How are you, Blanquita?"

"I want Jack"[13] was the frosty response. Ward, sensing matters were about to turn really ugly, put more distance between himself and the warring couple by taking up a new position alongside the baby grand piano.

"You can't have him," said Jack. "The court awarded him to me this month. I'm sorry; I do not want to discuss it further."[14] He swung his hands up, palms outward, in front of his chest, a characteristic gesture of his when he wished to end a conversation. Then he turned away from Blanca and

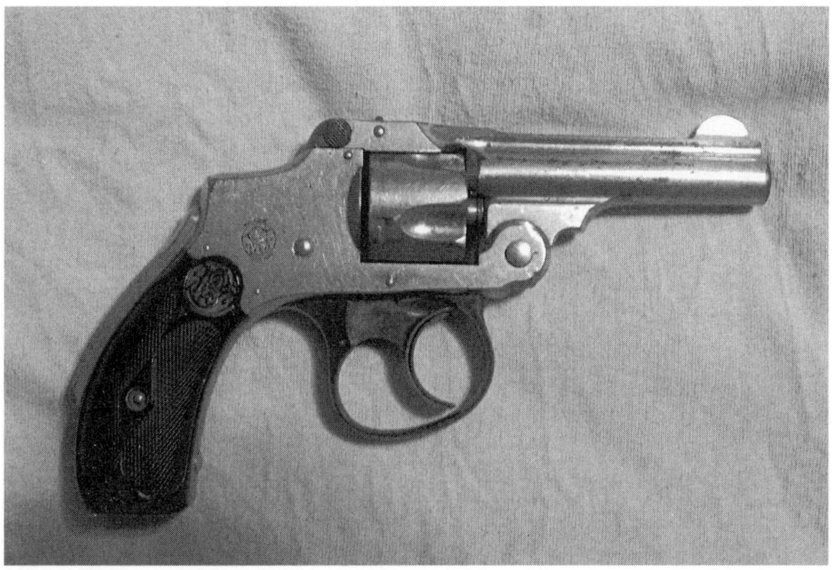

A .32 caliber Smith & Wesson "lemon squeezer" revolver, the kind Blanca used to kill Jack in the shooting

began staring out the French windows, emphasizing his decision by saying, "No! No! No!"[15]

Blanca didn't cry, or argue, or become hysterical. Instead she said, quite calmly, "Then there is only one thing for me to do."[16] She withdrew her left hand from her sweater pocket, revealing the .32 Smith & Wesson revolver that Jack had bought her for protection all those years before. In a steady, matter-of-fact voice, she said: "If I can't have my boy, take this."[17] The first bullet probably struck Jack in the side. He lurched toward the French windows, raising a protective arm. Four more shots ripped into his body, throwing him back into a chair.

For a second no one moved, frozen in time.

Then the room transformed into a blur of activity. Ward rushed over and grabbed Blanca by the arms. "It had to be done,"[18] she muttered.

An instant later, Hadamek raced in, and he and Major de Saulles helped the stricken Jack onto a couch. Hadamek looked up imploringly at Blanca. "Madam, what have you done?"

"I had to do it," said Blanca. "I couldn't stand it anymore."[19] Then she meandered into the hall, where she encountered Caroline, who grabbed Blanca's arm and cried, "Blanquita, Blanquita, what have you done?"

Those huge, dark eyes bore right through Caroline. "I'm sorry," said Blanca. "It had to be done."[20] Then, as an afterthought: "You might send for the police."[21]

Back in the living room, Ward was tending to the wounded man. Fortunately Jack's injuries didn't look that severe. "Where is the boy?" he whispered. Before Ward could answer, he said, "Don't let her get at me again."

In the immediate aftermath, no one knew what had happened to Jack Jr. Some time later, he was found upstairs, having fled to the safety of his bedroom, scared out of his wits by the gunshots.

Meanwhile, Jack was grimacing badly as he lay on the sofa. "Did you send for the police?"[22] he asked Ward. In the confusion, multiple phone calls for assistance were made, with Caroline, Ward, and Hadamek all later claiming to have phoned for a doctor. Until assistance arrived, Ward administered some rudimentary first aid.

The first medical man on the scene was Dr. Bryan C. Sword, in his capacity as ambulance surgeon for the Nassau Hospital. He examined Jack more thoroughly, frowning as he did so. These injuries needed emergency treatment. He told Ward, who ran upstairs and packed a pair of pajamas and a change of clothing for his wounded friend, thinking that he would be hospitalized for a week or two at most.

Oddly enough, the architect of all this commotion was the calmest person on the scene. After the shooting she walked into the front garden, accompanied by Suzanne, and sedately arranged herself on a seat in the shadow of a tall hedge. She was still sitting there when Hadamek next saw her. She called him over. "Jules, get me my boy."

"Madam, I cannot do it."

"Jules, what shall I do?"

"Madam, it is no use to run away."[23]

He was right. The police, in the bulky form of Sheriff Phineas A. Seaman, were already on their way. Unfortunately Seaman was a stranger to this heavily wooded section of the two-hundred-acre Ladenburg estate—it wasn't exactly a high-crime area—and he had no idea where The Box lay. What followed was a few minutes of pure Keystone Kops farce as the sheriff navigated the unfamiliar roads and lanes aimlessly until he chanced across an automobile parked by the side of the road.

"Where's The Box?" he shouted at the driver.

James Donner, curled up on his seat, was smoking a cigarette. "I don't know. There's a couple of ladies at a house up there—maybe that's it."[24]

At that moment a man appeared some way down the road, shouting and gesticulating toward them. Seaman accelerated toward him and followed the road around until he reached a large, brightly lit house. As he braked to a standstill, a glance at the property told him that these were obviously rich and probably influential people. A thread of unease wriggled in his stomach. Despite a lifetime in law enforcement—mainly as a detective—the bespectacled and mustachioed fifty-two-year-old sheriff of Nassau County had only been elected seven months previously; he needed to tread carefully. Alongside him was Constable Thorne, who earlier that day had taken Blanca's baffling call about the alleged garage break-in. Together, the two men marched in through the open front door.

They arrived at around 9:00 p.m. In the living room, Seaman saw de Saulles, prostrate on the couch, being attended by Sword and various family members.

"Who shot him?" he asked.

Jack's ex-wife, someone said.

"Where is she?"[25]

The family members exchanged bemused shrugs. In all the confusion Blanca's exit had gone unnoticed. Then someone recalled seeing her leave the house. Seaman's nerves began to twitch. An hour past sundown, tracking a fleeing suspect in these woods, in this light, would be a hellish ordeal. He ordered Thorne to take one side of the house, while he went around the other. But his fears were baseless: Far from fleeing the scene, Blanca was waiting calmly in the front garden, still sitting by the hedge, still in the company of her stunned maid, Suzanne. Seaman called for Thorne and then approached Blanca cautiously. "Are you Mrs. de Saulles?"

"I am. Are you an officer?"

Seaman replied that he was, and Blanca said quietly, "I suppose I've to go with you, then."[26]

"Yes, and I want the revolver you used."

"You will find it in the hall on the hat stand."[27]

Seaman nodded to Thorne, who backtracked into the house and located the gun where Blanca said she had left it, on the stand, between some hats and bags of golf clubs. He checked the chamber: five empty shell casings.

The roar of another combustion engine announced the arrival of the ambulance. The medics made Jack de Saulles as comfortable as possible and then stretchered him outside. Clutching the bag of spare clothing, Ward insisted on riding in the back of the ambulance so that he might comfort his injured friend.

Seaman tried to get a handle on what had happened. He took brief statements from the eyewitnesses, most of whom were reeling in a stupefied state of shock—although everyone agreed that it was Blanca who had pulled the trigger. These were the embryonic days of forensic investigation and the sheriff made no attempt to seal the crime scene or preserve evidence. Besides, it all looked open and shut. Instead, he busied himself with taking Blanca into custody as soon as possible. Suzanne, too. Good chance she might have been an accomplice. It was a very gentlemanly arrest: Neither woman was handcuffed. Seaman guided them gently to his automobile. Both got in the backseat while Thorne joined his boss in the front. Seaman then took the wheel and they drove off.

At the end of the driveway, they came upon Donner, still smoking and still waiting patiently for his fare. By this time the meter had ticked round to four dollars. Blanca asked Seaman to stop and coolly motioned the chauffeur toward her. "Take good care of the dog," she said. "Drive to Roslyn and see my maid, Louise, and she will pay you for the trip."[28] She added that she hadn't forgotten the promised dollar tip and that Donner should ask Louise for this also.

Seaman watched this exchange with open astonishment. Never had he seen a murder suspect act in so poised a manner. She exhibited no hint of panic and certainly no remorse, just the calm, imperious manner of someone used to giving orders and having them obeyed without question. Shaking his head, Seaman let in the clutch and pulled away.

Donner tipped his cap, watched them go, climbed back into the car, and retraced his journey to Crossways. When he arrived he handed the dog to Louise and explained what had happened. After giving Donner his fare and the dollar tip, Louise, incredulous, decided against waking the rest of the household. She knew that the butler, Noe Tagliabue, had waited until his usual bedtime and then cleared the table and retired not in the best of humors. As the head of staff he wouldn't appreciate being awoken at this late hour, as even in such extremis, the hierarchical proprieties needed to be observed. As a consequence, Tagliabue did not hear of the shooting until the next morning.

A few miles to the south, at the Nassau Hospital (now Winthrop-University Hospital), doctors were working feverishly on Jack's injuries. As they cut away layers of clothing and the full extent of the bullet wounds became apparent, Marshall Ward saw the physicians exchange anxious expressions. One of them shot Ward a grim look and shook his head, murmuring that Jack wouldn't live "fifteen minutes."[29] Despite this dire prognosis, Jack was prepped for surgery. At one point, according to Ward, Jack briefly regained consciousness on the operating table, opened his eyes, and whispered, "My wife shot me. I want you to have her arrested. She shot me."[30]

If true—and there was much about Ward's evidence that would raise doubts about his credibility—these were the last words Jack de Saulles ever spoke. At 10:20 p.m. surgeons gave up the struggle and pronounced him dead. He was thirty-nine years old.

In the meantime, oblivious to this development, Seaman continued his odyssey through the dark countryside. By now it was pitch black. During the course of this journey, Blanca began opening up to the sheriff, revealing the full extent of her animosity toward her ex-husband: "I shot him because he wouldn't give me my boy, and I hope he dies."[31] Seaman didn't say much, just listened.

Instead of driving directly to the Mineola jail, he took a detour south to the Hempstead Town Hall. Ordinarily, Seaman would have thrown his prisoners into the slammer and worried about the paperwork later, but this was no run-of-the-mill domestic tragedy. He needed to ensure that everything was done by the book. Justice of the Peace Walter R. Jones absorbed Seaman's retelling of the night's events. Like the sheriff, he was struck by Blanca's bored indifference and lack of remorse, and it didn't surprise him one whit when Seaman repeated her earlier remark about wanting de Saulles dead. He drew up an affidavit charging Blanca with felonious assault, which Thorne then signed. At the same time, Jones ordered Suzanne to be held as a material witness and set bail in the amount of one thousand dollars.

Formalities complete, Seaman marched his two prisoners back to the car. He was just about to drive off when Jones shouted for him to stop. A phone call had just come through from the hospital, he explained, and this changed everything. Seaman ordered his prisoners back into the town hall, where Jones addressed Blanca. "Madam, your wish is gratified; your husband is dead."

"Ah, I'm so sorry,"[32] Blanca replied, though to judge from her expression she was far from heartbroken. According to Seaman, "You might have thought, so far as she was concerned, that there was a party going on."[33]

On the strength of this development, Jones drew up a fresh affidavit, this time charging Blanca with murder in the first degree. With the revised paperwork in hand, Seaman took Blanca and Suzanne back out to his car. As they exited Hempstead, Blanca said to no one in particular: "Will they electrocute me right away?"[34]

All she got in reply was silence.

The bizarre journey continued. A short while later Blanca spotted a late-night roadside stand selling groceries.

"Stop!" she cried.

Seaman slammed on the brakes. Blanca then shouted for the vendor to bring her a bottle of milk. Once again sheriff and deputy exchanged disbelieving looks. When the milk arrived, Blanca handed over some money and told the seller to keep the change. Then, like some child sipping a bedtime drink, she settled down for the rest of the trip. Another strange interlude on this strangest of nights came when the vehicle chanced to stop near a graveyard. Blanca burst into fits of laughter. "How gruesome that we should stop at such a place at this time,"[35] she chortled. She was still chuckling when the automobile reached the Mineola jail.

Seaman led his prisoners to the north wing and up to the second floor. Blanca glanced about her at the barred cages and giggled that the place looked "like a zoo."[36] Her gaze lingered on a clothesline draped along the corridor. Seaman made a mental note to remove the potentially dangerous item. He placed Blanca and Suzanne in adjoining cells, two away from the cell that had housed Florence Carman. Because of Blanca's erratic behavior, Seaman had her examined medically that same night. He contacted the county physician, Dr. Guy Cleghorn. After a brief examination, Cleghorn recorded his conclusion: "Sheriff Seaman: On account of the extreme nervousness and mental condition of Mrs. Blanca De Saulles it would be unwise to confine her to a cell for her own safety. Guy Cleghorn."[37] Seaman promised to consider the suggestion.

Events would prove that the sheriff held some highly unorthodox views on incarceration, and throughout her time in the jailhouse Blanca would be treated more like a hotel guest than a prisoner.[38] Right from the outset Seaman gave her the run of the jail, and later that night she made a string of phone calls. One was to Murray Hill 7600, the Ritz-Carlton Hotel in Manhattan. She spoke to Jack's wealthy cousin, the art collector Captain Philip M. Lydig, and it soon became clear that the prisoner was tetchy in the extreme. Listeners who overheard portions of the conversation were able to piece together the gist: "I am in Mineola Jail. . . . For shooting Jack. . . . Because he wouldn't give me my boy."

The voice on the other end of the line was heard to repeatedly say, "My God! My God!"

After a minute or two, Blanca's eyes flashed angrily. "*My God! My God!*" she mimicked. "That's what they all say. Such talk makes me sick."[39] With this she slammed the receiver down onto the cradle and stalked off to her cell, leaving word that she would see no one except a representative of Uterhart & Graham, a high-powered law firm with offices in Manhattan and Hempstead. (One of Blanca's earlier calls had been to a lawyer friend, Frederic R. Coudert, and he had recommended the firm that had secured Florence Carman's acquittal.) However, the first lawyer on the scene was Leon Prince, who had represented Blanca during the divorce action. He arrived at the jail during the night and sent a note to her, but she had already decided on counsel and sent him packing.

During the remainder of that night, Blanca's biggest concern was reserved for Suzanne Monteau. She couldn't understand why her maid was being held in custody, and she offered to post bail for the terrified and wholly blameless young woman. For some reason the request was refused. Wearily, Blanca made her apologies to the distraught Suzanne, then settled down on her bed and fell into a deep sleep.

NINE

Let the Battle Commence

The next morning Blanca rose at ten o'clock, and daylight gave her a chance to familiarize herself with her surroundings. Her cell window overlooked the jail's graveled courtyard and an ivy-covered wall that was home to some nesting doves. Apart from that there was not much to see.

Beyond the wall it was a different story. News of the shooting had gotten around fast and already the streets encircling the jail were jammed with a constant stream of automobiles, from Chevrolets and Fords all the way up to gleaming roadsters. Every occupant, it seemed, was straining to catch a glimpse of the celebrity inmate. None succeeded.

Oblivious to the frenzy, Blanca dressed slowly in the white silk outfit that she had worn the previous night and sat down to a breakfast of special delicacies that she had ordered. The meal was cooked by the sheriff's wife, Estella, who also acted as matron of the jail. While the dishes were being cleared away, Blanca summoned a guard: "Please call my attorneys and ask them to see that I am released on bail at once. I must see Little Jack."[1]

She frowned as the guard explained apologetically that bail was out of the question for such a serious charge. Only then did the gravity of her situation seem to sink in. After some thought she asked to use a phone. Her first call was to the firm of Uterhart & Graham. Why, she demanded, had someone not been to see her? Because they had not yet been officially hired, was the answer. Blanca remedied this omission and was told that someone would be with her within the hour. After completing her phone calls, Blanca settled down with the morning papers.

The shooting of ex–football star Jack de Saulles was front page news not just in New York but across the nation. Murder in "400": Heiress Shoots Athlete, announced the *Tacoma Times,* while another paper boomed FAMOUS BEAUTY KILLS HER DIVORCED HUSBAND. What made this second headline so significant was that it was splashed in the

Los Angeles Times, a breakfast staple of just about everyone in Hollywood—including Rodolfo Guglielmi.

Mae Murray, another recent Golden State immigrant, tells how, with "heartbreak in his eyes and voice,"[2] Rodolfo showed her the newspaper, sobbing bitterly over what had happened. Like Blanca, he had seen the inside of a prison cell and knew the desolation that it could inflict. But his concerns hit closer to home. He had crossed a continent to efface the memory of his involvement in the sordid de Saulles divorce action and his subsequent arrest on trumped-up vice charges only to find that even at this distance his past was threatening to catch up with him. Not that he had much to lose. Since moving to Los Angeles, it had been tough sledding. Even in 1917, the City of Angels drew throngs of young, good-looking hopefuls, just like him, all fighting to get a foot in the door. So far Guglielmi had come up short. To make ends meet he'd been forced to fall back on that old standby: taxi dancing. That was degrading enough. Now this.

The biggest difference that money can buy in any criminal trial is time, and Blanca de Saulles and her family could afford boatloads of the stuff. Not for her some harassed court-appointed attorney, whose only interest would be in getting the case to trial as quickly as possible, pleading her out, and then moving on to pick up the next legal crumb on offer. Million-dollar defendants get million-dollar defenses, tailor-made, meticulously prepared over several months, with access to the very best (and most expensive) expert witnesses, and, most important of all, a superbly orchestrated PR campaign.

The man chosen to lead this crusade arrived at the jail just before midday. Most days of the week, Henry A. Uterhart spent his time unraveling tax or divorce problems, but he was also a top-notch performer in the criminal court. A giant of a man—he stood six feet four, and that was without the omnipresent brown derby—he had an intimidating presence inside a courtroom and out. Although clean-shaven in the modern style, he was disarmingly Victorian in dress, with a fondness for high-wing collars. Like most courtroom high-flyers, he was a shameless grandstander. In one case, acting on a dare from opposing counsel, he gulped down two sedative tablets to prove that he would be awake and active the next day in court, thereby proving that the testator in the case, a woman who had swallowed a single tablet, couldn't have been drugged when she made her will, as she claimed. He won his point. (Whether the court factored in the difference in stature between Uterhart and the pocket-sized testator is not recorded.)

On this morning Uterhart entered the Mineola jailhouse, his pockets bulging with money. He carefully peeled off a thousand dollars, enough for the bail that would free Suzanne. (It later emerged that the funds had been furnished by a Mrs. Roma M. Flint, one of Blanca's fashionable Park Avenue set.) After her release, Suzanne was besieged by reporters who bombarded her with questions about the fateful night.

"Mrs. De Saulles merely asked me to go with her," she said, pushing her way through the crowd. "I didn't know where or why she was going. I didn't know she carried a revolver."[3]

Then a waiting car whisked her away to Crossways. She stayed just long enough to pack a box of her mistress's clothes before returning to the jail. Also in the box was a photograph of Jack Jr. that Blanca set up on the little dressing table thoughtfully provided by Mrs. Seaman. Her duties complete for the day, Suzanne was then driven away to seclusion.

In her wake, Sheriff Seaman willingly fielded questions from the press. His sympathies were immediately apparent. "If the child is brought here to see his mother, she may see him and caress him all she wishes," he said. "The boy is all she seems to think about, and I certainly would not do anything to stop her seeing him as often as possible."[4]

Constable Thorne, too, seemed dazzled by the jail's star inmate. "The way she talked to me, I am sure she did not have the slightest idea in her head of shooting her husband."[5]

Up on the second floor, Uterhart was hard at work. His first consultation with Blanca lasted two hours. By meeting's end, the big lawyer had formulated a clear strategy. He would rely on a tried and trusted legal maxim as relevant today as it was in 1917: If you can't attack the evidence, attack the victim. This would be the linchpin of his defense, an all-out assault on the character of Jack de Saulles.

Sure enough, Uterhart emerged from the jailhouse spitting fire. His first move was to let slip a rumor that ten days before the shooting, Jack had savagely beaten Blanca, a beating so bad that it pushed her over the brink. Although not a shred of evidence existed to prove that such an assault ever occurred, it didn't matter. In criminal cases it's not truth that matters, it's perception; the denials or apologies could come later. Uterhart had the gloves off, ready to say and do whatever was necessary to blacken Jack's name and to sway public opinion in favor of a woman who had been "deeply humiliated and wronged."[6]

Defense counsel Henry A. Uterhart (right), with his partner, John G. Graham

Uterhart rumbled that all the facts of Blanca's tragic home life would be made public at the appropriate time. He also stated his belief that on August 3, pursuant to the court ruling, Blanca was entitled to custody of her son. De Saulles had given "his word of honor as a gentleman to a woman that the boy would be returned in the evening—early in the evening—and the boy was not returned. Mr. De Saulles broke his word."[7] Blanca, he said, was perfectly within her rights to attempt to claim him. She had devoted her life and the whole of her love to little Jack, and "the retention of the boy by De Saulles was the culminating blow and struck her very deeply. It was as if her troubles and anxiety reached the very breaking point."[8]

Uterhart then gave the sympathy button an extra push for good measure. Blanca was, he said, "practically a stranger in the country, with her relatives and friends in Chile, she could not bear the loneliness of her situation."[9] And he sighed that eliciting details of the tragedy from Blanca had been fiendishly difficult; her only concern was for the safety of her only child. Throughout their conversation, he said, her gaze rarely left the photograph of her son. Despite this distraction, she had managed to provide Uterhart with a lengthy and exhaustive account of the de Saulles marriage, dating from 1911 when the couple first met in Chile. Uterhart detailed five years of abuse and neglect for the scribbling reporters. At the memoir's conclusion, he was quizzed on the whereabouts of Jack Jr. The big lawyer professed ignorance but declared that, once the boy was tracked down, he would obtain visiting rights for him. Uterhart finished his first press conference on an upbeat note, repeating a promise he had made to Blanca: "I will throw away my license to practice law if any jury which hears your story does not free you."[10]

This was no idle boast. Uterhart had sentiment and precedent on his side. Just six years before in Denver, another society belle, the stunningly beautiful Gertrude Gibson Patterson, had also resolved a messy divorce by shooting her husband in the back. Conviction had looked a certainty. But, against all the odds and all the evidence, the jury set Gertrude free. The astonishing acquittal led a brother of the victim and himself a lawyer, to declare ruefully, "The verdict means that a pretty woman can commit murder and get away with it. I know from my practice that conviction of a woman criminal is almost impossible."[11] And that was Uterhart's trump card: the blinkered refusal of all-male juries in the early twentieth century to convict any attractive woman of murder. The male conscience, apparently, was unwilling to countenance the prospect of those winsome features being twisted and blackened by a hangman's rope or else seared by 2,200 volts of electricity.

Even though Uterhart proclaimed his confidence about the outcome—ergo the remark about relinquishing his law license—he wanted a slam dunk, and that meant digging up as much dirt on the dead man as possible. Assistance came in the shape of John E. Bleekman. Just one day after the shooting hit the headlines, the forty-seven-year-old civil engineer—he had helped construct the Union Depot in Cincinnati—motored the fifteen miles from his home at Elmhurst, Queens, to the Mineola jailhouse to offer his services to Blanca. He obviously bore a powerful grudge against de Saulles, most likely the result of having been bested in some business deal. In the event, Bleekman wasn't permitted to see Blanca, but he did throw the hungry reporters some tasty morsels.

For instance, he claimed that he could prove that in 1911 Jack had bragged of his intention to "marry a woman for her great wealth."[12] And then there was Jack's arrogant claim that he could "win any given woman with flowers in the morning, a ride in the afternoon, and a dinner in the evening."[13] Further allegations made by Bleekman went considerably beyond what any newspaper was prepared to print and far exceeded anything leveled by Blanca against the dead man. Clearly Uterhart didn't trust Bleekman's so-called evidence, as, after this interlude, nothing more was heard from the vengeful engineer. But some useful mud had been thrown; some of it was bound to stick.

When asked if temporary insanity would play any part in the defense, Uterhart nodded, saying it would enable him to get details of Jack's adultery into evidence.

"Do you think she was insane at that time?" one reporter asked.

Uterhart grew thoughtful. "Yes, I think so. Imagine her mother love and the purity of heart that she possessed—being so young and separated from her own family, and then the absolute possession of him being questioned."[14]

Then Uterhart dropped a bombshell: The "Richest Girl in South America" was nearly broke!

Reporters gasped. After all, just one day beforehand, a paper had declared Blanca to be "probably the wealthiest woman ever accused of such a crime in America."[15] What the hell had happened? All Uterhart would say at the moment was that thanks to de Saulles's wretched profligacy, Blanca's inheritance had been whittled down to a mere fifty-three thousand dollars, forcing her to scrape by on a paltry income of four thousand dollars per annum, plus the three hundred dollars in monthly alimony. Uterhart was playing on the biggest stage of his life, and no one needed to tell him the importance of getting the press on board. Massaging the flow of news was vital. Hence his visible annoyance when a pressman asked for a comment on reports that Blanca's mother had cabled friends in Washington to say that she was leaving on the first available ship from Santiago and that Blanca would be "amply supplied"[16] with funds to defend herself. Uterhart bristled and blustered as he attempted to downplay Blanca's wealth. He didn't want the world to hear about a spoiled society princess with a penchant for dancing, endless shopping sprees, and glittering society parties, who barely a year beforehand had offered to charter an entire steamship to transport her boy from America to Chile. No, he needed the public to get behind a poor, frightened young *girl*—Uterhart's preferred terminology—cowering in the face of a tyrannical husband.

Someone else wrestling with the problem of Blanca's public image was Charles R. Weeks, the fifty-one-year-old district attorney of Nassau County. A Republican known for his dry wit, Charlie Weeks had been elected the previous year, before which he had served seven years as a justice of the peace in North Hempstead. He knew the Long Island politico-legal machine inside out—the horse trading, the backroom deals, the egos, the vast wealth—and he knew that convicting Blanca de Saulles would take every ounce of his legal acumen, and probably a hefty slice of luck, as well. Having been the assistant prosecutor in the Carman trial, he harbored no illusions about the size of the task confronting him.

Weeks made his first visit to The Box one day after the shooting with Seaman as his guide. A horde of reporters trailed in their wake. The approaches to the house were full of somber-faced friends and family acquaintances who had called to give their condolences and learn about the funeral arrangements. Seaman frowned. Not because of the sympathizers, but rather the hundreds of jostling sightseers, who were pouring in on foot, by horse, and by automobile, and treating this murder scene like it was some Coney Island attraction. As the crush along Valentines Road reached suffocating levels, Seaman shouted for guards to be posted in the grounds.

Inside the estate, reporters ran rampant, trampling heedlessly across the billiard table lawns, notebooks poised, cameras snapping, ready to record

Prosecutor Charles Weeks (right), with co-counsel Lewis J. Smith at the time of the Florence Carman trial

every incident, every emotion, no matter how trivial or private. There was one scene of heartbreaking poignancy, Major de Saulles slumped over a table on the porch, snowy white head between his hands. Alongside him, Caroline attempted to comfort her almost comatose father, but he seemed beyond assistance. Halfway down the lawn, at a garden table with a great umbrella shading it from the bright sun, sat three friends of the dead man: the unfortunately named Captain Coffin, who was attached to the United States Army Aviation School at Mineola; Louis Stoddard, a polo-playing companion of Jack; and Charles Pettinus, who had been designated the family spokesman.

Pettinus said that the dead man's brother, Charles, who was working in Denver, was rushing back east as fast as the train would carry him. He also stated that Jack had been fully entitled to custody of the child—"the little chap was to stay with his father during this month"[17]—and he emphasized how Jack had provided healthy outdoor activities for the growing lad. Every so often, whenever a particularly tricky question came his way, Pettinus would retreat to the house to seek clarification before proceeding. The veteran press pack soon realized that they were being played. The battle for the hearts and minds of the public—vital in any criminal case but absolutely critical when high-profile protagonists are involved—was in full swing.

The next day impatient reporters who had been badgering Seaman for an interview with Blanca finally got their wish. She proved to be a natural. With her slender figure and chalky white face set off by a gingham dress with a large white collar that had more than a whiff of school uniform about it, she gave off the contrite appearance of a young student being summoned to the principal's office. Jack had married her, she said, purely for her money, believing that she had millions, only to cast her aside when he discovered the true level of her wealth. The Errázuriz-Vergara fortune had already been greatly dissipated by the time that Jack met her, so that the family possessed "but a shell of its former wealth."[18] Even so, immediately after the honeymoon he had started milking her depleted fortune, obtaining forty-seven thousand dollars from her by "stealth and false pretenses."[19] She described her ex-husband as a Jekyll and Hyde character, someone who kept all his good qualities for the general public and reserved his evil traits for the family home, where he brutalized her repeatedly in front of their son and the servants.

He had been a reckless father, taking Jack Jr. into barrooms and parading him in front of his numerous lady friends, especially Joan Sawyer. She recalled other incidents. Once, in South Bethlehem, Blanca found tailors' and milliners' bills in Jack's pockets for articles of women's apparel that she had not purchased. Jack had laughed off her concerns, saying a friend had asked him to pay the bills, but she hadn't believed him. She recalled telling the press when she first arrived in New York that "Americans are the finest men in the world. The Latins and French may have better manners and more polish, but the Americans are big, generous, and trustworthy."[20] But life with Jack de Saulles had destroyed that rose-tinged notion. She had tried to settle the dispute amicably, only to be badly let down by the judicial system.

So was that why you took a gun with you? asked one reporter.

No, said Blanca, it had been a reflex action because she feared traveling over "one of the loneliest roads on Long Island."[21]

She delivered her monologue in a flat, unemotional voice without any apparent rancor toward the deceased. Then Blanca made her excuses and retired to her cell. It had been an outstanding performance.

That same day the autopsy on the body of Jack de Saulles was performed by two Hempstead doctors, Henry M. Warner and Smith A. Coombs. They found four bullet wounds and possibly a fifth. The doubtful injury was a nick on the skin covering the knuckle of the index finger of the left hand. One bullet went through the little finger of the left hand and hit the ring finger, fracturing the knuckle; another entered the left arm below the elbow; another hit the upper arm. The fourth and lethal bullet entered the back on an upward trajectory, an inch and a half to the left of the spine, tearing the renal artery and lodging in the left lobe of the liver. The resulting massive hemorrhage led to death. Both doctors were of the opinion that all the shots had been fired either at the side or the back of the victim, who had probably raised his left arm to shield himself.

Later that day Uterhart was back at the jailhouse. He told Blanca that the Chilean Embassy in Washington had declined to offer assistance at the current time because when she married Jack she had renounced her Chilean nationality. However, since the divorce her situation was less clear, and lawyers were still seeking clarification. Blanca took the news in stride, along with everything else that had happened. And her appetite certainly wasn't affected. If press reports were to be believed, she had wolfed down the three hearty meals that Estella Seaman had cooked for her. Uterhart again spent considerable time cloistered with Blanca, mapping out tactics and promising that he would do everything in his power to arrange a visit from Jack Jr. as soon as possible. Blanca didn't look convinced. Uterhart soothed his client's concerns, promising that everything would be all right both in the short term and the long. As he later told the assembled pressmen: "If Mrs. De Saulles is acquitted the child must go to her; she is the only living parent and the only one who will have any right to him. And this afternoon I told her that, and I told her too that no jury of American citizens would convict any mother who was trying to save her child."[22]

Uterhart's efforts to generate support for Blanca were bearing fruit. That day she was visited by Miss Helene White, a daughter of banker Archibald S. White, who had been a business partner of Bleekman's on the Cincinnati railroad project. She arrived in a large, shiny red Rolls Royce. Two other women, obviously Latin American but annoyingly anonymous and determined to remain that way, also called to offer moral support for Blanca in her time of need. Frustrated by their inability to ferret out the names of these two visitors, reporters shifted their attention to Crossways, where Noe Tagliabue remained a steadfast model of loyalty. He told the press that Blanca was a devoted mother who spent all her waking hours playing with the boy and always taking her meals with him.

Tracking down Jack Jr. was proving to be a real headache. Following the trauma of the shooting—which he had not witnessed, contrary to some early newspaper reports, but undoubtedly overheard—he was cared for by Caroline Degener and his grandfather at The Box. However, after a visit from the family attorney, Lyttleton Fox, it was decided to spirit the lad away to some hiding place. After arranging this, Fox drove the short distance to Maurice Heckscher's summer home at Westbury to discuss various matters. Also present was Marshall Ward. They made arrangements for Jack's body to be removed to the Frank E. Campbell Funeral Church, undertakers to the rich and famous,[23] at 1970 Broadway.

More important, Fox told the others, round one in the PR battle had plainly gone to the defense. That day's newspapers had resurrected every detail of the divorce and in the process Jack had been painted blacker than pitch. The de Saulles family needed to fight back—and quickly. At Fox's urging it was decided to release a letter sent by Jack to Blanca just a few weeks earlier to demonstrate the dead man's kindness and thoughtfulness for his son.

My Dear Blanquita:

As you know, The Box is dedicated to little Jack. He had around him there all his pets, including his pony, dogs, etc. He seems to enjoy these attractions so much and they have kept him outdoors the whole day long.

It appears to me rather hard on the little fellow during these hot days to move him to some place where he will not have the freedom of the country life, such as he is having now at Westbury. Therefore, merely as a suggestion to you, I say that during this coming month of July, which period belongs to you, I will be perfectly willing to step out of the house and not return there until my period comes around again. I will further offer you my servants, which would be, of course, at no cost or expense to you.

Inasmuch as this property is solely for little Jack's use you need not consider me in the matter in any way, and at the same time I think that with Jack's interest uppermost in your mind you should put aside any little personal feeling that you might have had and let the boy continue to enjoy the magnificent life that he has been leading and which has kept him in the pink of condition.

Of course, this is all up to you. It is for you to decide, and should you care to take him away, he will be ready at the time appointed by the Court.

Hoping that you are well, and also that you are enjoying the summer, believe me, most sincerely

JOHN L. DE SAULLES[24]

It was a decent riposte—as good as the de Saulles family could muster in the circumstances—and demonstrated that Uterhart wasn't going to have it all his way in the battle for propaganda supremacy. Some newspapers, too, were already beginning to question Uterhart's strategy, with one saying that "an acquittal would be equivalent to writing into the statute book: 'A husband's adultery shall hereafter be punishable by death at the hands of the wife.'"[25]

The next day Blanca collapsed in her cell. When Uterhart arrived at noon, he found her prostrate on the bed, repeatedly muttering, "Why don't you bring my little Jack to me?"[26] Throwing aside the two Spanish novels he had brought as gifts, he shouted for medical assistance. While awaiting medical help to arrive, Uterhart relayed this development to the press corps. He also wanted to issue a clarification: "Mrs. De Saulles never said 'I'm glad

I did it' after shooting Mr. De Saulles, as reported."[27] This, said Uterhart, had been misreported. Then he began highlighting perceived weaknesses in the prosecution's case. For instance, the cartridges that had killed de Saulles were the same bullets he had put into the gun when giving it to Blanca two years previously. "A woman who premeditated murder would certainly have used fresh cartridges," declared Uterhart. "She could not tell whether the old ones were still good or not."[28] This announcement raised a few sardonic smiles among the gathered newsmen, none of whom could recall any killer being quite so fastidious.

The press was getting itchy. With no sign of the boy at the jail, a swarm of reporters descended on The Box, this time flattening some expensive shrubbery in order to press their noses against the windows. They saw Mrs. August Heckscher, mother of Jack's cousin and business partner, placing flowers in several vases in the front drawing room. Angrily, she stopped what she was doing and stormed out to the porch, chiding the reporters that such an invasion of privacy was outrageous and ordering them from the property. When one of the pressmen shouted a question about Jack Jr.'s whereabouts, Mrs. Heckscher snapped that she knew where the boy was but that "no one else has any right to know."[29] At that moment an upstairs window flew open to reveal the grizzled beard and thin white hair of Major de Saulles. In a voice shaking with passion, he shouted down, "I am the boy's legal guardian. . . . I know where he is. No one else needs to know anything about him."[30]

Nursing their discontent, the reporters trudged back to their cars and returned to the jail, to see what, if any, developments had occurred during their absence.

It had been surprisingly quiet. The way Uterhart told it that morning, Blanca had been knocking at death's door, and yet, for some reason, the requested medical assistance didn't arrive until 6:00 p.m. And it came in the form of not one, not two, but three doctors. There was County Physician Dr. Guy H. Cleghorn, who normally tended prisoners at the jail and had examined Blanca at the time of her arrest. Alongside him were two physicians from the Long Island College Hospital, J. Sherman Wight and Louis C. Johnson. They examined Blanca and found her to be "thin almost to emaciation,"[31] tipping the scales at a scant one hundred pounds. Blanca disclosed details of her medical history, especially the sunstroke she had suffered some years previously, since when her health had been fragile. The doctors were united in their belief that the prisoner should be granted bail.

When Weeks heard this he almost choked with disbelief. "I will oppose any application for bail."[32] Nor did he think that Blanca was "as ill as some persons would have us believe."[33] And he assured the citizens of Long Island that they would get full value for their tax dollars when it came to prosecuting Mrs. de Saulles. "The fact that she is reputed to come from a wealthy family does not entitle her to any more consideration than that accorded to [Dominick] Damasco,"[34] also being held at the Mineola jailhouse.

The doctors' findings also came as a shock to others at the jail, most of whom were astonished at just how well Blanca had been bearing up during her ordeal. But there was no stopping Uterhart. He trumpeted that the doctors had described his client as "a very sick girl,"[35] and that her (as yet undiagnosed) illness resulted more from "her sufferings for several years past"[36] than to the shock and reaction from killing her husband. Uterhart's hyperbole did take something of a hit with Cleghorn's observation that Blanca was "one of the most remarkably normal women"[37] he had ever examined, more composed and calm even than Florence Carman, whom he also had treated. His finding was borne out by Sheriff Seaman. He said he had "never seen so even-tempered a woman as Mrs. De Saulles."[38] The sheriff was obviously smitten. "When I see her I can only think of a tiny bird. I never saw so bird-like a human creature."[39]

Uterhart fought to regain control of the situation, only to falter when queried about his client's alleged financial distress. He admitted that, yes, she did pay a season's rent of two thousand dollars for Crossways—approximately half her stated income—but this was beyond her means. Her sole reason for such extravagance was because she felt she had to compete with her husband for little Jack's affection. Uterhart's usual ready smile faded notably when another pressman asked if it was true that the unusual custody terms agreed during the divorce resulted from a threat by Jack to file a countersuit, naming "a dancer often in company with Joan Sawyer."[40] Uterhart blustered that the terms of the decree had come as "a great shock and surprise"[41] to everyone.

For the first time Blanca had been publicly linked with Rodolfo Guglielmi, and Uterhart was visibly rattled. Earlier, questions about Blanca's wealth had forced him onto the back foot; now he needed to regroup again to project her as a young, vulnerable girl driven to homicide by the heartless manipulation of a callous husband, not some giddy social butterfly with a fondness for footloose tango dancers. All he could manage was a clutch of letters written by members of the public, wishing Blanca well. One came from a man who claimed to be chargé d'affaires at the American Legation in Chile in 1912, when he met Blanca. "I beg you to consider me at your orders in whatever way I can assist you. I beg you to believe me your faithful and devoted servant, who kisses your feet."[42] Uterhart declined to identify the author of the letter, which was in Spanish, other than to say it was written on stationery from the Princeton Club.

Another, from Mrs. Jennie B. Jones, living in Milwaukee, offered sympathy to Blanca and attacked Jack's character because of business relations he'd had with her husband.

My Dear Mrs. De Saulles:

In our morning paper I read of the dreadful predicament you are in, and I cannot resist the temptation of writing you. You know how my heart goes out to you in this hour of anguish. I know of no way that I can help you, but if I can I stand willing. I can't help the tears coming to my eyes when I think of what you must be going through. It was an awful price to pay—he was not worth it. I know you did it from a sense of duty.[43]

Mrs. Jones claimed to have known de Saulles from several years previously when he was living at Long Beach, where his riotous house parties "were all affairs only whispered about."[44]

It was all very titillating and all entirely fictitious. Within twenty-four hours, relatives of Mrs. Jones, including her husband and sister, issued a statement that, while she might have written a letter of sympathy to Blanca, she had never met the dead man and there was "not a particle of truth"[45] in claims that she knew details of Jack's private life.

In releasing this so-called sympathy letter, Uterhart had miscalculated; he fought to regain lost ground by emphasizing Blanca's plucky stoicism. He said that the first her family knew of her marital discord came when a friend, Dr. Van Schroeders, visited his brother in New York in the months preceding her divorce and met with Blanca. He wrote to Amalia that Jack was "drinking heavily"[46] and that it was no longer safe for Blanca to stay with him. Within weeks Amalia had arrived to comfort her ailing sister.

While Uterhart worked the press, Blanca was being moved. It might not have been the hospital ward recommended by her doctors, but she was able to swap an eight-by-twelve-foot cell for a well-ventilated, comfortable room in the sheriff's private wing. Next door sat a piano that Seaman said Blanca could play if she wished. To celebrate the change, Estella Seaman was dispatched to New York City to buy some fresh apparel for the prisoner.

Suzanne Monteau was also proving her worth. Her daily visits followed a set regime: First she dressed her employer's hair, and then she attended to her toilette before going outside to face the press. She had been well coached. Her announcements invariably included some mention of her employer's history of ill-health. Ever since suffering sunstroke four years previously, whenever the weather turned hot Mrs. de Saulles complained of "a queer feeling in the head."[47] And yes, her mistress had been stricken by just such a feeling in the days preceding the shooting.

Later that afternoon, Blanca received another visitor, the Chile-born Mrs. Aida Iglehart, whose husband she had phoned just before the shooting. Details of their conversation, conducted in Spanish, never made it out to the press corps, who were far more interested in an expensive automobile that was slowly passing the jail. As the newspapermen dashed forward to identify the occupants, the female passenger hastily drew a veil over her face, while the man driving turned his face away and floored the gas. Some thought they recognized the two as Caroline Degener and Charles Pettinus. Quite why they wished to see the jailhouse was a mystery. What is certain is that, later that same day, Lyttleton Fox issued a statement on behalf of Major de Saulles:

> *It is a matter of great regret to me that Mrs. De Saulles, having taken the life of my son, now chooses to heap calumnies upon him. Those calumnies will do no permanent harm, for the whole truth is certain to eventually come out. I know my son as he was and as few fathers can. Thank God, others know as I did and hold his memory green and clean in their hearts. His faults he had in common with many other good men, but very few could justly claim to equal him in his splendor and his fineness. Jack was a man, every inch of him. I deeply resent the campaign of unjust attack that seems planned.*
> *ARTHUR B. DE SAULLES*[48]

The battle lines were being drawn.

Meanwhile, the de Saulles family had postponed Jack's funeral to allow his brother, Charles, to arrive from Denver. Ever since the body had been moved to Campbell's Funeral Church, they had been inundated by mourners wishing to pay their last respects. Many were Yale alumni, unified in their condemnation of Blanca. Jack, they insisted, had been a devoted father, extremely careful in his tending of Jack Jr., someone who would not dream of taking his son anywhere inappropriate. While the insults flew back and forth, Justice of the Peace Walter R. Jones announced, out of respect to the family, that the inquest would be delayed until after the funeral.

After several frustrating days, the teams of reporters that had been combing every inch of Long Island in an effort to track down the missing boy finally got a break. Uterhart had received a tip-off that Jack Jr. was holed up at the Heckscher's summer place, two miles from The Box. Corroboration came from Maurice Heckscher. "There is no mystery and never has been in respect to the whereabouts of little Jack De Saulles. He is at my house at Westbury, under the care of his aunt, Mrs. Rudolph Degener, and of my wife."[49]

Uterhart got busy, saying that, while he was happy for the child to remain in the custody of his grandfather, he would appeal to the de Saulles family to allow Jack Jr. to visit his mother. Although technically Blanca was the legal guardian, Uterhart conceded that the practicalities of keeping a child in jail overrode the law. With a sorrowful shake of his head, he passed along Blanca's comment that, if custody of Jack Jr. were denied to her, she had "no desire to live."[50]

Then it was back to trashing the dead man's reputation. The letters Blanca had received from the public, Uterhart said, provided clear evidence that Jack was not, as he had been dubbed, the "most popular man along Broadway."[51] Nor was he unanimously adored in Washington, where one female columnist blasted Jack as a "promiscuous libertine," accusing him of being "lax in habit and universal in taste."[52] Such criticism was music to Uterhart's ears, and he kept stirring the pot by contrasting Jack's hell-raising lifestyle with the selfless actions of his ex-wife. Why, Blanca had even taken a fellow prisoner under her wing. According to Uterhart, "Happy Lil,"[53]as Blanca called her, had fallen into "evil ways,"[54] but thanks to Blanca's counseling she had resolved to make a new start in life when she left jail. Uterhart said that Dr. Wight had completed his official report on Blanca, and he quoted from its conclusion: "The woman is psychopathic and is in a distressed state. She has been seriously ill for at least a year and is still on the down track."[55]

Mrs. Seaman also expressed concern about Blanca's mental state. "If only we could do something to bring her out of this apathy. I am afraid if she continues in this frame of mind she will be seriously ill."[56]

Newspaper editors, rubbing their hands in glee over the boost to their circulation numbers, targeted anyone who could keep the story running. Next on the journalistic hit list came Alfred B. Nathan, Blanca's divorce lawyer, who was tracked down to his vacation home at Schroon Lake in the Adirondacks. The lawyer remained closemouthed, reluctant to discuss the divorce terms because he feared it might prejudice Blanca's chances in the upcoming trial, which would be "a long, hard fight."[57] He characterized as "ridiculous"[58] suggestions that he had cut a deal for Blanca on the custody issue in return for a blanket being thrown over certain of her actions. However, he did admit to having previously acted for Joan Sawyer, and he refused to explain how Blanca came to retain his firm as counsel. Some of the questioning made Nathan uncomfortable.

"Why was no appeal filed in Mrs. De Saulles's behalf after the divorce decree gave her husband almost equal rights to the boy?" shouted one reporter.

"Because she did not instruct us to appeal."

"Was she satisfied with the provisions of the decree?"

"Well, as I said, she made no attempt to appeal."[59]

It later emerged that, before being run to earth by the press, Nathan had interrupted his vacation, returned hurriedly to his Lower Manhattan office, picked up the de Saulles divorce file, and then hightailed it back to Schroon Lake. One possible reason for Nathan's sudden and hasty action may lie in a cryptic comment from an unnamed employee at the Heckscher office, who predicted that "the trial will develop a tremendous sensation in favor of Mr. De Saulles."[60] Although he refused to elaborate on this intriguing forecast, it seems clear that the employee was hinting at the rumors about Blanca and Rodolfo.

This provided uncomfortable reading for Uterhart and very uncomfortable reading for Rodolfo, who combed each day's copy of the *Los Angeles Times* for the latest developments. There are claims that Rodolfo attempted to contact Blanca during this period. If he did—and it's easy to imagine someone of his romantic nature at least trying—then much the greatest likelihood is that he was told to keep his head down. The last thing Blanca needed at this trying time was any contact with Rodolfo Guglielmi.

On August 7, the train carrying Charles de Saulles from Tulsa steamed into Penn Station. From there a car whisked him to Jack's business premises on

West 42nd Street, where he and Maurice Heckscher were closeted in a long conversation. The second leg of his journey took him to Jack's apartment. There, Charles gazed down at the ruined body of his brother in its bronze casket. He shared his grief with a column of naval and military officers from various countries who filed solemnly past the open casket in a mark of respect. Charles dutifully shook hands and thanked everyone for their kindness and consideration. Then he and Heckscher left for The Box.

They arrived to some jarring information: Blanca's family had left Chile en route to New York. The journey might take several days, but the financial firepower that the Errázuriz-Vergara dynasty was bringing to the fight would be awesome.

TEN

The Funeral

Not even sizzling heat and a blanket of humidity could quell public interest in the funeral of Jack de Saulles. Originally the service had been scheduled for Grace Church on lower Broadway, but the venue later shifted to Jack's apartment on West 57th to afford greater privacy. That was the plan; it didn't succeed.

Crowds began gathering just after dawn, and by eleven o'clock, the time of the funeral, the blistering sidewalks so teemed with an estimated two thousand spectators that twenty-five policemen, many on horseback, were called in to control the crush. Despite family requests for a private funeral, a few rubberneckers slipped through the police cordon and sneaked in to the building. Across the street two "over-dressed" women took in the commotion with knowing nods. "Jack sure was a spender," said one. "He spent it as fast as he made it."[1]

One of the few funeral vehicles brave enough to negotiate the crowded street bore Major de Saulles. As he stepped out and saw the size of the throng, his haggard expression turned grayer still, and his knees buckled. His elder daughter, Georgiana, and the chauffeur dashed forward, grabbing hold of the ailing major and helping him inside. The major's other daughter, Caroline Degener, had volunteered to remain with Jack Jr. at the Heckscher's residence. So many floral tributes filled the apartment that it scarcely had room for the mourners. Most were male, either old friends from Yale or business associates; others came from the political world. A blanket of white roses covered the casket, banked at both sides and at the back with masses of flowers. A single wreath of lilies of the valley dominated the display.

The Right Reverend Bishop Ethelbert Talbot of the diocese of Eastern Pennsylvania and Dean Frederick Beekman, rector of the Church of the Nativity of South Bethlehem, shared the duties of the service. They gave no sermon, just the Episcopal service for the dead and a few hymns, including

"Peace and Lead, Kindly Light," performed by a quartet from Grace Episcopal Church. After the brief service, the funeral cortège made its way through the heaving crowd, bearing Jack de Saulles to his final resting place.

It was originally thought that Jack would be buried in South Bethlehem, but this was changed to Green-Wood Cemetery in Brooklyn. Here he would lie among the likes of newspaper publisher Horace Greeley; the fabulously crooked William "Boss" Tweed, who stole an estimated two hundred million dollars from New York taxpayers; noted abolitionist Henry Ward Beecher; and Leonard Jerome, grandfather of Winston Churchill. The honorary pallbearers included Marshall Ward, Dudley Malone, the Collector of Internal Revenue "Big Bill" Edwards, Rear Admiral Louis Gomez of the Chilean navy, Captain Philip M. Lydig, Maurice Heckscher, French naval officer Captain Raymond Michel, William F. McCombs, and Lyttleton Fox.

Major de Saulles did not attend the gravesite. After his near collapse at the service, his family thought it unwise for him to go to the cemetery. His wife, Catherine, tiny and white haired, did make it to Green-Wood, but the strain of it all overwhelmed her. She broke down completely and had to be helped away.

After the funeral, Charles de Saulles held a press conference at his brother's real estate office to announce that attorney George Gordon Battle had been engaged to investigate the charges against Jack and to vindicate his name. Charles was shaking with indignation as he handed out copies of a prepared statement. After denouncing the attack on his brother as "grossly and incredibly false,"[2] he tore into Uterhart: "I should have thought that even the malignity of a hired slanderer would have waited until after the funeral of his victim. But this Mr. Uterhart has been so zealous in his efforts to traduce and defame the memory of the dead that he has not observed even that measure of ordinary decency."[3] Charles then read out a lengthy statement:

> *I should greatly prefer to say nothing in this matter and to await the proper processes of the courts, which will in good time disclose all the facts and vindicate the good name of my brother. But Mr. Uterhart's extraordinary conduct in continuing to make these charges renders it necessary for me, in justice to the memory of my brother, to state very briefly some of the salient facts. Mr. Uterhart has stated that the decision of the Supreme Court of this state giving the custody of my nephew, little Jack De Saulles, to his mother for seven and to his father for five months, was a surprise*

and a disappointment to Mrs. Blanca De Saulles. The fact is that this division of custody was pursuant to a written stipulation, signed by Mrs. De Saulles and her attorney, and approved by the Referee who heard the case, and by Justice Finch of the Supreme Court, who granted the decree. Furthermore, it was expressly agreed by letters between my brother and his wife that she should have the boy in July and he should have him in August. And she expressed herself in her letters as perfectly satisfied with this arrangement. So that there can be no shadow of pretext that my brother did not have every right, legal and moral, to the custody of the boy in August.

And it has been stated that my brother misused a part of his wife's fortune. This charge is entirely without foundation. My brother not only did not misuse any of her private funds, but was most generous in his financial dealings with her, spending large sums to gratify her expensive tastes and to pay her debts. As to their married life, I shall not follow the example of Mr. Uterhart. I shall make no charges or recriminations, but I shall say that my brother was a devoted and loving husband in the earlier days of their married life, and that it is the opinion of her friends, as well as of his, that the change in their marital relations was due to her conduct and her treatment of him.

I have it in writing over her own signature that their domestic differences were chiefly due to her own fault. It is certain that her friends continued to like and respect my brother after the divorce proceedings. I can mention no better illustration than the fact that the Ambassador from Chile, an old friend of Mrs. De Saulles and her family, had dinner with my brother only a few days before the tragedy.

Nor do I believe that her act was caused by an overpowering affection for the boy. She had agreed to a division of custody and even when she had him in her charges she did not spend all her time with him by any means. During the divorce proceedings she went abroad for several months, leaving the boy in this country. And the fact that she shot his father in the back, firing five shots in the presence of the little boy, my aged father, and my sister, seems to me to indicate that the welfare of the boy was not in her mind at the time. What more dreadful heritage could she have bequeathed him than that memory? The cold deliberation of her act: her statement immediately after the shooting: "Now send for a policeman," and her whole conduct seems to show a mind moved by cold fury and not by sudden anger.

But all these things will transpire in due time. I do not wish to bandy recriminations, but I must protect my brother's name. He was not free from fault, but he was always generous and kindly in his treatment of her. He was loved by hosts of friends, and his memory will always be dear to them. I hope that the rage which caused his death will cease to pursue him in his grave, and that it will not be necessary for me as his brother again to defend his memory.[4]

When details of this diatribe reached Uterhart, he wasted no time in drafting a response:

With respect to the extraordinary statement of Mr. De Saulles, I will only say so far as it concerns myself, that one of the most ancient devices known to the law is contained in the rule, "When you have no case, abuse the opposing counsel." Mr. De Saulles glosses over as a matter of no importance the undisputed fact that it has been judicially determined that John De Saulles was an unfaithful husband and that his wife was granted an absolute divorce in this State upon the ground of his infidelity. If this constitutes Mr. De Saulles's conception of "devoted and loving husband" he is welcome to his opinion.

The most important of the charges of Mrs. De Saulles against her husband were, in part, that he married her for her money, grew cold toward her when her fortune did not come up to his expectations, got $47,000 of her fortune of $100,000 by deceptions, became unfaithful early in their married life, took women companions into their apartment, and took the boy out with them, treated her brutally and contemptuously in the presence of her son and servants, and tried to destroy the boy's affection for her.[5]

As reporters struggled to digest this torrent of words, one of them threw Uterhart a curveball. If Blanca had such a skimpy income, how could she afford to rent a swell place like the Crossways for the season? Uterhart repeated the same story he had offered a day earlier: that in her fight to retain the affection of her boy, she was forced into "reckless expenditure . . . to offer him attractions equal to those which De Saulles, backed by the Heckscher millions, could offer."[6]

Uterhart, visibly nettled, steered the exchange back to Blanca's worsening mental state, saying she had spent the day in bed, eating almost nothing and constantly asking to see her son—but the questions kept coming. Why did Mrs. de Saulles carry a gun with her on the fateful night? Uterhart's response—"Because many women had been held up or alarmed by highwaymen in the lonely roads of Nassau county"[7]—fooled no one, least of all District Attorney Weeks. The outlandish assertion of "highwaymen" roaming the byways of Long Island brought forth a snort of contempt. The prisoner, Weeks said, "went there to shoot her husband. The killing of John De Saulles was a deliberate murder."[8] He added that his department had uncovered all the evidence it needed to proceed, and he was confident of the outcome: "The State can put its case in less than forty-eight hours."[9]

Blanca had no complaints about her jailhouse treatment. "I have done everything possible for the comfort of Mrs. De Saulles," said Mrs. Seaman, who was acting as personal chef and factotum to her celebrity inmate.

> *Her physicians have told me that she is very frail and that care should be taken to prevent serious illness; so I feel it my duty to personally supervise the treatment accorded her. Besides, it is a real pleasure to be able to do anything for the poor child, she is so deeply grateful for the smallest attention. I have never known a more refined and sweet-tempered young woman.*[10]

Mrs. Seaman further reported that when she asked Blanca if she wanted a priest, the latter had replied, "During my residence in the United States I have had no active connection with the Church, and I do not wish to have it appear that I think of such matters only in time of trouble."[11]

But everybody wanted a share of the de Saulles limelight. In San Francisco, actress Ruth Shepley resurfaced to claim that she had been secretly "affianced" to Jack, and she sprang to his defense. "When they call Jack De Saulles the most popular man on Broadway it makes me want to cry 'unfair,'" she told a reporter as she curled up in an armchair in her suite at the Palace Hotel on Market Street. "Jack had the personality to be the most popular man in New York, not in the sense that 'Broadway' popularity is usually taken to mean."[12] She insisted that she and Jack had intended to marry. "I loved him as much as a woman can love a man," she said, adding elliptically, "and a woman can love a man like him more than any tongue can tell."[13]

On this same day, Marshall Ward also entered the verbal fray. At a hastily convened press briefing, the dead man's business partner declared that Jack "was no Lothario. He was as clean and straight and honest a fellow as ever lived. Of course, to defend her they must throw mud at him."[14] Then Ward twisted the knife. Blanca had attended the Carman trial, and it was that travesty of justice that gave her the idea that "a woman might commit a murder and come to be regarded as a heroine."[15] Nor was it any coincidence that Blanca had appointed the same law firm that had defended Mrs. Carman. Ward toned down the rhetoric to tell how one day after the shooting Jack Jr. came to him and asked, "What did you do with my dad?" Ward said he had been unable to find the words to tell little Jack what had happened, but the lad had pressed, "You are going to tell me." Ward said that his father had gone to the hospital. "Not for good?" asked the boy.

"No, he'll be back soon, Jack," Ward gently lied. "He'll be all right."

Their exchange seemed to comfort the little boy, who "adored his father."[16]

That night and the following morning, the dead man's relatives and their lawyers thrashed out the details concerning visitation rights for Jack Jr. When asked earlier, Charles de Saulles had said, "No decision has been reached to refuse or consent, so far as I know. I will try to do . . . what is best for the boy's welfare, and just what I believe my brother would have done and what he would want me to do."[17] At meeting's end, an announcement conveyed that Jack would visit his mother for the first time since the shooting. District Attorney Weeks, when advised of the decision, had no objection.

But first there was the business of the inquest into Jack's death. It convened at the Old Mineola Courthouse, with Justice of the Peace Walter R. Jones acting as coroner. A frisson of excitement hung in the air, even before testimony began, from the revelation that overnight someone—smart money was on some press employee—had broken into Crossways and stolen a set of photos of Jack Jr. Testimony began at 2:00 p.m. with Dr. Harry G. Warner, who performed the autopsy. De Saulles had died from hemorrhages caused by several bullet wounds, he said, and he had extracted two of the bullets in his examination. Weeks brought out that the murder weapon was a five-chambered revolver, confirming that Blanca, in her rage, had emptied the revolver into her ex-husband.

Marshall Ward gave a graphic account of the shooting that didn't differ materially from anything previously reported. After him, Sheriff Seaman and Constable Thorne described the circumstances of Blanca's arrest. With these formalities observed, Jones called Suzanne Monteau. There was no response. Jones tried a second time, still no response. The maid was nowhere to be seen. Bemused court officers shrugged, and Jones, fighting back frustration, adjourned the inquest until a later date. When news of this development reached Uterhart—who hadn't bothered attending the inquest—he protested

The Mineola Courthouse staged the "most sensational" trial in Long Island history, but a fire in 1981 destroyed the records and transcripts.

that Miss Monteau's absence followed a simple misunderstanding. She was, he said, in the jailhouse with her mistress—"not more than 75 feet from the room in which the hearing was held"[18]—and would have been perfectly willing to testify had she been made aware of the court's wishes in advance.

Having satisfied the court on this score, Uterhart went back to working the phone. All day long he had been conducting intense negotiations, and at 5:10 p.m. his efforts finally bore fruit when a large black touring car left the Heckscher home in Westbury. Twenty minutes later it pulled up outside the long, low, ivy-covered jailhouse in Mineola. Out stepped Ernest B. Tracy, a friend of the de Saulles family, with a private detective hired to safeguard the car's third passenger. The two men lifted Jack Jr. from the backseat and walked him up the steps.

Flashbulbs popped to record the moment. The press had its first view of the innocent cause of this tragedy: a chubby lad, large for his age, smartly turned out in a white sailor suit, his mop of brown hair tucked into a straw boater. Jack Jr.'s arrival had been expected, so a uniformed turnkey swung back the main door without being asked. Inside, the boy cried, "Where's mamma's room? I want to see my mamma."[19] Directed toward a flight of iron stairs, he scampered up, shouting, "Mamma! Mamma!"[20]

Blanca stood in the doorway of her room. The boy ran up and threw himself into her waiting arms, almost knocking her over and sending his straw hat flying. Blanca smothered him with kisses; her frigid exterior melting instantly. For the first time since her incarceration, she wept.

Watching the scene, Estella Seaman also wiped away tears as the little boy asked, "How long are you going to be here, mother?"[21] Blanca was evasive. "A long time, I fear . . . but you mustn't mind. Mother will come back to you."[22] Throughout the half-hour visit, Blanca balanced Jack on her knee, not once letting him out of her sight. Every second of the reunion took place under the watchful eye of two witnesses—and a handful of carefully selected reporters. The only awkward moment came when the little boy asked, "Where's daddy?"[23] and Blanca couldn't find the words to answer. But Jack Jr. didn't stop beaming the whole time he was with his mother, turning moody only when told it was time to leave. Blanca clutched him to her bosom for as long as possible and only surrendered him with the greatest reluctance, begging the boy to come again soon.

Earlier that day, before news that her son was on his way had revived her, Blanca reportedly had relapsed so severely that the sheriff once again called Dr. Cleghorn. The doctor found her in a state bordering on "collapse"[24] and "still losing weight at an alarming rate,"[25] something of a surprise considering the platefuls of food that Blanca was demolishing on a regular basis, according to Mrs. Seaman. He wanted to X-ray her, he said, to diagnose the mysterious malady from which she was suffering. Without much improvement in her health, he doubted that Blanca would be fit enough to stand trial. But Jack Jr.'s visit had wrought a miraculous change. Mrs. Seaman could scarcely believe the transformation. "She seems like a different woman. You would not know her."[26]

Two more developments rounded out the day. First came the surprise news that Jack had died without signing a will. For months his lawyers had urged him to remedy this oversight and had prepared several documents, only for him to postpone signing the instrument. His counselors first drew up the paperwork during the divorce proceedings, but Jack kept fiddling with the details, mostly as they applied to his son. The will indicated that he should attend public schools until he reached age thirteen, then a prep school, then Yale. While no details of the estate were released, estimates put his business income at more than fifty thouand dollars a year.

Then, as dusk began to fall, a cablegram brought the announcement that, owing to ill-health, Señora Errázuriz-Vergara had delayed her journey to America, and would not now be departing until Saturday, August 11. It was anticipated that Amalia would be traveling with her.

The next day saw the resumption of the inquest. Uterhart accompanied Suzanne Monteau to the DA's office in the courthouse, where she gave a deposition, describing her version of events on the night in question. Weeks asked why Blanca seemed in such a hurry that night. "She told the taxi man to drive as fast as he could to The Box, because she said we would be able to get the baby and get back before Mr. De Saulles returned from the club."[27]

"Tell what happened when you got to The Box."[28]

"When we got to The Box we left the taxi not very far from the house and walked to the front door. We saw his sister on the stairs with the baby."[29] Blanca then said, "I want to see Mr. De Saulles"[30] and was directed toward the living room. As she entered the room, Jack stood up and came toward her. Blanca said, "I don't think it is nice for you to keep the baby so long and not let me know anything about it. I don't think that is nice."[31]

"Blanquita, you can't have the baby now or ever."[32]

Aware of the importance of this evidence—especially in light of rumors that it would form a cornerstone of the defense—Weeks asked if de Saulles had definitely used this phrase. Suzanne swore that this was the case. Then, Suzanne continued, Blanca approached Jack. He didn't move. "He looked terrible. . . . Oh, my! His eyes were terrible. He looked as if he would jump on her."

"Did he look as if he would strike her?"

Weeks's question was astonishing. That a district attorney would ask a leading question so favorable to the defense defied belief.

"Yes."[33]

"How far was his wife from him when you noticed this look?"[34]

About eight feet, said the maid. Mrs. de Saulles approached until she was about two feet away, then stopped. "She took the revolver out and shot him. He didn't move. He had his face toward her. She shot him in front three times, and then he turned. Nobody said anything. Nobody moved. Everybody was there. She put the gun on a table and said: 'Now call a policeman.' We waited a few minutes, and the police came."[35]

After the inquest was adjourned, Uterhart declared himself "elated" at Suzanne's testimony, which he regarded as the "strongest possible evidence for the defense."[36] Weeks, too, was satisfied. He thought that Suzanne's assertion that Blanca looked "absolutely calm"[37] weakened defense claims that hers had been an act of passion.

But public support, at least according to Uterhart, was continuing to build behind the beleaguered young woman, and it was coming from all sectors of society. A US sailor, born in Chile, had visited the attorney's office and laid five five-dollar gold pieces on the desk. "I want to give this toward Mrs. De Saulles's defense fund,"[38] he was reported as saying. A clerk thanked the man and returned the money, assuring him that no such fund was needed or existed.

Mrs. Seaman also drip-fed details of Blanca's health to the press. It had improved considerably following the visit of her son, said the sheriff's wife, and for first the time she had some color in her face. Doctors Wight and Cleghorn, on the other hand, still had concerns about their patient's health, and that afternoon an X-ray machine was wheeled into the jail. All Wight would say as he left was that his patient was suffering from "great exhaustion."[39]

Disappointment, too, played a part. Blanca had heard that Jack Jr. would be making a second visit that day, but as the hours ticked away so did her hopes of seeing her son. At one point she stood forlornly at the second-story window of her neatly furnished room, watching the roads for the auto that would bring Jack Jr. In the streets below, excited onlookers pointed at the window. It was the first time they had seen Blanca, the whiteness of her face accentuated by her dark hair, pulled straight back from her forehead. She quickly withdrew, eluding the press photographers who had set up their bulky cameras at the front entrance in hopes of grabbing more shots of the boy as he entered the jailhouse.

During the afternoon two visitors arrived. One was a fashionably dressed elderly woman, the other a Mr. Cutan, a young Chilean who had known Blanca as a girl in Valparaíso. They stayed for a few minutes only, then drove off together. Half an hour later Cutan returned, alone, bearing a copy of *Town Topics,* which he handed to Blanca.

Blanca's vigil lasted until 9:00 p.m., ending only when a jailer shook his head and told her that Jack Jr. definitely wasn't coming.

August 11

In his daily press briefing on Saturday, Uterhart first repeated his claim that Blanca always felt entitled to full custody, only to backtrack hastily when a reporter pointed out that she had agreed to the 7–5 split. "I cannot discuss that," Uterhart said. "It is too close to the issues of the trial."[40] Grizzled veterans of the crime beat had noticed that any mention of the divorce settlement made Uterhart uneasy. They wondered why.

Weeks also had a couple of tidbits to keep the front-page pot boiling. Although coy about divulging details, he declared that, in his view, the deposition of the taxi driver, James Donner, greatly strengthened the state's view that Blanca had gone to shoot her ex-husband deliberately. So, what are your chances of getting a guilty verdict? he was asked. He paused. "I think there is no doubt that the murder was premeditated. I think we have a strong case. But I am too old a campaigner to predict a victory," he replied and then added wryly, "remember, she's a woman."[41]

With Blanca under lock and key and likely to remain so for weeks if not months, the press needed another angle to keep the story running. They found it in the de Saulles family's finances. According to one newspaper, just before his death, Jack had begun work on a polo field, five hundred by nine hundred feet, at the rear of The Box. Two large sheds had already been erected to stable his eight polo ponies, and the turf was rapidly being readied for play. Estimates put Jack's outlay at six thousand dollars so far, and the work was far from complete. He also had engaged a firm of landscape architects to prepare a tract of land adjacent to the property of Maurice Heckscher, with a view to building a home there in the near future. Such expenditures, said family friends, made a mockery of claims that Jack relied on Blanca for money.

They also trashed those stories about Blanca being forced to live in relative poverty. She had taken Crossways, they said, because it gave her the space to build an elaborate playground for her son, and the rent for the property was actually $3,500 for the season, not $2,000 as the press had reported. Bearing in mind Uterhart's claim that Blanca's annual income was $4,000 a year, plus maintenance of $300 a month, one newspaper quoted sources as saying it would have been "impossible"[42] for her to live in the extravagant manner that she did without receiving financial assistance from her family in Chile.

Another paper gleefully reported that details of the sealed divorce decree would "probably figure prominently"[43] in the trial. This announcement once again forced Uterhart on the defensive, sparking yet another indignant denial that, in a countersuit allegedly threatened by de Saulles, Blanca's name had been linked with "a cabaret dancer."[44]

Uterhart was far more comfortable relaying details of Blanca's health and demeanor. Dr. Cleghorn had told him that she had been able to sit up during the day and was feeling "very much better."[45] Cleghorn had added, "Today, for the first time, I feel optimistic about Mrs. De Saulles"—until sounding a cautionary note: "But she is still very ill."[46]

August 12

Despite intense public interest, Blanca was exercising caution. When a group of women arrived at the jail, claiming friendship with the prisoner, they were peremptorily turned away, with word that Blanca would see no one except legal counsel and close friends. The women, apparently, returned to the city "much disgruntled."[47] But no such frostiness greeted Suzanne Monteau. Each day she arrived at the jail, bringing not just companionship but regular changes of clothing and "a few delicacies to eat."[48]

A rather different kind of visitor showed up on the afternoon of August 12. A large automobile was seen to slowly drive past the jail. Nothing unusual there. Since the shooting practically everyone with a car on Long Island had taken time to visit the jailhouse. Inquisitive reporters routinely scrutinized each car's occupants, and most were quickly dismissed as non-newsworthy. On this occasion, though, they spotted Major de Saulles in the backseat, his eyes fixed on the window of the second-story room where Blanca was being held. He didn't stay long. As soon he saw the press pack begin to gather, he barked at the chauffeur, and the car raced off.

Earlier that day, a band of evangelists had held a religious service in the jail directly beneath Blanca's window. They sang "My Faith Looks Up to Thee." Blanca showed no interest in them. Nor did she have time for a priest who called to offer spiritual guidance; he was dismissed with word that she had made alternative religious arrangements.

The day's most significant development, so far as the defense was concerned, came with news that the J. Doll Construction Company of New York had filed in the County Clerk's office at Mineola a lien for $2,383.51 against John de Saulles and Mrs. Emily Ladenburg, from whom Jack bought The Box. The lien was for nonpayment of work done on the polo field between July 19 and August 7. For the first time, a chink had appeared in the claims that Jack had no need of Blanca's money. Perhaps in light of this development, District Attorney Weeks announced that he was forgoing his vacation to better prepare the case against Blanca.

August 13

More headaches lay in store for Weeks when it became known that the defense once again had consulted Max D. Steuer. Fortunately for the state, the formidable attorney's participation was restricted to matters relating to that contentious divorce settlement. But even so, when Steuer spoke, others listened, and he stated that several weeks prior to the divorce hearing the couple had signed a preliminary agreement.

> *Following the court decree another agreement was made by Mr. and Mrs. De Saulles which modified the court order that prohibited the mother taking her son to Chile during the period of the war. The original stipulation provided that Mrs. De Saulles was to have possession of her son seven months each year and his father was to have him for the other five. But as these periods were divided so that each parent had the boy alternate months, Mrs. De Saulles said she could not take her son to Chile to see her relatives and return in a month.*
>
> *I suggested that she should have the boy for a continuous period of seven months and the father for five, and a petition to that effect was made to the court. While that was pending I took the matter up with Mr. Fox and former Judge Morgan J. O'Brien. They finally agreed to this arrangement, and I understand that the agreement was put in writing by attorneys for Mr. De Saulles and by Prince & Nathan, who were attorneys of record for Mrs. De Saulles.*[49]

According to Steuer, this agreement was made after the initial hearing and before the referee's final judgment, yet, for some reason, it was not acted upon. Had both parties signed the agreement, Steuer hinted, this tragedy might have been avoided.

Steuer took no further part in the case, much to Uterhart's relief. All this talk of dubious divorce settlements was deflecting attention away from Uterhart's primary goal: swinging public sentiment in favor of his client. Her condition, he warned, was declining again, and could only be ameliorated by another visit from her son, and yet the de Saulles family was playing hardball over access. Uterhart professed himself disgusted by their intransigence and baffled by Jack Jr.'s continued absence from the jail. Caroline Degener scoffed that there was "no mystery"[50] about the boy's whereabouts. "He is with Mrs. Heckscher and a nurse."[51]

August 14

The clearest demonstration yet of the public support for Blanca came from a most unexpected quarter. Out of the blue, Joan Sawyer offered herself as a sacrificial lamb for the defense. In an open letter to the press, she wrote: "I am very sorry Mrs. De Saulles is in this deep trouble, and if I can help her by having my name and reputation blasted publicly, I am at her service."[52]

Such apparent selflessness probably owed more to a craving for publicity[53]—since the divorce Joan's career had nose-dived—than from a genuine desire to help her former rival. Especially as, tacked on the end of Joan's statement, was this barbed threat: "If the counsel for the defense will look into the matter more carefully I think they will find it agreeable to save me from more unjust and unpleasant notoriety."[54] Joan seemed to be saying: *Go easy on my name during the trial. You don't know what I might reveal about the defendant.* Understandably in the circumstances, Uterhart refused to be drawn out, continuing instead to bang the drum about his client's frail health. According to him her pulse was now "barely discernible."[55]

At long last the warring parties thrashed out an agreement over the issue of regular visitation rights for Jack Jr. In a letter from attorney George Gordon Battle to Uterhart, he stated, "I am directed by Charles A. H. De Saulles to inform you that John Longer De Saulles Jr. will call tomorrow, August 15, at Mineola Jail, at 11 a.m., for the purpose of visiting his mother, Mrs. Blanca De Saulles. I am further directed to say to you that the boy will visit his mother at any reasonable time she may desire . . . if she will manifest this desire in writing to me at least twenty-four hours before such visit."[56]

This was a major victory for Blanca, and more good news followed, this time from Chile: Señora Errázuriz-Vergara, her son Guillermo, and other daughter Amalia had left Valparaíso aboard the steamship *Palena* for New York. The family had also been pulling strings on the diplomatic front, with the announcement that the Chilean Embassy had commissioned Guillermo as a special attaché, which gave him official standing in America, thereby materially aiding his efforts on behalf of his imprisoned sister.

August 15

The next day, as promised, Jack Jr. was brought to the jail. In the car with him were Caroline Degener and Mrs. Heckscher. To avoid the scrum of reporters, they pulled up at the rear entrance. Also with them was private detective Harry V. Dougherty, who carried Jack Jr. to his mother's room while the two women remained in the car. Blanca was lying on the bed but didn't rise to greet her son. Jack Jr. kissed her and then played for half an hour in the room, fascinated by a brass birdcage that his mother had bought. Once again, reporters viewed the meeting from a distance. Sheriff Seaman shook his head and expressed worries about Blanca's deterioration, saying that she now ate little and spent most of her time in bed. The press lapped it up. One report claimed that since her incarceration—just eleven days—the prisoner had lost forty pounds!

But the visit from Jack Jr. obviously provided a tonic, and over the next few days Blanca's health improved. She was sleeping better, and her demeanor became brighter, more cheerful. Under Dr. Cleghorn's tutelage, Blanca began a course of calisthenics. For the first time in a couple of days, she was able to leave her bed and, with Suzanne's assistance, waded through the estimated fifteen hundred letters she had received. Some came from cranks, but the vast majority was from well-wishers, offering support. The letters came in such abundance that Sheriff Seaman had to place three large boxes in Blanca's room to accommodate them all. Never in the history of Nassau County, said Seaman, had any prisoner received so much correspondence. Nor did interest in the case limit itself to America. Across the Atlantic, the London *Daily Mirror* splashed images of the photogenic Blanca de Saulles, her late ex-husband, and son, telling readers that the prisoner was "an immensely wealthy woman."[57]

Such coverage gave Uterhart palpitations. But that was nothing compared to the devastating blow he received on August 25, when his longtime partner, John J. Graham, died at his home on Jericho Road in Syosset. His health problems began while he was representing Florence Carman. The strain of that case, it was said, had played havoc with his heart. He collapsed at the Belmont racetrack and had been ill for several months, but no one suspected the seriousness of it. Uterhart must have wondered if defending Blanca de Saulles would have a similar effect on him.

ELEVEN

Indictment

As summer faded into fall, the custody battle heated up.

On September 4, Charles de Saulles obtained an order from Surrogate[1] Robert Fowler directing that Blanca show cause why he shouldn't be appointed general guardian. Uterhart's disdain was palpable. "Of course the petition will be opposed,"[2] he told reporters. Moreover, he feared that serving the papers might cause his client to break down. "Mrs. De Saulles took the matter very hard, but had recovered somewhat before I left her at 6 o'clock."[3]

He explained that earlier that day Blanca had shown a greater interest in the admittedly cramped world around her, staring out from her jailhouse window at the lines of soldiers from the newly established Camp Mills being drilled on the plain. Overhead, fragile biplanes from the nearby Hazelhurst Aviation Field skittered and wheeled in the crystal clear sky, grimly heralding a new frontier in warfare. According to Uterhart, as Blanca watched all of this, her mood darkened. Then came the hammer blow of the de Saulles family's petition.

"My client will insist that I oppose this application," he announced, "and I shall do so on the ground that a proceeding is unnecessary at this time. . . . There is less reason for changing the guardianship of the boy at this time, as he is being well cared for by his father's other relatives."[4] The dry legalese frustrated the press pack, who drifted away, wondering how best to placate impatient editors who demanded personality-driven pieces in order to maintain public interest. It turned out they had just twenty-four hours to kill before the next big development.

The following day, after weeks at sea, Señora Errázuriz-Vergara disembarked in Havana and made immediate preparations for the second leg of her journey, from Key West to Washington, on Henry Flagler's recently completed Overseas Railroad. Once in Washington, she was expected to confer with the Chilean ambassador and other friends. The family's millions were already being put to good use, as Uterhart announced that another Long Island legal heavyweight, former Nassau County judge Lewis J. Smith, had joined the defense team. Significantly, Smith had been the prosecutor in the Carman case, a chastening experience that gave him invaluable insight into the difficulties of convicting a wealthy defendant. Uterhart also told the press that he intended to greet Señora Errázuriz-Vergara in New York when she arrived.

The lawyer held true to his word. At 3:55 p.m. on September 10, he was standing on the platform at Penn Station when the train carrying the party from Chile wheezed to a halt. The señora—two days behind schedule, owing to a busy round of arm-twisting in Washington—looked elegant as always. Clean-cut Guillermo, in his gray lounge suit and tennis shoes, could have been on his way to the club for a game of squash. Only Amalia, her light brown suit badly wrinkled by travel, showed any ill-effects from the three-week journey. Comparisons to her younger sister inevitably followed, and the best that anyone could manage to describe her appearance was "wholesome."[5] Uterhart guided the family to his vehicle and then chauffeured them to Crossways, where they would remain for the duration of the ordeal. An unruly caravan of reporters chased them every yard of the way. At Crossways, the señora refused interview requests but, after some hesitation, turned to Uterhart. "Tell them this," she said in a flawless English accent, "that I am here to do for my daughter all that a mother can do. That is all I will or can say at this time."[6]

Shortly afterward, Señora Errázuriz-Vergara and Guillermo were driven to the jail. Amalia motored instead to the East Williston home of the Igleharts, who had visited Blanca regularly since her incarceration. At 5:30 p.m. the auto carrying the señora and her son drew up at the rear of the jail, and they hurried in. The señora, dressed in black and wearing a heavy black veil, was said to be in mourning for a relative who had died recently. She seemed frail. On the steps she required assistance from her son as she stumbled and nearly fell.

Inside, Sheriff Seaman bowed and scraped and led the way to Blanca's second-floor room. Curiously, before the reunion, the señora, overcome again, had to rest to compose herself before seeing her daughter. Accounts of their meeting are sketchy, but it doesn't appear to have been excessively warm. Señora Errázuriz-Vergara had never forgiven Jack for that frightful scene in Paris, which she blamed on Blanca's reckless liaison with such an obvious fortune hunter. Today, though, was all about pragmatism: getting the full details of the crime and determining how best to clean up this humiliating mess. She and Blanca huddled together for more than two hours. The relationship must have thawed a little because, as she left, the señora pointed to four doves on the coping over Blanca's cell window and radiated delight, taking them as a good omen.

Two days later the matriarch returned to the jailhouse, this time with Amalia. Blanca hugged the sister she hadn't seen since her seclusion at the Hotel Majestic during the divorce hearing. The meeting lasted several hours, and at its conclusion Blanca was said to be in much better spirits, despite not having seen her son for two weeks. Once again the de Saulles family was quibbling over the contentious visitation rights. Their grievance harked back to August 15, when Battle had laid out the stipulation of a twenty-four-hour notice for each visit. At the time Blanca stated that she wished to see her son every day from ten o'clock to noon. Battle sniffed that daily visits were not "reasonable,"[7] countering that the family felt that twice a week would be appropriate. The two sides met at the Bar Association to hammer out a compromise, but the meeting ended in discord. Blanca's refusal to comply with their condition of a written request for each visit meant that she hadn't seen her son since August 28.

More frustration came with the agonizing slowness of the judicial process. Because of a shortage of available Supreme Court justices, no grand jury could be called in September. Therefore an indictment would not be returned until October at the earliest. A further delay would follow until a trial date was set.

But until then, Blanca had other battles to fight. To no one's surprise, Uterhart went to court to oppose Charles de Saulles's guardianship application. When the date of Blanca's trial was set, he declared that he wouldn't oppose the appointment of Mrs. G. Maurice Heckscher as temporary guardian—but until such time Blanca was the child's legal guardian and entitled to regular visits.

Former US senator James A. Gorman contended, for the petitioner, that Blanca had "incapacitated herself"[8] from acting as her son's guardian. Because her relatives were aliens, the boy's relatives on his father's side should be appointed. Furthermore, upon the death of his father, Jack Jr. had inherited a house and nine acres in Nassau County, reason enough, said Gorman, for a guardian to be appointed.

Uterhart countered, quite reasonably, that Blanca must be considered innocent until found guilty, but he worried about the adverse impact of all this bickering on his client.

> *I do not think the case of Mrs. De Saulles should be prejudiced in the eyes of the community and of persons likely to be called on the jury, through having newspaper headlines state that the Surrogate has taken this mother's boy away from her. . . . I do not believe it fair for the court to exercise discretion by appointing as guardian the bitterest enemy of the mother. If the court insists on appointing a guardian, we would not object to Mrs. G. Maurice Heckscher.*[9]

When Gorman cried foul, Uterhart argued that the boy should remain in "a woman's care."[10] Also, if Blanca were acquitted with the boy in the custody of the de Saulles family, Uterhart feared that she might have trouble reclaiming her son. The presiding adjudicator, Surrogate Robert Fowler, reserved his decision.

Elsewhere on Long Island others had clearly followed the de Saulles case closely. When Robert Carbone of Cedar Manor filed for divorce from his wife, Constance, a professional singer, on the grounds of adultery, she applied in the Supreme Court in Manhattan for an order allowing her to see her two sons. Carbone said he had no objection to any visitation, but he was wary of ceding custody because he feared that she would remove them from the jurisdiction of the court. Also, he was scared. "She has threatened me, not once, but a dozen times," declared the plaintiff, "that if I did not give up the children she would shoot me, as she had a precedent for such action in the recent De Saulles case."[11] Justice Samuel Greenbaum, not about to deny an enraged mother access to her children, ordered the quaking husband to let his wife see the boys.

On October 11, after much legal heel-dragging, the Nassau County grand jury finally began considering the case against Blanca de Saulles. The state's star witness, according to Weeks, would be Julius Hadamek. This move surprised the defense. They felt that the valet's assertion by phone that de Saulles wasn't at The Box strongly supported their view that she had no intention of killing him. Weeks promised to quash that misapprehension. Among others called to testify were Caroline Degener, Marshall Ward, Suzanne Monteau, Constable Thorne, Dr. Warner, James Donner, Noe Tagliabue, and two gardeners who worked at Crossways.

Unlike a trial, evidence to a grand jury is given in camera, so there are no reports detailing what was said. All we know is that Weeks presented his case in a single day and the grand jury said it would announce its verdict later. As grand juries exist mainly to rubber-stamp a district attorney's wishes, it came as no surprise when, on October 15, an indictment was handed down, charging Blanca with murder in the first degree. If convicted, she faced the electric chair.

Two days later Blanca left the jailhouse for the first time since the night of the shooting. At 2:00 p.m., flanked by Uterhart and Lewis J. Smith, she walked through a darkened tunnel that led from the jail to the courthouse and into the court of Justice Jaycox. Standing in the shadow of the towering Uterhart only emphasized Blanca's childlike frailty. She was immaculately turned out in a frock of green and white checks, with a large black bow, all topped off by a matching black hat.

When the clerk of the court said, "Blanca De Saulles, you are indicted by the Grand Jury on the charge of murder in the first degree. How do you plead?"[12] she looked utterly bewildered. Uterhart spoke for her. "We plead not guilty, your honor."[13] Blanca sank into her chair and, her hands clasped in her lap, remained mute and still. For the most part she kept her head downcast, but when she did lift her face it showed the benefits of the exercise that she had been taking recently. Her eyes had a sparkle previously lacking, and some color had returned to her cheeks. A trial date was set for the latter half of November. Not having uttered a word, Blanca and her phalanx of lawyers reentered the tunnel. As she exited the darkness a press cameraman set off a flashbulb, startling her. She stifled a scream and clutched hold of Uterhart's arm. After steadying herself, she walked, unassisted, back to her room, where reportedly she collapsed on her cot.

Now it was a matter of waiting.

During this hiatus Uterhart held all the aces. A steady stream of press releases flowed from his office, all scripted to present Blanca in the most favorable, caring light. He let it be known that his client was raising a little flower garden on the sunny side of the jail, assisted by her constant companion, Mrs. Seaman, who was doing everything in her power to make Blanca's time behind bars as comfortable as possible.

The Errázuriz-Vergara family also played its part. Every day her mother and sister brought huge bunches of flowers. Those that Blanca couldn't fit into her room she distributed among the other inmates. Indeed, Blanca was turning into a regular Elizabeth Fry,[14] judging from her concern for the welfare of her fellow prisoners. When a Polish woman, arrested for not sending her children to school and unable to afford the ten-dollar fine, was jailed for ten days, Blanca stepped into the breach and paid it for her. The grateful mother heaped "blessings on her benefactor,"[15] and, praying for Blanca's speedy release, left the jail as quickly as possible. Amy Felix, another inmate, also benefited from Blanca's largesse. Life had been tough for this young woman, but she was fighting back. A junkie at the time of her arrest, Amy had kicked the habit during her six months behind bars. Blanca had taken her under her wing, and just before Amy's walk to freedom she, too, received ten dollars and an assurance that if she fell on hard times she should get in touch. Uterhart's strategy owed nothing to subtlety, but, judging by the glowing press coverage, it was working wonders.

After further wrangling, the announcement came that Blanca's trial was provisionally scheduled for Monday, November 19. It all depended on the murder trial of Dominick Damasco, slated to begin the Monday previous, which could overrun a couple of days. Weeks said he was ready, no matter what, and he intended calling about fifteen witnesses. Uterhart, bursting with confidence, boasted that he could make do with half that number. One person unlikely to testify was Major de Saulles. Since the shooting his already frail health had taken a serious turn for the worse, raising concerns that he might not even attend the trial.

During the interim, Blanca's legal team won a significant victory on November 8 when Surrogate Fowler handed down a decision refusing to appoint Charles de Saulles as Jack Jr.'s guardian. "I do not quite understand why the Supreme Court originally saw fit to deprive the mother, being the innocent party to the divorce action, of the sole custody of her infant, under fourteen, ordinarily granted to the innocent parties." He added darkly, "No doubt there were good reasons."[16] Fowler held that the death of Jack de Saulles had nullified the divorce decree and that, in the normal course of events, he would grant the application of the uncle. But because accusations had been made that Charles de Saulles was "not a fit and proper person and that his ordinary residence has been the scene of debaucheries in times past," Surrogate Fowler deferred the matter for the taking of testimony "in order that I might inspect the parties and their witnesses."[17] He intimated that even if the application were granted he would insist that Blanca be allowed to see the boy whenever possible.

Responsibility for conducting the trial lay in the hands of Supreme Court Justice David F. Manning. At age sixty, Manning was long on experience and notoriously short on patience. He conducted his trials briskly, always with an eye on the clock and the taxpayer's dollar; time wasters received no mercy. But other factors were beyond his control. On November 13, it was announced that the judge had received a threatening letter. Scrawled in pencil and unsigned, it forecast that Justice Manning would face a "dire fate" unless he "did his duty"[18] and ordered the jury to discharge Mrs. de Saulles and allow her "to return to her baby."[19] Manning dismissed the letter as the work of a "religious crank"[20]—the note was larded with biblical references—but it was noted that two officers accompanied him when he entered court for the Damasco trial.

In matters of courtroom decorum, Justice Manning ran a tight ship: no cameras and definitely none of the frippery that marred the trial of Mrs. Carman, in which rows of knitting women had raised the specter of Madame Defarge with her clacking needles in the shadow of the guillotine. Court would open promptly at 10:00 a.m., lunch would be taken between 12:30 and 1:30 p.m., and the court would adjourn at 4:00 p.m. Because of the crank letter, Justice Manning placed a strict embargo on anyone standing in the corridors, nor would any spectators carrying bundles be admitted to the public gallery. He also ordered extra policemen to be drafted in with instruction to admit only those who could be seated. Anyone without a seat would have to wait outside the courthouse.

Justice Manning's circumspection was well placed. According to one newspaper, interest in the trial "eclipses anything that has been encountered before in the criminal history of Long Island."[21] Applications for seats were oversubscribed threefold. Because of the limited seating capacity and the wide public interest, the clerk of the court first issued tickets to newspapermen and others with business in the court, and the remaining 175 seats were made available to the public on a first-come, first-served basis. Society friends of the de Saulles family had made numerous applications for seats, but Justice Manning ruled that none except those directly involved in the case should receive favor.

Both sides made last-minute preparations. In a curious and surprising move, it was reported that the defense team would do "all in its power" to prevent the unveiling of Jack's "Broadway career"[22] during testimony. Such a decision can only have been driven by trepidation. If the defense did open that can of worms, it would allow the prosecution similar license to dig into Blanca's background, and, clearly, there was something buried there that Uterhart didn't want exhumed.

Weeks declared himself confident that the prisoner would be convicted. "The case is a simple one," he said. "The wife came to the house and shot her husband, from whom she was divorced. Eyewitnesses were standing within a few feet of her. I don't know how that can be explained away."[23]

But as trial day drew closer, Uterhart continued feeding the insatiable press hunger for news about his client. The latest update outlined Blanca's intention to provide Thanksgiving dinner for all sixty inmates of the jail. Dinner would consist of roast turkey, cranberry sauce, and all the trimmings of a regular Thanksgiving feast. The jailhouse cook—said to be "some chef"[24]—would prepare it, and Uterhart promised that the meal would be served regardless of the jury's verdict.

On the eve of the trial, Weeks drafted two late additions to the prosecution team: Charles I. Woods and Elvin N. Edwards. The stage was now set. After three months of waiting and millions of words in the press, the young lady from Chile was about to face a jury of twelve good men and true.[25]

The Trial, Day 1

November 19, 1917

The crowds flocked in from every fashionable corner of Long Island. Fancy automobiles jammed the streets around the Old Mineola Courthouse; horns honked, and irate drivers shouted as chauffeurs unable to find a parking spot on the wide expanse of paved highway in front of the building were steered into the nearest available field. For most it was a wasted trip. Justice Manning had mandated that members of the public be excluded from the voir dire process. As a result, only journalists were on hand as Blanca entered the Mineola courtroom at 9:45 a.m.

She was deathly pale, thin to emaciation. A plain white silk blouse fastened with pearl buttons, a short skirt of black cloth, and low, patent leather shoes accentuated her schoolgirlish appearance. The outfit was stylish but understated. Flouting current fashion, she wore no hat, which allowed spectators to see the mane of dark hair pulled back in a thick coil at the nape of her neck. Her steps were faltering, and at times she seemed almost to stumble and might have fallen had the ever-present Mrs. Seaman not held her arm. Blanca took her seat at the defense table, immediately adjacent to the jury box, and where she was bookended by Uterhart and Smith. She folded her arms and spoke only to whisper occasionally to her attorneys.

The courtroom artists quickly got to work with their chalks and pencils. Elsewhere, an army of "sob sisters,"[26]—regular fixtures now at every major trial—began recording Blanca's dress, expressions, and hand gestures, trying to read her soul, to probe beneath the facade, to discover what drove such a fragrant young woman to the ultimate act of violence on the night of August 3. At a time when millions were dying in trenches on the Western Front, some found their presence ghoulish and repugnant. "The sob squad had gathered, not as you might suppose at the bunting draped mounds of the heroes," one sarcastic newspaper editorial began, "but at the Mineola courthouse where Blanca De Saulles, otherwise Blanquita De Saulles, the 'Fragile Flower of Far Off Chile,' the 'Vision of Loveliness,' the 'White Widow,' the 'Dainty Little Child Wife Who Is More Beautiful Than a Picture,' and, incidentally, the murderess, is on trial for her life."[27]

A few rows behind her sat Amalia and Guillermo. Although ill health had absented their mother, her presence was still felt, thanks to rumors that she was prepared to spend her entire fortune, "estimated at $20,000,000,"[28] to free her daughter and secure custody of Jack Jr. With numbers like that in play, the press was forecasting "the world's most expensive murder trial."[29] Amalia and Guillermo sat imperious and stoic. They offered no obvious words of encouragement to the prisoner, who, if she noticed them at all, didn't show it. Across from them, on the other side of the gangway that divided the spectator seating, the de Saulles clan sat in icy silence. All wore deep mourning, and none spared Blanca as much as a sidelong glance when she entered. Deacon Murphy, a former district attorney of New York County and a reputed expert on jury selection, was protecting their interests.

At 10:00 a.m. Justice Manning took his place on the bench before an enormous American flag that covered the wall behind him, and the business of jury selection got under way, a process expected to take two days. As both sides began quizzing the panel of 150 prospective jurors, it became clear from Uterhart's questions that insanity would figure prominently in the defense strategy. Justice Manning caught the drift and reminded the court that, if this were the case, the onus would fall on the state to prove the prisoner sane.

One by one the veniremen took the stand. Many excused themselves on conscientious grounds, citing an opposition to the death penalty. Those who cleared this first hurdle then had their their prejudices and bias exposed to public view. The case already had polarized opinion among potential jurors. One Oyster Bay resident, John Rader, said he was convinced of Blanca's innocence, and when asked by the judge if any evidence could change that impression, he replied, "There's no evidence that can wipe it out."[30] At the other end of the spectrum, Charles W. Smith of Great Neck said, "According to what I have read in the papers, there is no question about her guilt."[31]

And so it went. By lunchtime, not a single juror had been empanelled.

In the early afternoon, at the fourteenth time of asking, they finally found a juror acceptable to both sides. By virtue of being chosen first, John C. Bucken, a sixty-one-year-old bookkeeper for the banking house of J. P. Morgan & Co., automatically became jury foreman. Asked if he had any objection to the death penalty, the square-jawed Bucken replied, "None whatever!"[32]

Later that afternoon the pace picked up somewhat as Bucken was joined by Philip H. Ohm, fifty-three, a retired grocer; Edward K. Pietsch, sixty-eight, an electrical engineer with an enormous white beard; and Louis J. Comellas, a Freeport realtor, just one year shy of his fiftieth birthday.

When Justice Manning closed proceedings for the day, the state had used seven peremptories, the defense three. The four chosen jurors were placed under the guard of Sheriff Seaman and driven to the Garden City Hotel[33]—a couple of miles south of the courthouse—where the jury would be sequestered until the trial ended. Outside, on the courthouse steps, Uterhart refused to disclose his strategy, other than to forecast some "emotional testimony."[34]

That night Blanca ate a light supper and retired at nine o'clock. According to Mrs. Seaman, she slept like "a tired little child."[35]

The Trial, Day 2

When Blanca walked into court on the second day, journalists noted that she was wearing the same outfit as the day before. A few smiled and exchanged knowing winks. Uterhart didn't want his client turning up each day in some brand new haute couture masterpiece from Paris; keep it classy, but keep it quiet. As for Blanca herself, she looked a little brighter than the previous day.

Just putting on a brave face, said Uterhart, in reality she was yearning to see her boy. To help resolve the impasse, Uterhart and Weeks put their heads together. Their discussion ended with the DA consenting to Jack Jr. being brought into court the next day. Justice Manning immediately called a sidebar. Citing the inflammatory effect such a move might have on potential jurors—and mindful of any possible future appeal—he overruled Weeks's concession. In the middle of this legal horse-trading, Blanca remained "the quietest, most dispassionate person in the Mineola courtroom."[36] At other times, especially during Weeks's questioning of potential jurors, she showed signs of displeasure, pouting when referred to as "the defendant." In a flabby climbdown that would characterize his trial conduct, Weeks agreed to soften his reference to "this young woman,"[37] which appeared agreeable to Blanca. The questioning continued.

As the morning dragged on, the soporific atmosphere was briefly electrified when Dr. Wight spotted that one of the reporters had smuggled a camera into court and had focused it on the prisoner. He signaled to Sheriff Seaman, who grabbed the culprit by the collar and hauled him from the court. In their wake, Manning warned the remaining reporters of the risks of violating the rules he had laid down. Blanca watched without any obvious interest. At lunch, she restricted herself to one glass of hot milk, on doctor's orders.

Another flurry of excitement came during the break when a woman brought a young boy into court. Excited reporters swarmed, thinking that Jack Jr. had indeed arrived, only to back away when they realized that the newcomer was the son of an unrelated family. Their disappointment didn't last long. Just before the afternoon session commenced, Señora Errázuriz-Vergara swept into court. She looked both regal and intimidating. Over a black tailor-made suit she wore a cloak of the same somber hue, buttoned to the neck, with a fur collar. A black silk mushroom hat and matching spotted veil rounded off the ensemble. Reporters reached for superlatives. One overawed observer wrote that she was "remarkably young looking and distinctly handsome. Her regular features, her radiant hair and supple figure prove at first glance that the classic beauty of the daughter was the child's born heritage."[38] Alongside the señora sat the Chilean consul general at New York, Carlos Castro-Ruiz, and Dr. Wight. When one of her attorneys informed Blanca, who didn't see her mother enter, "a ghost of a smile stole across her pale features."[39]

Before entering the court the señora had complained to reporters that she had been permitted to see her grandson only once and only in the presence of two servants. Now she was escorted to the front row of the spectators' seats, a few feet directly behind her daughter. One row farther back sat Amalia and Guillermo. At no point did Blanca turn around to acknowledge any family member; she maintained the same dull, glazed look that had been her default expression since voir dire began.

The only note of animation in an otherwise tedious afternoon came at two o'clock when Señora Errázuriz-Vergara suddenly swooned while a potential juror was airing his views on capital punishment. Dr. Wight rushed forward to administer smelling salts, and, under his guidance, Señora Errázuriz-Vergara was removed to the judge's chambers and given a cup of tea. Taken to the sheriff's quarters, she was allowed to rest on a bed.

In the meantime, Justice Manning's famed temper was getting shorter with each rejected juror. "I could go into the courtroom and find twelve men without trouble,"[40] he barked and ordered both sides to cut back on unnecessary objections. His admonition had some effect. By the end of proceedings, four more men had joined the panel: William P. Jones, a sixty-year-old realtor; John A. Ellard, fifty, a superintendent; and two retirees, Herman H. Beers, fifty-four, and William H. Jones, sixty.

At the conclusion of the day's business, Blanca met her mother briefly in the sheriff's quarters. She seemed brighter, cheered up by news that she would be allowed to see her son. Uterhart boasted that he had "forced"[41] this concession from relatives of the dead man. Nonsense, the de Saulles family retaliated, their actions had been entirely voluntary and with the best interests of Jack Jr. in mind. Justice Manning, still wary of possible attempts to influence the jury, reiterated his order that under no circumstances would the boy be allowed into court.

As the courtroom slowly emptied, Sheriff Seaman was frowning heavily. The pressmen gathered around him. In an announcement that showed just how much he had allowed personal attachment to cloud professional responsibilities, the sheriff expressed bemusement at just having learned that the prosecution planned to call him as a witness.

The Trial, Day 3

The promise of a visit from her son at day's end seemed to buoy Blanca on the third day of jury selection. When she entered the court, followed by Amalia and Seaman, her cheeks showed a tinge of color previously absent. She also had made her first fashion change of the trial, a cream-colored crepe de chine waist open at the throat. Amalia, too, appeared more animated. Not quite as tall as Blanca, she wore a black turban with a bow of black ribbon at the side and a dark blue coat with a wide rolling collar and white cuffs. Like Blanca, she shied away from any jewelry.

Earlier that day, the already selected jury members went for a long walk that took them close to The Box, and in the afternoon they enjoyed an automobile ride. To a man, they seemed delighted with the way the state was accommodating them. Upon their return to their hotel, they found that their numbers had been swollen by two. Harry Livingstone, a forty-nine-year-old railroad superintendent, and Nicholas Schneider had satisfied both sides. At age thirty-seven, Schneider was the youngest person selected thus far.

As soon as court adjourned at 4:00 p.m., rumors that little Jack was en route emptied the press box. A quarter of an hour later, an open-topped gray auto belonging to Mrs. August Heckscher pulled up outside the jail, and Harry Dougherty emerged, carrying the chubby youngster in his arms. A volley of flashbulbs lit Dougherty's path as he carried Jack through the small courtyard and up to the main gate. "They're all after me for my picture,"[42] the youngster cried delightedly as Dougherty set him down in the jail corridor. For most it was the first time they had heard the youngster speak and they were surprised that, like his mother, he had an English accent.

Inside the sheriff's quarters, Blanca and her son played together for two hours. As the visit drew to a close, Jack was brought a cup of chocolate that he gulped down. At 6:15 p.m., after he had hugged his mother good-bye, Amalia led him to another vehicle from the Heckscher fleet, a closed sedan. He shouted back, "Goodbye; I'm coming back Saturday and then I'm going to stay all the time."[43]

Another barrage of flashbulbs temporarily blinded the child, who needed help getting into the auto. Amalia lingered for a moment, hands deep in the pockets of her belted, blue box coat, and chatted comfortably with the press. She said that little Jack's visit had greatly cheered his mother. "Of course, we are all confident she will be acquitted."[44] Like the rest of her family, she, too, had an impeccable English accent, and she knew how to push all the right buttons. "We are all very grateful to all the dear people who have been so kind to us. You know, you can just feel that everyone is sympathetic. . . . When the truth is told no one will ever hold my sister guilty."[45]

More good news came on another front. Friends of Blanca were said to be "jubilant"[46] over news that an investigation launched by the de Saulles family into Blanca's private life had failed to unearth any skeletons. The inquiry had focused especially on the time that Blanca checked into the Majestic Hotel under an assumed name, when it was rumored that she had found comfort in the arms of a certain cabaret dancer.

If Rodolfo Guglielmi got wind of this latest development he must have shuddered. After almost a year of scuffling around in Hollywood, knocking on agents' doors, and most of those doors slamming in his face, he had finally landed a part as a dress extra in *Alimony.* The job paid only five bucks a day, but one casting director at least had noticed the young actor with the elegant moves and the moody good looks.

He was also making useful contacts elsewhere. Among his fellow extras in *Alimony* was a delicate young beauty named Alice Taafe. The couple hit it off immediately and often went out dancing. In time she would change her name to Alice Terry and become one of the silent screen's most accomplished leading ladies—but she didn't forget her young dancing partner. Just a few years later, when cast by her husband, the director Rex Ingram, in *The Four Horsemen of the Apocalypse,* she mentioned that Rodolfo, with his dark appearance, would be ideal for the leading role. The rest, as they say, is movie history, but for now the last thing that the struggling actor needed was any connection with the most sensational murder trial in a decade.

The Trial, Day 4

But the bad news kept on coming.

The next morning's newspapers announced that Deputy County Clerk William B. Selden, of New York, had been served with a subpoena from the Nassau County district attorney's office, requiring the production in court of all papers and records connected with the divorce action brought by Mrs. de Saulles against her husband. The required papers were sent to Mineola in the custody of a court messenger. Weeks, convinced there was something buried in these documents that would weigh heavily against the defendant, dropped heavy hints to reporters that he might introduce details of the divorce at the conclusion of the state's direct evidence.

Blanca clearly wasn't fazed by this news as she entered court that morning. On the contrary, she had a glow about her that acquaintances attributed to the visit of her son the previous evening. At eleven o'clock the eleventh juror, George Siles, sixty-one, a decorator, was selected. When asked if he worried that Siles, unlike all the other jurors, was childless, Uterhart laughed and said that he liked Mr. Siles's face "particularly well" and was sure he was a man of "human sensibilities."[47] An hour later, the final juror, Alexander S. Norton, a fifty-four-year-old retired firefighter, joined the panel. As he took his seat, Blanca nodded slightly, as if in approval. Although both sides expressed their happiness with the jury's makeup, a glance at the avuncular, silver-tinged jury and then at the gamine defendant left no doubt in observers' minds that in the vital battle of jury selection the state had been decisively routed. Some of these men had grandchildren almost as old as Blanca.

After the twelfth juror was sworn in, the court took a lunch break. An hour later, everyone returned to the packed room, and District Attorney Weeks stood to make his opening address. The *Atlanta Constitution* had forecast A Murder Trial that Will Rival [Harry Kendall] Thaw's.[48]

It was time to test the accuracy of that prediction.

TWELVE
Someone's Lying

The Trial, Day 4

Reports that a jury had finally been selected and that the trial proper was about to begin galvanized the crowd milling on the courthouse steps and caused a stampede for seats in the public gallery. But before anyone gained admittance to the court, court attendant William B. Purcell searched them for weapons, irrespective of social standing. This extra layer of official security resulted from yet another threatening letter to Justice Manning, this time warning him to be "prepared to meet your God if this young woman is not acquitted."[1] Manning might have shrugged off the letters as being of "no serious import,"[2] but, judging by the heavily armed presence in the corridors and around the courthouse, someone was taking the threat seriously. Despite these delays, the court quickly filled, mostly with fashionably dressed women. Given the crush and the unseasonably mild weather, it was fortunate that this was one of the few courts to be ventilated by fresh air from open windows.

Amalia and Guillermo resumed their customary position immediately behind Blanca. Next to them sat Suzanne Monteau and Dr. Wight. Across the courtroom sat the de Saulles family, grim-faced, steeling themselves for the battle to come. Against doctors' orders Major de Saulles had struggled into court, maintaining his soldierly appearance, determined not to succumb either to his physical pain or the bitter pangs of loss from which he was so evidently suffering. He had arrived from South Bethlehem the previous day but was so weak that he'd had to retire early, and was attended through the night by his daughters. On this day, Caroline, in deep mourning, her face shrouded in a thick black veil, was acting as nurse in attendance.

As soon as the lunch break ended, Weeks rose to make his opening speech. He didn't have a flowery delivery, and in twenty minutes of rapid, somewhat perfunctory narrative, he outlined the state's case. It hinged on one simple question: Why had Blanca taken a gun with her? He looked directly at the jury. "We intend, gentlemen, to prove to you that the defendant committed murder in the first degree when she killed John Longer de Saulles"[3] because it had been a clear case of premeditation.

He took the jury briefly through the prisoner's turbulent marriage and then, in greater depth, through the terms of the divorce decree. "Bear in mind that this was the legal agreement. In April of this year, as the time approached when the boy was to go into his father's custody, Mrs. De Saulles started proceedings."[4] To placate her, Jack de Saulles agreed that "in alternate months, May, July, and September, she was to have the boy and the father was to have him in June and August."[5] It was also stipulated that either party could have the boy for three hours by mutual consent at any time during the other's period of custody, provided it didn't interfere with the boy's welfare. This became known as the "Three-Hour Agreement."[6] Weeks made a great play of stressing that out of the 378 days preceding the shooting, Jack had only had custody for 66, and that "on August 3 the boy was properly in the custody of his father."[7]

All through this opening, Weeks could barely get a sentence out without being interrupted by the defense. The trial-savvy Uterhart's strategy was plain: break up the flow, don't let Weeks settle into a comfortable rhythm, keep the jury distracted. In this disjointed fashion, Weeks outlined the events of the evening of August 3. First came the phone call that Blanca made to The Box and her being told that her ex-husband was out at his club. The response hadn't fooled her in the slightest, said Weeks. She had "sensed"[8] that Jack really was at home, and she was determined to confront him. Every act that night was carried out in a deliberate and methodical fashion: the urgent phone calls to the taxi company, the fast drive to The Box, taking care to park some distance from the house where she couldn't be seen. "She had the chauffeur turn the taxicab around and then walked toward The Box, and as she walked she held her hand under her sweater this way."[9] Weeks mimicked the gesture as he spoke.

For some reason this act of pantomime startled Blanca. Previously her attentiveness had varied between bored and catatonic, but now she sat upright and, turning in her chair, leaned forward to better watch the district attorney. Weeks warned the jury that the defense would claim that Blanca drove to The Box that night in the belief that Jack was not at home, and yet her first words to the valet were: "'Where is Mr. De Saulles?' If she had believed he was not there, there would have been no reason to ask for him."[10] It would have been a telling point, had not Weeks overlooked one factor: Blanca had already seen Jack's car parked in the driveway, reason enough for her to surmise that he was still at home.

Weeks continued. He described how, having cunningly smuggled a gun into the house, Blanca entered the living room and confronted her ex-husband. A brief argument broke out, and "she shot him in the back and said she hoped he would die."[11] Weeks paused for effect and then pointed at the prisoner. "She used servants, automobiles, and money. Her revolver had a safety catch. It was necessary to release this catch before firing each shot. But she did it. She fired five shots, and she knew what she was doing."[12] Moreover, Blanca's actions after the shooting only added to the state's contention that this shooting was not the irrational act of some unhinged mind. Consider her remarks to the valet, the arresting officers, the chauffeur, and Thorne, telling him where she had left the gun.

And there were plenty of other incidences to demonstrate that here was a woman in full control of her faculties and aware of the consequences of her actions. For instance, on the journey to Mineola jail, she had made the remark about the electric chair. She had also asked the driver to stop so she could buy a bottle of milk from a roadside seller, whom she told to keep the change, and she drank this milk quite calmly while the car was still in motion, even joking, "How gruesome that we should stop at such a place at this time,"[13] when the auto stopped near a graveyard. At the jailhouse she had acted in a similarly normal fashion, trying to obtain bail for her maid, and she also phoned Crossways to arrange for clothing to be delivered. All this, according to Weeks, showed that Blanca was perfectly sane at the time of the shooting. He finished by saying, "The people, accordingly, will ask that you find a verdict of murder in the first degree."[14] As Weeks made his demand for the death penalty, Blanca "raised her head defiantly and glared at him."[15]

Weeks called his first witness. George A. Fairfield, a surveyor, had drawn up a huge floor plan of the house that showed the hallway, living room, and location of the telephone, as well as the surrounding grounds. Uterhart objected to the floor plan, saying it didn't represent the condition of the property on the night of the shooting. He was overruled, as he expected, but he was continuing his policy of disrupting the prosecution's flow at every opportunity. Bad law: good advocacy. Fairfield was allowed to proceed. He described The Box as lying in a lonesome spot in a sparsely populated neighborhood. The distance, he said, from Valentines Road, where Blanca had left her cab, to the front porch in a direct line was 240 feet, and from the porch to the shrubbery where Blanca was arrested was another 300 feet. A murmur greeted these numbers; it was the first indication for many in court of just how large the de Saulles estate was.

Next came William H. Pickering, who had taken photos of the house a week after the shooting. While the various diagrams and photographs were being displayed and argued over, Blanca sank back into her semistupor. Nor did she display any curiosity or, indeed, abhorrence when Dr. Henry M. Warner described what he had found during the autopsy. He produced, identified, and catalogued each of the five bullets. Then, with the aid of a lead pencil and a court policeman, he indicated the course followed by each projectile. All the shots had been fired either at the side or the back of the victim, who had probably raised his left arm to shield himself. During this testimony, Uterhart bounced up and down like a jack-in-the-box, repeatedly disputing the witness's evidence that the victim had been shot in the back. In the end, a weary Justice Manning gaveled Uterhart to silence, saying that Warner's evidence had entered the record and was going to stay there, no matter what defense counsel might think.

When Warner's findings were corroborated by Dr. Smith A. Coombs, who had assisted at the autopsy, Uterhart argued that Coombs had changed his testimony since the coroner's inquest. "Isn't it true that you and Dr. Warner first agreed that the bullet struck the middle finger and then passed to the ring finger and that you afterward changed it to make it that the bullet passed through the little finger and then struck the ring finger?"

"No, sir."

"Doctor, aren't you in the habit of changing your diagnoses?"

"No, sir."[16]

Uterhart cocked an eyebrow. He crossed to the defense table and read from a paper that dealt with the witness's evidence in *Killilea v. Morgan* (1916). In 1915, Michael Killilea had worked as a dairyman on the Glen Cove estate of millionaire banker J. P. Morgan, when Eric Meunter, a German language teacher, broke into Morgan's mansion and shot him twice. Morgan survived, and Meunter was taken into custody (where he committed suicide). In the days following this attack, a rope was strung across a bridge leading to Morgan's house to prevent cars from entering the grounds. Killilea, unaware of this precaution, happened to be riding his bicycle at night and hit the rope, throwing him off and hitting his head. The injuries he sustained had doomed him to a life of total blindness, and he filed suit against his employer.

On February 4, 1916, a jury awarded him damages in the sum of twenty thousand dollars. During that case, Coombs had testified on behalf of Morgan, as Uterhart now reminded him. "Is it not a fact that in that case, after having made a diagnosis of concussion of the brain, you afterward changed it and testified that there was nothing wrong with the man?"[17] When the witness denied doing any such thing, Uterhart waived further cross-examination until he could obtain from the county clerk the record of the case referred to. (Uterhart never did recall Coombs, and probably never intended to do so. He merely wanted to plant doubt in the jurors' minds about the witness's veracity.)

Then Weeks called Raymond Hamilton, who operated the taxi service in Roslyn. "Are you acquainted with this defendant, Mrs. Blanca de Saulles?"

"Not personally. I am acquainted with her by telephone."[18] He told how on the evening of August 3, at some time between a quarter to seven and a quarter to eight—he refused to be more specific—he had received a telephone call from Blanca, requesting a taxi immediately at Crossways. Hamilton promised to send a cab, but because he was short-staffed that night a delay ensued. This had greatly upset Blanca. Twice more, Hamilton fielded irate phone calls from her. After the second of these follow-up calls, he had dispatched James Donner to Crossways.

Donner took up the story. He told of picking up the defendant—"she seemed angry because I was late"[19]—and another woman who had hold of a bulldog on a leash. At this point, Suzanne Monteau was asked to stand up, and Donner identified her as Blanca's traveling companion. He described the harum-scarum journey to The Box, how Blanca kept urging him to go faster and take shortcuts along unfamiliar roads. When eventually they reached their destination, Blanca and the maid alighted, telling him to stay in the car and tend the dog. "She walked across the lawn in a direct line toward the house, with her right hand held against her side, like this."[20] Donner stood and demonstrated how the hand was held awkwardly against her person. After that he did not see Blanca until much later that night, when she left the house in the custody of the sheriff. She said, "Take good care of the dog. Drive to Roslyn and see my maid, Louise, and she will pay you for the trip."[21]

On cross-examination Uterhart seized upon a point in Donner's testimony. Earlier the chauffeur had said that Blanca told him, "I'll give you a dollar if you get me there in time."

"If you got her there *in time?*" Uterhart repeated, emphasizing the last two words.

"Yes—if I got her there in time,"[22] replied Donner. The inference was clear: Blanca wanted to reach de Saulles's home before Jack returned from the club, although Donner made no direct testimony to that effect.

Weeks called his next witness, Julius Hadamek. A rustle of expectation ran through the court. In press accounts Weeks repeatedly had trumpeted his belief that the Austrian valet would serve as the jewel in the prosecution's crown, and everyone was eager to hear his testimony. Hadamek—stockily built, dark, and low-voiced—was clearly nervous. Weeks gave him the kid-glove treatment, gently teasing out details of the witness's background, before turning to the events of August 3. "Did you get a telephone call from Mrs. De Saulles that evening?"

"Yes. She called about 7. She wanted Mr. Jack. I said I'd find out if he was in. Mr. Jack was standing at my elbow. I whispered who it was and he said, 'Well, I'm out.' I told Mrs. De Saulles so."

"Was anything further said?"

"She told me, 'Don't say to Mr. Jack I called.'"

"Did Mr. De Saulles say anything about going to the club and being back in about an hour?"

"Yes."[23]

Hadamek only admitted these details with the greatest reluctance. Discussing his master's affairs in public felt like a betrayal of the servant's code, and it showed. And whether by design or accident, his faltering English and hesitant manner robbed his answers of the impact that Weeks had wanted. The lawyer struggled to extract details of the crucial phone call. Hadamek said that Mrs. de Saulles had asked after the boy's whereabouts, and he replied that Jack Jr. was in bed. When she had asked why they were keeping him so long, he had fumbled to offer any reasonable explanation. Finally, she had told Hadamek to bring the boy over to Crossways, and he replied that this was not possible.

Weeks moved along. Had the witness seen Mrs. de Saulles later that evening? Yes, she had come to the front door and "asked if Mr. Jack was in."[24] He told her that Mr. de Saulles was in the living room. At this point Mrs. de Saulles had rebuked him sharply. "What is the meaning of it that you keep Jack here? It is my time to have him."[25] Hadamek's voice became lower still as he told the court that before he could say anything else, Caroline Degener had appeared on the stairs and confirmed to Blanca that Jack was in the living room.

Just then, much to Hadamek's relief, the phone had rung. It was while answering that call that he heard gunshots. He dropped the phone, ran into the living room, and quickly surveyed the scene. Blanca was standing over her prostrate husband, holding a pistol. "Madam," he asked Mrs. de Saulles, "what have you done?" She had turned to him and said, "I had to do it. I couldn't stand it any more."[26] In all the confusion, Hadamek lost track of her whereabouts, and he next saw her some time later when she was sitting in the garden with her maid. Weeks had no further questions.

Uterhart began his cross-examination slowly. "Hadamek, when Mrs. de Saulles called you on the phone, wasn't the first question she asked, 'Where is Jack?'"

"Yes, sir."

"Didn't she mean the boy?"

"Yes, the boy."[27]

Uterhart reminded the witness of his earlier testimony, an admission that he had been instructed by Jack de Saulles to say that he was at the Meadow Brook Club and would be there for an hour. "That was a lie, wasn't it?"

"Yes, sir." This answer came in such a subdued tone that the judge admonished the witness sharply to "speak up, so the jury may hear you."[28]

Uterhart continued. "You told it because he was your master and told you to do it, didn't you?"

"Yes, sir."[29] As Hadamek spoke he looked to Charles de Saulles for support. None was forthcoming. Charles and the rest of his family sat frozen-faced. Thus far, Hadamek had served as an excellent witness for the defense.

Uterhart wanted clarification of the actual words used by Blanca that night on the phone. "Didn't she say to you, 'Don't say anything about my ringing up; I'll be right over to get Jack'?"

Hadamek gave it some thought, before replying, "Yes, sir."[30]

A hum rippled through the court. If true, Hadamek's testimony provided strong evidence that Blanca *had* gone to the house merely to get her son. Not that the prisoner seemed to notice. All through Hadamek's time on the stand not once did her eyes stray toward the witness. Nothing could disturb her lethargy, or so it seemed.

Someone else similarly afflicted was prosecutor Weeks. Throughout the cross-examination he had remained astonishingly mute despite Uterhart's flagrantly leading questions. And he saw no reason to break that silence as the big defense counsel pressed on. "Now, brush up your memory again, and tell what was the very last thing you heard Mr. De Saulles say to the defendant."

"I heard him say to her 'No, no, no.'"

"Did he say that firmly, emphatically?"

"It wasn't so very loud, but he said it as if he meant it."[31]

"Who was in the living room when you went there after you heard the shots?"

"Only I and Major De Saulles."[32]

"Where were Mrs. Degener and Marshall Ward?"

"I don't know—they may have been in the dining room."

"Are you positive Ward was not in the room?"

"Yes, sir."[33]

The court collectively gasped. At the prosecution table, Weeks must have listened to this exchange in a state of numb disbelief. Hadamek's testimony had hit him like a lightning bolt. In press interviews, at the inquest, and at the grand jury hearing, Ward claimed to have witnessed the shooting, yet here was direct evidence that turned his claim on its head, effectively branding him a liar. Worse still, this accusation came from a fellow prosecution witness. Courtroom disasters didn't come much bigger.

Uterhart paused for a moment to let the jury absorb Hadamek's allegation. He told the valet to look at the defendant as she sat with her chin resting upon her hand, her elbow on the table. "On the night you have been describing," he asked, "did not Mrs. De Saulles appear to you like a very ill woman?"

At long last, Weeks pulled himself upright to object. The witness, he said, wasn't qualified to pass such an opinion, as the defense well knew. Justice Manning sustained the objection and reprimanded Uterhart over such egregiously inappropriate questioning. Uterhart clucked an apology and turned back to the witness. "Well, would you say that after the shooting that evening she looked as pale or paler than she looks now?"[34]

"I do not remember, but after the shooting she was very pale."[35]

"Much paler than she is now?"

"Yes."[36]

The court rustled again, observers wondering how anyone could possibly look whiter than Blanca at present. Uterhart readied himself for one last broadside.

"Marshall Ward didn't hold her by the hand or wasn't near her and didn't help put Mr. De Saulles on the couch after the shooting, did he?"

"No."[37]

Uterhart sat down with the air of a wholly satisfied man.

Weeks, on the other hand, looked almost shell-shocked as he struggled to salvage something from this shambles. "You pretend to say that Ward was not in the living room when the shots were fired. You weren't there, were you?"

"No, sir. I was in the hall."

"Then you don't know, do you?"

"No, sir."[38]

Weeks had phrased these two questions artfully. At no time had Hadamek said that Ward wasn't in the room at the time of the shooting, only that he was not present a few seconds later. Weeks had twisted the testimony to his own advantage. But it had come at a high price; casting doubt on your own witness is a strange turn of events for an attorney.

As Hadamek left the stand, he exchanged a bleak smile and a word with the defendant. No one could hear what Blanca said, but the valet's grave response was in keeping with his position: "Very good, madam."[39]

Uterhart might not have landed any knockout blows, but when court was adjourned for the day there could be little doubt as to which side would most enjoy the evening meal.

THIRTEEN

Amnesia

The Trial, Day 5

There had been no letup in the volume or virulence of the threatening letters received at the courthouse, with most taking dead aim at Justice Manning. Proof that these were still being taken seriously came the next morning when the judge arrived at the Mineola railroad station to find two burly court officers waiting to accompany him to court. Despite the drab, drizzly weather, a large crowd had gathered on the courthouse steps long before the doors opened. As they entered the court, everyone—including the press—submitted to a search. When Blanca appeared, she nodded politely to the jury, all of whom nodded back, and took her seat. Because the court was so dark, it was necessary to illuminate the bench with electric light, a garish intrusion that gave Justice Manning the appearance of being the central figure in a stage set.

Today, Weeks intended to play his best cards. The first witness was Marshall Ward. The reporters sharpened their pencils and their scorn. "Pasty-faced,"[1] one called him; another lampooned him as "a symphony in blue. He wore a blue serge suit, blue polka dot cravat, blue shirt and had a blue-bordered handkerchief displayed at his breast pocket."[2] After Hadamek's damaging testimony the previous day, Ward obviously posed problems for the state, but while the "dapper little man"[3] might have looked foppish, he had genuine steel in the way he went about mounting a recovery mission. At Weeks's urging, Ward presented a lengthy and largely uninterrupted account of the fateful day's events: lunch with Jack and his father at Sherry's, then a drive to The Box, where Caroline had just arrived. Aided by diagrams and a plan of the lower floor of the house, Ward pointed out where the furniture stood in the living room. After dinner, he said, the family and guests listened to the phonograph in the living room until Caroline took the child up to bed. While she was gone, a loud knock came at the front door.

"The Major was lying on the couch in the living room. Jack was lying by the wall at his father's feet, and I was on a stool near. I heard a voice say, 'I want to see Mr. De Saulles,' then I looked up and saw Mrs. De Saulles. She had stepped through the door into the living room. Jack and I got up.

"Jack went over and put out his hand and said 'How are you, Blanquita?' I went over to the mantelpiece."[4]

Ward described the tense confrontation between Jack and Blanca. As it grew more heated, he left his place by the mantelpiece and inched his way toward the piano. "They were standing about three feet apart," he said. "When Jack said he wouldn't argue with her, he turned his back upon her, and she said, 'Then there's only one thing to do.' I saw the flash of the gun, and I heard four shots in rapid succession. I saw Jack stagger forward, but I did not see him fall. As soon as I could collect myself I went over to Mrs. De Saulles and seized her arms. She said, 'It had to be done.'"[5]

Listening to this evidence, Blanca's eyes blazed angrily, then creased into a sardonic smile as Ward spoke of tending his stricken friend. But her brittle contempt faded as fast as it had appeared, and she lapsed back into her customary stupor.

Ward continued: "I went to the telephone to call a doctor and after that went back to the living room to see what I could do. Then I called up the doctor again to see why he had not come and went out on the porch to watch for the headlights of the automobile."[6] He described seeing Blanca outside the house a short while later, just moments before the ambulance arrived. "I went to the hospital with Mr. De Saulles and stayed there until he died."[7]

Thus far Weeks had given Ward his head, and it had been smooth sailing. Now the district attorney had to navigate trickier waters. "Did you see Julius Hadamek at the time of the shooting?" Ward replied that he had not. In its own way this testimony was just as damaging as Hadamek's had been a day earlier. Now Weeks was hamstrung by two prosecution witnesses, both of whom had, allegedly, run to de Saulles's assistance, yet neither would admit to having seen the other. Weeks fought hard to paper over the ever-widening cracks. "Was anyone with Mrs. De Saulles?"

"Yes, a woman, her maid, stood by the door."

Reluctantly, Weeks returned to the subject of the vexatious valet. "When *did* you see Julius Hadamek?"

"I saw him in the hall and living room after the shooting."[8]

With this Weeks handed the witness over to the defense.

Uterhart took his time, slowly raising his commanding bulk from the desk before approaching the witness. He soft-pedaled his opening, with a few general questions about the witness's eighteen-year friendship with the dead man, including how Ward had used Jack's Manhattan office as his business headquarters and his connection with the New York Cotton Exchange. Then, without pause, he switched smoothly to the night of the shooting. "When Mrs. De Saulles came, you didn't want to hear what she said, did you?"

"I got up to meet her, but when I heard her mention little Jack I would have left the room if I could: I didn't want to hear a family quarrel. I could not pass her to get to the door."

"There was a door by the piano; why didn't you go out that?"

"I didn't think of it."

"But you could have gone out on the porch without brushing past Mrs. De Saulles?"

"Yes, but I didn't think of it."

"As a matter of fact, you stayed where you could hear every word of the family quarrel, didn't you?"

"Not intentionally. I don't know whether I heard every word or not. I don't know what I missed."[9]

Ward was negotiating the cross-examination like a seasoned campaigner and growing in confidence until, without warning, Uterhart struck like a rattlesnake. Pointing an accusing finger directly at the witness, he shouted, "Have you ever been convicted of a crime?"

Ward shifted uneasily in his seat before muttering a barely audible, "No."[10]

"Do you swear that?"

"Yes."[11]

"I'll show you a paper, and possibly I can refresh your memory."[12]

Uterhart produced a transcript made from the records of the West Side Police Court in Manhattan, detailing how Ward had been fined ten dollars and costs for intoxication and fighting in a restaurant. He looked up from the document and skewered the witness with a defiant stare. "Weren't you convicted of using loud and boisterous language and refusing to leave Rector's while intoxicated?"[13]

"No, I was convicted for disorderly conduct. I was arrested for fighting at Rector's." Ward shifted uncomfortably in his seat, fingering his lips as he spoke.

"And committed to jail because you couldn't pay your fine of $10?"

"Because I didn't have any money with me. I was committed until I got the money."[14]

It was scarcely a capital crime, but, filtered through Uterhart's hypercritical prism, the minor incident took on a decidedly menacing air. And there was worse to come as Uterhart dug even deeper into Ward's past. "Have you ever been accused of defrauding a dressmaker named Miss Mary Riley?"

"This is the first I've heard of it."[15]

Uterhart affected surprise and then read out details of a suit brought when Ward worked for the Paul J. Rainey Pier Co. and reportedly sold Miss Riley bonds worth thirty thousand dollars. The charge alleged that Ward, in his desperation to get his hands on the client's money, used his mother's name and made false representations.

"Does that refresh your recollection?"

"It does not."[16]

"Don't you know that you sued the Rainey company for commission and that their defense was that you had been guilty of fraud in selling the bonds?"

"I know they lost the verdict after the jury was out ten minutes."

"—and that the Appellate Division reversed the decision?"

"On a point of law, I understood."[17]

Uterhart sighed and read from the decision of the Appellate Division, which found that, although Ward *had* misrepresented certain facts regarding the bond sale to Miss Riley, other factors obliged them to overturn the lower court's decision. When he finished, Uterhart turned to the witness and snapped, "That's all for you, Mr. Marshall Ward."[18]

None of these revelations had a jot of bearing on the shooting of Jack de Saulles, but they did have a devastating effect on Ward's credibility, portraying him as a shifty operator, not to be trusted. Ward's stupidity beggared belief. In first denying and then admitting various offenses that he knew to be in the public record, he had handed the jury a gold-plated reason to disbelieve him. Clearly, this round had gone to Uterhart. As the newspapers made plain. Counsel had given Ward "a very miserable half hour,"[19] wrote one, while another said that Uterhart had used Ward "very roughly."[20]

Weeks struggled to limit the damage. On redirect, he asked Ward to explain the circumstances of the fight at Rector's. "The persons at the next table were being very annoying. I remember that we did have a fight and that after we got over to court I was held there for about three quarters of an hour before I could get the money."[21] After this Ward was allowed to leave. He slunk back to his seat, having learned firsthand that the witness stand can be the loneliest place on earth.

Fortunately for Weeks, the next witness was a far more imposing and credible character. Caroline Degener, dressed in deep mourning, swept past Blanca like she didn't exist as she made her way to the stand. Once seated, she raised her veil to show an angry, dark face and hair slightly tinged with gray. Her eyes were sharp, and her voice displayed a flinty bitterness when she spoke. She gave her answers promptly and concisely and confined herself to exactly what she knew.

On the night in question, at approximately eight o'clock, she had taken her nephew upstairs to put him in his pajamas and ready him for bed. She was coming down the stairs with Jack Jr.—"to say goodnight to his grandfather"[22]—and was about four steps from the bottom when Blanca entered the hallway. Caroline had halted involuntarily and said, "How do you do, Blanquita?"[23] She noticed that "Blanquita had her hands in the pockets of her jacket."[24]

"Did you notice how Mrs. De Saulles was dressed?"[25] asked Weeks.

"She was dressed in white and had her hands in the pockets of her sweater.[26] Blanca then said, 'Good evening, Caroline. I wish to see Mr. De Saulles.' I called Longer—that was the name I always called him by. She went on into the living room and I heard her say, 'I want my boy,' and I heard him say, 'You can't have him. It's my month. That's all there is to it.'"[27]

Then she heard the shots. Caroline instinctively dashed toward the living room. At that moment Blanca emerged. "I seized her by the arm and said 'Blanquita, Blanquita, what have you done?' She said 'I'm sorry. It had to be done.'"[28]

After this, Caroline ran upstairs "to see about the boy. I don't know how he disappeared. I think he ran up when he heard the shots. . . . I did not see Mrs. De Saulles until twenty minutes later, after I had telephoned for an ambulance and the police."[29]

Weeks asked when the witness next saw Blanca. "I went out on the porch and saw her. She was seated on a bench. I did not speak to her and she did not speak to me. I noticed that there was some dark-complexioned woman with her. This woman came to The Box with her and stood in the hall. I have since learned that this woman was her maid."[30] At no time, Caroline said, did she speak to Blanca while the latter was waiting for the police to arrive.

On cross-examination Uterhart attempted to trip up Caroline over the exact time of the shooting. To every question she replied, "I cannot tell you."[31] But Uterhart was like a dog with a bone, constantly chewing away at the timeline. Caroline's patience finally snapped. Fixing Uterhart with a fearsome glare, she snapped that she was unable to say exactly what happened at what time as she was *too busy* trying to soothe Jack Jr., *too busy* arranging for the ambulance, and *too busy* telephoning the police! Uterhart reeled back, startled by such vehemence, and, realizing that there was no more to be gained, released her.

Contrary to pretrial rumors, Arthur Brice de Saulles was well enough to testify. Since the shooting, the seventy-six-year-old's health had deteriorated badly, and he looked broken in body and spirit as a valet assisted him to the stand. With his snowy white hair and a mustache to match, he evinced an air of patrician stolidity and Victorian integrity. But even this old soldier wasn't expecting Weeks's first question: "Do you know Mrs. De Saulles?"[32] He looked first at the prosecutor and then at his former daughter-in-law. "You mean Mrs. De Saulles, John's wife?"

"Yes; do you know her?" Weeks asked again for the sake of legal formality.

"Well, I think I ought to,"[33] the major replied in a quavering voice that shook with emotion. Under gentle prompting, he gave his account of Blanca entering the room and then opening fire. He asserted that as she shot Jack she exclaimed, "If I can't have my boy, take that."[34]

"What was your son's position at the time she shot him?"

"He had turned so he was facing the windows."

"Was his back toward her?"

"Completely toward her."[35]

This was the response that Weeks had been after and he stressed it for the jury's sake.

"What did your son do after the shots were fired?"

"I saw him stagger and ran to his side as he fell. I began to search for the wounds, but I couldn't find any, though I saw that the arm was broken. Then the valet came, and he and I carried the poor boy to the couch."[36]

It was powerful stuff, made more so by the major's tightly controlled delivery. The patriarch of the de Saulles clan, although struggling with his emotions and his health, was determined to do right by his son. Inadvertently, however, his testimony proved a boon to the defense. Singularly lacking from Major de Saulles's version of events was any mention of Marshall Ward being present at the time of the shooting, dealing another hammer blow to Ward's credibility. In the circumstances, Uterhart wisely decided not to cross-examine, and the major, in a state of near collapse, was escorted from the court. Relatives and family friends rushed to his side as he was taken into an adjoining room where a doctor administered medical treatment.

The prosecution moved at a fast pace. Next came Constable Leonard Thorne. He told how he and Sheriff Seaman had placed the defendant under arrest and had asked her where the revolver was. She had directed them to a stand in the hall. Thorne said he had recovered the weapon from the hall, and he held the .32 Smith & Wesson aloft for the jury to see. Weeks did his best to milk the moment, but it was noticeable that when he showed the misshapen bullets to the jurymen, most averted their eyes, with some preferring to look at the ground. Blanca did neither. Not a flicker of emotion clouded her face when the gun or bullets were produced. Thorne told how, when they were driving Blanca to be committed, he had asked, "Why did you shoot your husband?"

"Because he wouldn't give me my child; I hope he dies."[37]

Once inside the jail, he said, Blanca had asked to make a phone call to the Ritz-Carlton hotel. She had spoken to Captain Lydig, in an attempt to get bail for her maid, but his incredulous response had infuriated her. She snapped peevishly, "All this, my God, my God, that makes me tired."[38] (The state had wanted to add Captain Lydig to its list of witnesses, but his duties with the army made him unavailable to testify.)

Uterhart kept his cross-examination brief. He needed the jury to gain some sense of Blanca's physical condition on the night of the shooting and Thorne readily obliged. "She hadn't any color."[39]

Sheriff Seaman took the witness stand next. Before the trial, showing scant regard either for the law or his official duties, he had professed astonishment that the state intended to call him as a witness. This was scarcely surprising, as since Blanca's incarceration he had acted more like a considerate uncle than an officer of the law. As his testimony unfolded, it became clear to everyone in court that the sheriff seemed more of an accomplice than a witness. The low point came when Weeks said, "Did you hear Mrs. De Saulles ask while coming from Hempstead to the Mineola jail: 'Will they electrocute me right away?'" All he got from the sheriff was a long, noncommittal pause.

Weeks waited.

No answer.

He asked the question a second time. This time Seaman did respond, "Somebody said that while we were in the car, but I don't know if she said it."[40] Weeks was almost speechless. The sheriff's treachery—there could be no other word for it—had stunned him. Rather than let this debacle slide further out of hand, Weeks whispered that he had no further questions.

Unusually for a prosecution witness, Seaman appeared far more comfortable during cross-examination. Like Thorne, he stressed Blanca's extreme pallor and cool attitude, and the jury was visibly fascinated by the sheriff's description of Blanca's mental state. "In my judgment she was far from being a well woman," he said. "She walked into the jail with her hands in the pockets of her sweater and said that the place looked like a zoo. She gave a funny little laugh every once in a while. There was a clothesline in her cell and I took it out. I was afraid she might make away with herself."[41]

Under Uterhart's gentle coaxing, Seaman continued: "I didn't think she was quite right and phoned for Dr. Guy Cleghorn, the jail physician. After he had examined her he advised me to have her removed from the cell to a room. I got a certificate from the doctor which said that the removal should be made on account of her extreme nervousness and mental condition."[42] At this juncture, Uterhart asked for the certificate to be entered into evidence. Over an objection from Weeks, Justice Manning allowed it.

"Since she's been in jail," said Uterhart, "has Mrs. De Saulles ever asked for her boy?"

"Many times,"[43] said Seaman. After this, Seaman was excused.

The next witness, Justice of the Peace Walter R. Jones, also took particular note of Blanca's unusual self-control when he questioned her after the shooting. "She told me she was sorry to make so much trouble, and I said she was not half so much sorry for me as I was for her."

"What was her physical appearance?" asked Uterhart.

"She was very white and so calm that she amazed me."[44]

On this note, Justice Manning called a halt to the morning's proceedings.

After the resumption, the state called Captain William A. Jones of the New York Police Department. The studious-looking Jones had helped pioneer the study of firearms identification and ballistics. Just recently he had played a part in the sensational case of convicted killer Charles Stielow, who once came within minutes of the electric chair before a temporary stay averted what would have been a grotesque miscarriage of justice. Thanks in large part to Jones's evidence that Stielow's .22 pistol couldn't have been the murder weapon, the German-born farmhand saw his death sentence commuted and later quashed.[45]

It had already been a busy day for the fifty-four-year-old Jones. That morning in a Brooklyn courtroom for the trial of Charles Lynch, charged with murdering Patrick L. Shields, Jones had thrilled spectators by firing several bullets into a bucket of wadded cotton to demonstrate that rounds fired from this particular automatic—found in Lynch's possession—matched bullets recovered from the body. The clinching evidence, Jones explained to the jury, was that the automatic had a defective barrel that left distinctive marks on each bullet.

After leaving Brooklyn, Jones had driven up the Motor Parkway to Mineola. He took the stand with a confidence born out of many years of courtroom experience. An excellent witness, he coolly and professionally explained how the .32 caliber hammerless Smith & Wesson worked. "It has a safety lock and requires pressure of the hand to be discharged," he said. "At the same time you have to grip the case with the hand and press the trigger with the fingers to fire it. Pressure must be exerted for each shot."[46]

Justice Manning interjected. "Do you mean . . . it requires two distinct motions of the hand to discharge it each time?"

"Yes,"[47] said the witness. Despite Uterhart's best efforts, he couldn't make any headway with the gun expert and soon released him from the stand.

Next came Dr. Bryan C. Sword, the ambulance surgeon, who testified that he was called by phone to The Box, where he found Mr. de Saulles dying. Sword accompanied the victim to the hospital, but nothing could be done to save him.

The final witness was James Garriety, an orderly at Nassau Hospital, who testified that he helped carry de Saulles into a ward, where he undressed the wounded man. After de Saulles died at 10:20 that night, Garriety moved the body to the morgue adjoining the hospital.

As promised, Weeks had taken fewer than forty-eight hours to present the state's witnesses. But he still had one final piece of evidence to present, a lengthy letter written by Jack to Blanca on May 2, 1917. This letter, said Weeks, demolished Blanca's claim that custody of the boy on the night of the shooting was rightfully hers.

> *Our one thought in life must always be for Jack's welfare, for we have made his start bad enough as it is. Therefore, in order to give you an opportunity to take a trip or trips to Chile with our boy, I agree that, so long as you obey the terms of the final decree, in spirit and letter (as I have no doubt you will), I will waive certain of my rights under it, and under our stipulations. In order that there may be no misunderstanding now or in the future as to what rights I waive, I now set the matter out in detail as follows . . .* [48]

Over several densely worded paragraphs, Jack outlined his willingness to set aside the court's ruling and allow Blanca to take their son to Chile from November through May if she so desired. Until that time he proposed that they split custody, with Blanca having the boy during the months of May, July, and September 1917, while he retained custody during the months of June, August, and October 1917. He ended by saying, "If you will write to me assenting to this and promising that you will abide by it, then we will consider the arrangement in effect."[49] Under the circumstances, it seemed a generous offer, and Weeks told the jury that in a reply, dated May 3, Blanca described this arrangement as "entirely satisfactory," promising to carry out "the entire agreement"[50] and to return the boy from Chile at the proper time.[51] Such an agreement on Blanca's part, said Weeks, not only confirmed that on August 3 Jack Jr. was legally in the custody of his father but demonstrated that the defendant's main aim on the night in question was not the recovery of her son but the cold-blooded murder of her ex-husband.

At 1:50 p.m., the state rested its case.

It had been confidently expected—and the defense had done nothing to counter the expectation—that Uterhart would plead his client not guilty on account of insanity. After all, back in 1906, when Harry K. Thaw, the multi-millionaire coal and railroad baron, was charged with shooting love-rival Stanford White, his team of high-priced attorneys had dreamt up the novel defense of "dementia Americana" to explain their client's actions. Apparently the chief symptom of this hitherto unknown ailment was an overwhelming compulsion on the part of the sufferer—exclusively male, red-blooded, and American—to avenge himself on any man who had violated a woman's chastity. It worked. After two stunningly expensive trials, Thaw was found not guilty by virtue of insanity and committed to an asylum.[52]

Before beginning his opening address, Uterhart had one request: that Blanca be excused from giving testimony on the coming Friday afternoon. She was in very poor health, he said, and needed a weekend's rest to prepare for her ordeal on the witness stand.

Justice Manning agreed.

Then Uterhart began to speak. Unlike Weeks, he belonged to the old-school theatrical style of advocacy, one that targeted the heart more than the brain. Even so, his opening wrong-footed everyone in court. He made not a single reference to insanity, nor did he assert that de Saulles's mistreatment of his wife had caused this tragedy. Yes, de Saulles had been a scoundrel whose conduct toward Blanca defined the essence of cruelty from day one of their marriage, but only by inference did Uterhart dangle the possibility that de Saulles had contributed to his own demise.

No, said Uterhart, something altogether different had instigated this tragedy: a physical complaint that caused Blanca to shoot her husband! The testimony of three physicians would prove that the "mental confusion"[53] that had numbed the moral sense of the young woman on the night in question was induced by a combination of physical factors. Uterhart ticked them off: the sunstroke that Blanca suffered a few summers previously at Deal Beach; a depressed fracture of the skull, one and one half inches in diameter and three-eighths of an inch deep, caused by a fall in Chile in 1902; and a second accident in 1915, which fractured the bone anew. Uterhart told the jury that Blanca had been X-rayed. "You will see the actual photograph of Blanca's skull; you will see the depression and you will see the crack which is still ununited."[54] This depression still exists, said Uterhart, because the bones had not united, leaving a fragment of skull pressing down on one of the frontal lobes of the brain—"the place where all the highest faculties of the brain exist, judgment, reason and control."[55]

The cumulative effect of these injuries—aggravated by the brutal heat wave in the week that de Saulles was killed, a week of stupefying headaches for Blanca—had flicked a switch in Blanca's brain, said Uterhart. On the fateful night she had taken the gun to protect herself on the lonely road. Then, when de Saulles refused to relinquish the boy, a feeling overcame her that he was about to do "something particularly mean and vicious"[56]—a feeling inspired by a look in his eyes that she knew of old.

"She felt as if she had been struck a tremendous blow on the top of the head."[57] Uterhart's voice rose high as he painted a picture for the jury and an enthralled courtroom. "She felt a tremendous pain in her brain. All went blank. She knew nothing more until she awoke in the jail. She was as a dead woman."[58]

Since being incarcerated, Blanca had been examined by various doctors, all of whom found her dazed and listless. "She complained of severe pains in her head," said Uterhart. "Her temperature was low, way below normal, and they could scarcely feel her pulse beating. Her face was ghastly white."[59] The physicians, mystified by these symptoms, went looking for the cause. Uterhart gave the jury a penetrating stare. "And they found it, gentlemen. They found out that for some time she had been suffering from a disease which affects the nerve centers and the brain, and which rendered her irresponsible and brought on the mental confusion on the night of the shooting."[60]

Hypothyreosis—the word rolled easily from Uterhart's lips—was a term new to almost everyone in the courtroom. He described it as a condition of the thyroid gland that affects the nerve centers of the brain and which, if not checked, ends in hopeless mental infirmity and death. "On that night she was not responsible. She knew not the nature of her act or that she was doing wrong. She was not a criminal, but an invalid."[61]

This was too much for Weeks, who had listened to Uterhart's opening with a mixture of incredulity and utter disbelief. "Objection! Objection!" he cried. His argument—that the jury not regard this emotive address as evidence—received a bizarre response from the bench. Justice Manning said Uterhart could continue and that he, the judge, would instruct the jury later as to how much was to be considered as evidence. Manning's directive flabbergasted Weeks. By then the damage would have been done, he protested. But the judge, whose frequent and favorable glances at the defendant had not gone unnoticed by the press, refused to budge.

"I also object," said Weeks, "to the ungentlemanly way in which Mr. Uterhart referred to 'old Mrs. De Saulles.'"

"Probably he did not mean it: it was probably made in the heat of the argument,"[62] said the judge. Weeks slumped back in his chair. The trial was turning into a farce.

Unruffled, Uterhart continued on his merry way. "This defense is founded on a question of responsibility. The shooting of Jack De Saulles on August 3,

1917, is not disputed, nor is it disputed that the defendant's hand held the pistol. But you mustn't think that means the defendant is guilty. You who have had experience in civil cases understand that after a plaintiff proves his case and the defendant says there is no dispute about the facts, there still may be other facts to consider. You may hold my promissory note, with my signature on it, but I may prove that I gave a house and lot which discharges the note. That brings us to the line of defense we shall present.

"By reason of other facts, the fact of a killing may be recognized under the law as justifiable and excusable—a defendant may be excused for an act otherwise criminal."[63]

In a shrewd move, Uterhart lavished extravagant praise on the physicians whom he intended to call to the stand. "These doctors are not experts," he said. "They are not brought into the case for the purpose of testifying. They are the doctors who were called in because she needed medical care and advice. They are the doctors who treated her and who are now treating her and are now curing her of the very conditions which I have described."[64] Uterhart picked up the pace. "Our defense does not consist of anything like brainstorms or emotional insanity, or the so-called unwritten law."[65]

No, said Uterhart, instead, "We are going to prove this woman innocent under Section 1120 of the Penal Law, which says that no person shall be held responsible for an act which was committed under such a defect of reason that the person did not know the nature or quality of the act, or that it was wrong."[66] He elaborated. "Many people think that a person to be so excused must be a raving lunatic, with no more reason than a wild beast. That is not the law. The object of the criminal law is not to take revenge, an eye for an eye, a tooth for a tooth; it is to deter evil persons. We expect to prove that this defendant was not responsible mentally or legally within the language of the Penal Law."[67]

Blanca's actions on the night of August 3 were rooted in her traumatic marriage, said Uterhart, and he made a solemn promise: "The things I tell you, you will hear largely from the lips of the defendant herself. I merely outline the facts to which I expect her to testify."[68]

Then came a blistering attack on the life and morals of Jack de Saulles. It took the form of a chronological account from the time that Jack met Blanca, how de Saulles had been a ruthless fortune hunter only to discover that his heiress wife was nowhere near as rich as he hoped or thought. "It was in South Bethlehem that her heart and spirit were broken,"[69] as she came to realize that Jack had married her for money. And Jack's heartlessness toward Blanca was mirrored by his callous parents. "The old folks did not like her and did not hesitate to say so,"[70] said Uterhart. "The mother constantly asked Blanca how long she was going to stay and when she would leave—saying it was unfair for Jack to saddle them with the care of a foreign girl and a baby."[71]

Uterhart portrayed Blanca as the devoted wife, staying home with the baby while her husband was out every night drinking and bedding the good-time girls of Broadway. And on those rare occasions when he did consent to a home visit, he constantly let Blanca down, promising to show up and then not arriving. But de Saulles's most shameful acts involved money. Uterhart recounted the incident in which Señora Errázuriz-Vergara refused to advance Jack the necessary funds to close a real estate deal in Chile. "Blanca de Saulles was already in a condition when the cruelest of men are kind to women. Yet on receiving this reply her husband dragged her away to Paris."[72] As Uterhart piled on the emotion, some jurors were seen to wipe away tears.

According to Uterhart: "On July 1, De Saulles called her at the Hotel Wentworth: he wanted the boy sent out. She said she wanted to keep him all the minutes she was entitled to. She said: 'If I let you have him for the first three days of July, will you let me have him for the same time in August?' De Saulles gave his word of honor that he would do this. On July 6, De Saulles sent her the boy and on the same day he wrote her that the boy was hers until August 6." At this point Uterhart pounded the table. "This letter will be introduced in evidence,"[73] he roared. This was the first public suggestion that such a letter existed. Then he sat down.

Weeks jumped to his feet immediately, demanding that medical experts for the state be allowed to examine Blanca. "If you had made that request at a reasonable time it would have been granted," Uterhart replied sweetly. "But coming after she has been five days in this room it must be refused."

"I made the request some time ago," protested Weeks.

"You never did until yesterday."

"Your word against mine."

"I'm sorry, we have to disagree"[74] was Uterhart's parting shot as he sat down.

The courtroom buzzed. Uterhart's line of defense had completely thrown the prosecution and everyone else present. It had been confidently expected that an insanity defense would be mounted—as per the Thaw case—but the claims of a fractured skull and the thyroid atrophy were described as "amazing innovations."[75]

Suddenly, Uterhart's strategy became blindingly clear to Weeks: If Blanca were acquitted by virtue of insanity her chances of gaining custody of Jack Jr. would be zero. At the very least she would spend time in a mental institution, and that would be long enough for the de Saulles family to gain control of the boy. As Weeks packed his papers in readiness for the weekend, he knew that Uterhart was pinning all of his hopes on a clean acquittal.

FOURTEEN

Blanca Takes the Stand

THE WEEKEND WAS A TIME FOR ALL SIDES TO REGROUP. FOR BLANCA—THE "white widow"[1] as the press was now calling her—it meant a rare opportunity to see her little boy. At twenty minutes before noon on Saturday, Jack Jr. arrived, shepherded by his perennial bodyguard, Harry Dougherty. A few minutes later they were joined by Señora Errázuriz-Vergara, Amalia, and Guillermo, who arrived at the jail bearing lunch in a basket. There was almost a carnival atmosphere in Blanca's room as she and her son played together. Unlike in court, where her cast-iron self-possession never wavered for a moment, Blanca permitted herself the occasional faint smile as she gave her son some picture books, two toy boats, and a drum. He, in turn, handed her a large red rose before going off to sail his little boats in a tin bathtub. The party went on until 4:30 p.m., at which time Dougherty returned the boy to the custody of Mrs. August Heckscher. According to Amalia, everyone had a "dandy time,"[2] and, if the doctors had their way, it was an exercise that would be repeated regularly. Frequent visits, they thought, would greatly benefit Blanca's still fragile health. But the lawyers were unbending. They had agreed to a rigid timetable that allowed for visits on Wednesday and Saturday only, and there would be no deviating from this provision.

The jurors also enjoyed a welcome break from their duties. On Saturday morning the fine cold weather tempted them out for a long walk as far as Westbury, although their guards were careful not to let them get a sight of The Box. In the afternoon they had an auto ride, and after all that it was back to a roaring log fire at the Garden City Hotel.

Not everyone had an enjoyable weekend. Charles Weeks was still seething over Sheriff Seaman's volte-face on the stand, convinced the lawman had deliberately tried to sabotage the state's case with his fuzzy vagueness about the "will they electrocute me right away" comment. Weeks made it clear to reporters that one day after the shooting, Seaman had told him, unequivocally, that Blanca made the remark. All the press could say was that Seaman's testimony had been a "distinct disappointment"[3] to the district attorney. Off the record, Weeks cursed the sheriff's betrayal in terms that no newspaper dared to print. And he promised not to extend any special consideration when Blanca took the stand. "She will have to undergo the same cross-examination that any other defendant would under similar circumstances. I do not intend to be unduly harsh, but murder has been done; the people must not permit such crimes, and I propose to get all the facts."[4] He then ruminated on the difficult task that confronted him: "I will not spare her. I must do my duty and try to obtain her conviction in the first degree of murder. I am as chivalrous as the next man, but I must fulfill my oath of office."[5] He intended to show that Jack's alleged marital abuse was fictitious, a figment of Blanca's malevolent imagination, and he also threatened to call the older Mrs. de Saulles to dash claims that she had ever mistreated her daughter-in-law.

Although unable to admit it, Weeks had been totally blind-sided by Uterhart's assertion that Blanca's actions on the fateful night were fueled by a long-standing medical condition. And now he was hamstrung by the defense's refusal to allow Blanca to be examined by the state's medical experts. All Uterhart would say—smirking as he did so—was that he had been disposed to allow it, only to be overruled by the attending physicians. Uterhart's intransigence meant that Weeks spent most of the weekend rounding up his own team of doctors, who would have to form an opinion of Blanca's physical state based only on an examination of the skull X-rays. Ordinarily in a criminal trial, it is the state, with its awesome reach and bottomless pockets, that holds all the big cards. But for the first time in his career, District Attorney Weeks found himself in the unusual position of being comprehensively outgunned at every turn, by an opponent with equal, if not greater, financial firepower, and his confusion was beginning to show. From the outset the state's entire case had been predicated on a defense plea of insanity, and in Weeks's blinkered view this was still the way the trial would pan out. Nothing else could explain his bizarre statement that weekend: "We will contend that she was sane at the time of the shooting and never was anything else but sane."[6]

Over in the other camp, Uterhart was exploring the possibility of adding yet another string to his bow—a plea of self-defense. It derived from Suzanne Monteau's testimony at the inquest, when she had said, "Oh, he

[Jack de Saulles] looked terrible. I thought he was going to jump at her. Then she shot."[7] After studying all the witness statements, Uterhart decided against complication. He had enough in the medical bag to win this one, he was sure. Besides, his team of physicians was also mightily skilled in the black art of spin doctoring. Even if Blanca were acquitted, they told the press, her life was still not out of danger; it would take a "dangerous operation"[8] to remedy the unhealed fracture of the skull. This would consist of removing a section of the bone said to be pressing against her brain and substituting it with a sliver of bone taken from elsewhere. Without this operation, the prognosis was gloomy. There was a danger that the condition of the skull would eventually destroy her reason completely and might cause her death.

November 25

Sunday saw a long caravan of cars pull up outside Mineola jail. Old friends, casual acquaintances, and rubberneckers whose only contact with Blanca had been via the press all attempted to gain admittance to see the state's most illustrious inmate. Only two made it to Blanca's room; her mother and the tennis-playing playboy Count Otto Salm,[9] whose Chilean-born wife was a girlhood friend of Blanca's. Coincidentally—or perhaps not—Count Salm was also a close friend of Rodolfo Guglielmi. The two men had met in 1914 when Salm, who was also an excellent dancer, helped Rodolfo gain admittance to the inner circle of New York nightclub society. And it's possible that on this day Salm was acting as a courier, carrying a message from Rodolfo to Blanca, as years later Mae Murray stated that Rodolfo, utterly distraught over Blanca's predicament, repeatedly attempted to contact her during the trial. If true, then much the most likely intermediary would have been Salm.

For now, though, Salm and Señora Errázuriz-Vergara had Blanca to themselves, as no other visitor made it past the jailhouse front gate. Most observed the proprieties of good society, leaving their cards for Blanca in the manner of someone paying a house call. There were ulterior motives at work. Tomorrow was the big day, when Blanca was expected to take the stand, and demand was heavy for tickets to the public gallery. Sheriff Seaman blocked every request. Only those who can find seats will be admitted, he said, herding the disappointed callers from his jailhouse steps.

The jurors were not the only trial participants ensconced at the Garden City Hotel. Uterhart had also made the hotel his base and the venue for his daily press briefings. When asked to comment on Weeks's reaction to Seaman's surprise testimony, the big lawyer affected surprise. "I cannot understand Mr. Weeks's attitude. It would seem by this statement that he is anxious to keep out testimony that might not be favorable to the defendant. This is not the duty of a public prosecutor."[10] Then overconfidence got the better of him. "Long before I was retained in this case, Mr. Weeks secured all the telephone slips bearing the record of Mrs. De Saulles's calls on the night of the shooting. One of these slips shows that she called D. Stewart Iglehart, which is part of our defense to show that the shooting was not premeditated. Mr. Weeks has not attempted to use these slips and when Judge Smith asked for them he refused to give them up. I shall demand them in open court tomorrow."[11] Because Uterhart was hired within twelve hours of the shooting, any comments about events "long before I was retained in this case" were frankly ridiculous.

And Uterhart was not out of the woods yet. For some obscure reason in his opening address he had mentioned a letter written by Jack in which he said that Blanca "hated America and Americans,"[12] and intended upon obtaining a divorce, to take Jack Jr. back to Chile, where he would be educated. Now Uterhart was forced to backtrack. Blanca had since told him that she intended to remain most of the time in America, and would have her boy educated exclusively in the United States and reared as a US citizen. Uterhart said that Blanca "liked America and Americans, and that many of her best friends were Americans."[13]

Uterhart bristled when asked about reports that Weeks would halt the trial and establish a lunacy commission to decide upon Blanca's sanity, much as had been done in Thaw's first trial. There were several reasons why Weeks would be prevented from making such a motion, he snapped. Uterhart's indignation was buttressed by co-counsel, Lewis J. Smith, who expressed doubts that Blanca would be able to survive her ordeal. "She may get through all right," he said gravely. "But she is a very sick woman."[14] Despite regular visits from her doctors, he said, her unnatural weight loss had not been arrested.

Uterhart concluded what had been an uncomfortable press conference with the revelation that he was putting the finishing touches to a hypothetical question that he intended addressing to each of the defense physicians. Again, this was a strategy lifted from the first Thaw murder trial. On that occasion the question had run to some fifteen thousand words. According to rumors, Uterhart's interrogative was expected to exceed that word count by a third, much to the displeasure of Justice Manning. This trial was taking far longer and costing the Nassau County taxpayers far more than it should, and although barred from ordering the court to sit on the upcoming Thanksgiving Day, he now raised the specter of a Saturday sitting, unless both parties speeded up their snail-like progress. Justice Manning also clarified one other matter: the vexatious issue of whether Jack Jr. would testify. Under New York law it was left to the judge's discretion to decide whether a child under the age of seven could testify in a criminal trial, and in this instance he decided against having the child's story go before the jury. Even the appearance of Jack Jr. in court might prejudice the state's case, and he ruled, "That boy must not be permitted to appear in court under any circumstances."[15]

The often lurid press coverage of the trial was provoking a strange backlash, with some finding in this tragedy a parable for modern times. "The De Saulles case is a product of the selfish, pleasure seeking spirit of New York," the Rev. Dr. Christian F. Reisner told his flock at Grace Methodist Church, located at 104th Street in Upper Manhattan, on this Sunday morning. "Thousands follow it greedily, but few pay the price in the open that has been exacted here. . . . 'Whatever a man sows that shall he reap.' And neighboring hearts must also be torn by the thorns. Little 'Jackie' will never get away from the Cain mark."[16]

The Trial, Day 6

On Monday morning, an hour before the Mineola courthouse opened, the surrounding streets were choked with fancy automobiles and idle chauffeurs, who stood around smoking while their fashionably dressed, mostly female employers—one observer put the ratio at four women for every man—jammed the narrow corridor leading from the entrance of the building to the court so tightly that attorneys and newspapermen had to squirm through cellar passageways to reach their places. When the courtroom doors finally did open, a perfumed tidal wave of warm fur surged forward, knocking some court officials off their feet as spectators jostled to gain the best vantage point. Ordinarily, many of these society matrons—spearheaded by the acknowledged queen of Long Island's elite set, Mrs. Reginald C. Vanderbilt—would have already retreated to winter homes in Palm Beach and elsewhere, but the de Saulles trial was proving an irresistible draw.

For most, this was their first day at the trial and a hum of excitement filled the public gallery as the warring factions lined up. First came the de Saulles family, led by the stalwart major and his lawyer, Almuth C. Vandiver, together with Caroline and other relatives. They arranged themselves with quiet dignity on one side of the courtroom, to the left of the defense table. Moments later it was the turn of Señora Errázuriz-Vergara to make her grand entrance, accompanied by Amalia and Guillermo and a number of Chilean and American friends. They took up a position just behind the defense table. Some in the press had likened the two feuding families to the Montagues and Capulets. They had a point. This was intense drama and the stakes could not have been higher. But everyone was agog, waiting for the star player to make her entrance.

Blanca did not disappoint. She entered the court with head erect and staring straight ahead as, accompanied by the ever-present Mrs. Seaman, she took her seat at the defense table. Many were surprised at her relaxed composure. Certainly there was nothing in her demeanor to suggest that a nervous breakdown was on the cards, as the defense had warned the previous day.

Once Justice Manning called the court to order—fifteen minutes late because of the crush—Uterhart rose, bowed to his client without speaking, and gestured toward the witness chair. Blanca stood, disappeared along the aisle at the rear of the jury box, then reappeared to take the witness stand. She was simply dressed in a sand-colored sweater with a large collar of a darker brown and a skirt. Her hair was drawn back over her ears and fastened in a large knot behind. According to one mesmerized observer, she looked "paler and more beautiful than ever."[17]

Unlike her impassive performance while listening to other witnesses, she was animated, restless even, when she first took the stand. She glanced from her lawyer to the judge, and then to the jury, before sweeping the courtroom with her huge brown eyes, as if mentally sizing up the battlefield. Uterhart began by asking her name, and then where she lived. "In the Mineola jail"[18] came the barely audible reply. Justice Manning asked her to raise her voice. Blanca promised she would try. After the first few questions, she fell into a mechanical, monosyllabic routine that she maintained throughout, using as few words as possible. Her manner brightened noticeably whenever Justice Manning intervened, as he did frequently, framing questions in a manner that seemed both paternal and profoundly empathetic. On these occasions she became much more vibrant, even smiling at the judge, who seemed greatly flattered by such a reaction.

Uterhart asked Blanca about her various head injuries. She told how, as a little girl, she had fallen in the fireplace and banged her head on an andiron.

It had affected her so much that she never fully recovered. "I believe I was kept in bed for some time."[19]

"Were there any permanent results of that injury?"

"Only pains in the head." She pointed to an area just above her forehead. "The pains come and go."[20]

Uterhart then asked what had happened when she and Jack moved into the lonely house at Larchmont. For her protection, she said, Jack had bought her a revolver. Uterhart handed her the nickel-plated .32 Smith & Wesson.

"Is that the one?"

"Yes, that's the one."[21] She took the gun without flinching in the least.

Uterhart next dealt with various letters Blanca had written to Jack, ones that displayed affection—a desperate attempt, according to Uterhart's opening address, to save her crumbling marriage—and then compared them to the letters she had written to Nurse O'Neill, which, he said, revealed her true emotions. Blanca agreed that this was the case, embellishing the second string of letters with harrowing descriptions of her torrid home life, none of which, of course, could be corroborated. Across the court the de Saulles family sat with "incredulous expressions"[22] and compressed lips as Blanca piled on the opprobrium. Caroline, in particular, glared venomously at her former sister-in-law.

Uterhart drew from Blanca an account of her life as an innocent manipulated by a deceitful, grasping husband who, even after discovering that his heiress wife did not have the fabulous wealth that everyone assumed, still managed to swindle her out of forty-seven thousand dollars. Further financial details followed, all designed to reveal the level of Jack's duplicity.

After two hours of testimony, Justice Manning ordered a recess for lunch. The Long Island society set adjourned to the basement cafeteria to discuss the morning's events. Over sandwiches and coffee, there was high admiration for Blanca's courtroom demeanor. Very impressive. During this break it was Dr. Wight's turn at the defense PR helm. He informed the pressmen that Blanca was bearing the strain better than he had expected, while the señora, oozing confidence and charisma, added that her daughter had taken "a little rest"[23] and was ready to continue her evidence upon the resumption.

The opening of the afternoon session saw an astonishing scene in court. As the doors were thrown open, scores of women surged forward, fighting "madly and shamelessly"[24] to secure a spot in the public gallery. Three women fainted and many were hurt. They "shrieked and howled so loudly"[25] that Justice Manning, red-faced with anger, stormed from his chambers. "This is simply disgraceful,"[26] he roared, pounding his fist on the bench. "This is not a performance. This is a solemn trial.... Sheriff, I want that hall and corridor cleared entirely. Make everybody get out except reporters and those who have passes properly accredited."[27]

Easier said than done.

Seaman and his staff were simply overwhelmed by the mob of "frenzied women,"[28] most of whom laughed when the court officers gave them orders to leave and fought their way back into the room. Another woman swooned and had to be carried out; others were trampled underfoot. Even veteran reporters had never witnessed such scenes; indeed, so bad did it become that some pressmen had to squeeze through windows to gain admittance to the court. After fifteen minutes of bedlam, Seaman was finally able to clear all the corridors.

When some semblance of courtroom decorum was restored, Blanca, who had sat through the commotion totally unaffected, resumed her testimony. Uterhart wanted to know more about the automobile accident in Chile. "Do you remember what kind of a motor car this was?"

Blanca smiled ruefully. "A Ford."[29] This sparked laughter in court, with most struggling to picture the affluent defendant in such a vehicle. She described being thrown from the car and landing on her head, and then being aware of nothing until she awoke later, under the care of physicians. She was told that the accident had caused a depressed fracture of the skull, leading to pressure on the brain. Afterward she had been confined to bed for two days with "severe headaches.... I was dizzy and nauseated."

"Where is that fracture?"

"Right here." She lay a hand on top of her head, near the forehead. "I can feel the depression. Whenever I combed my hair it pained terribly and every time something disagreeable happened my head hurt fearfully. Sometimes I can't see and everything before my eyes gets blurred."[30]

Uterhart was Blanca's best audience. Every answer that she gave received some kind of accompanying gesture from the big lawyer, a sorrowful shake of the head or an encouraging smile, and with his towering bulk he had a way of leaning over her that gave him the air of protector rather than advocate. And judging from her testimony, this was a woman in desperate need of protection. After moving to The Box in May 1916, said Blanca, her husband's callousness reached a new, more terrifying pitch. "He told me one day that if I did not like it I could get out—he said that more than once. He said the father knew best about what was good for the boy."[31]

And always there were other women. One in particular. A frisson rippled through the public gallery. At last! This was the kind of juicy detail that most had come for. Blanca told how Jack Jr. had returned from an outing to the zoo, saying that his father had another woman with him, one whom he had been instructed to call "Miss Jo." "I almost died when I heard that. It was a terrible shock to me. I afterward learned that the woman the baby talked about was Joan Sawyer."[32] There was another coo of pleasure from the court. Blanca said that she'd learned of the affair from John Milholland, the brother of Inez Boissevain, the noted suffragist who had recently died and "whom I knew very well."[33] He told her that "everybody knew about it."[34]

When she had confronted Jack about his affair with Joan Sawyer, he had rounded on her viciously snarling, "Do you think you are the only woman who has ever been in love with me?"[35] Asked by Uterhart for her reaction, Blanca simply said, "I nearly died."[36] She described her husband as an abusive drunk who, most nights, stayed out till three and four o'clock in the morning. "He said he could not help the kind of life he was living as he was not made to settle down."[37] Blanca realized that she had become a figure of society fun when, at the Arrowhead Inn, she was publicly humiliated in front of a crowded restaurant.

The final straw came when she read the notorious edition of *Town Topics,* with its sensational coverage of the yacht party thrown by the Duke of Manchester and Jack de Saulles. How did that make you feel? asked Uterhart. "I was terribly scandalized,"[38] she whispered. Life was becoming unbearable, made worse by Jack's erratic behavior on his frequent visits to London. In a string of telegrams he would first beg her to join him, only to break her heart with a succession of last-minute rejections. She explained how a "peculiar trick of fate"[39] had prevented her from taking passage on the *Lusitania* on its fateful trip. Only a misunderstanding of her husband's wishes had prevented the trip, she said, adding, "When I heard of its going I wished I was on it."[40] A sigh from the public gallery reinforced Blanca's witness-stand sadness. Such comments might have made for good theater, but Weeks noted the remark with grim satisfaction. There was an opening here.

Further humiliations followed, said Blanca, with Jack squandering her fortune on a succession of loose women. When Uterhart tried to explore details of the divorce, he was abruptly halted by Justice Manning, with a reminder that under the terms of the settlement, each party was sworn to silence. "The law sealed her mouth,"[41] said the judge. Uterhart knew this, of course. But his intent was to fix in the jury's mind the notion that, because of some legal constraint, he was prevented from revealing even more damaging details about Jack de Saulles's colorful sex life.

Blanca *was* allowed to describe the aftermath of the divorce, how she had not dreamt that Jack Jr. would be taken from her, until her lawyer warned, "You know you are a foreigner and the child is an American citizen. No judge would permit you to remove the boy from the country to be brought up other than as an American."[42] Because of this, she agreed to the split custody. Only later did the full implications of the agreement sink in. "I felt as if the world was coming to an end when I realized what this meant to me."[43]

Blanca's head lowered as she spoke. Her distress was mirrored in the jury box, where several members dabbed at stray tears. Even Justice Manning, with all his years of experience on the bench, was visibly affected. Uterhart, who came from the old school of lawyering that believed a face full of tears was worth an ocean of evidence, and who had been mopping his cheeks lavishly ever since the beginning of Blanca's testimony, now blew his nose noisily and contented himself with waiting in gentlemanly fashion until the witness composed herself. With the court at an emotional fever pitch, he decided that the time was now right to lay the groundwork for his defense. "Do you remember the week of July 30?"

"Yes."

"The weather was hot, wasn't it?"

"Yes."[44]

Right on cue, Uterhart produced a weather record for that week that showed temperatures in the range of eighty-three to ninety-three degrees. On the day of the shooting the mercury stood at eighty-three degrees and the humidity had reached a soggy 86 percent, its maximum for this period. These were, said Uterhart, the hottest days of the year. "I know," grumbled Justice Manning, "I was holding court at the time,[45] and, taking over, he asked Blanca if she suffered from the heat.

"Terribly,"[46] she replied. "I felt on fire. I was terribly sleepy, but couldn't sleep. I tried to keep cool with showers. The pains in the head were almost unendurable."[47] Her memory had lapsed two or three times. And there were physical problems, as well; for instance, her fingernails broke off and her hair fell out, both symptoms, she now knew, of her previously undiagnosed thyroid condition.

Skillfully, Uterhart created the impression that because of this long-standing medical condition, on the night of the shooting, Blanca was not responsible for her actions. And the defendant played her part to perfection. Mostly, her answers were brief and she wisely avoided creating the impression of being a vengeful harridan. Her actions were inevitable and unavoidable, a view shared by many in the public gallery judging from the sympathetic expressions on the faces of the women who craned their necks to better hear her softly spoken answers.

And she also had plenty of allies among the sob sisters. One of these, Mrs. Wilson Woodrow,[48] struggled to keep her own emotions in check as she described the defendant: "Is she real? Is she flesh and blood, or some being woven of moonbeams? Women of her type, if normal, do not commit murder in hot blood or cold blood, either. They are statuesque, gentle, docile, and obedient."[49] Then came a dash of pseudo-Freudian insight—very popular at the time—the murder, declared Mrs. Woodrow, "was the irrational act of a woman mentally irresponsible for her deeds. There is no question of a sudden brainstorm or temporary insanity. Her condition is obvious. She is a melancholic subject in a state of fixed apathy. Her place is in a hospital and not in a courtroom."[50]

As the electric light in the courtroom took over from the fast fading afternoon, Blanca, who had been on the stand for several hours, began to wilt. She turned to Justice Manning, placed a hand on the judicial bench, and addressed him in a voice that barely carried to the first juror. "I'm so tired, please."[51]

Justice Manning turned to Uterhart and suggested that she continue by telling the story in her own words, "If it isn't too long."

"It is quite a story," said Uterhart.

"It won't be if you let her tell it herself,"[52] the judge replied tartly. Uterhart gave a gracious bow and sat down.

"Where shall I start?"[53] asked Blanca. Uterhart told her to just outline the events of August 3. She began with frustration over the phone calls, how she thought that Jack was manipulating the situation. Even when giving her responses in narrative form, her delivery was truncated, not verbose at all, just a few sentences at a time, followed by a pause. Whenever Uterhart tried to intervene, he was silenced by the bench; Justice Manning was adamant that he wanted this story told in Blanca's own words. The witness screwed her face into a frown, as if struggling to recall. Finally, she remembered making a phone call. "I told Mr. Iglehart that I was going to get the boy and I wanted him to go with me. He said it was too delicate a matter. . . . He offered to send his car, and I do not remember much of what he said."[54] Here, her voice trailed off, as if she was having trouble concentrating. Every pause only increased the tension in court. At times the breaks were so long that the only sound to be heard was the occasional rumbling of a radiator. No one, though, was distracted. Everyone seemed to be straining for the next word. Blanca continued.

"The maid and I started from Crossways and we took the dog. I wanted to take my baby right away with me and I didn't want Jack to know"—this was the first and only time that she addressed her ex-husband by his Christian name—"so I ordered the taxi to stop a little distance from The Box on the roadway. As the maid and I got out I saw De Saulles's car standing outside. I was surprised to see it there, as I had not supposed he would yet have returned from the Meadow Brook Club, where they told me over the phone he had gone to dinner."[55]

The jury's eyes were riveted on Blanca as she neared what they suspected would be the dramatic conclusion. "As I went into the house I saw my baby coming downstairs with Mrs. Degener, De Saulles's sister. I wanted then to take the baby and run."[56] At this point Blanca paused to sweep a nervous hand over her brow, as if struggling to remember what happened next. "But then Mr. De Saulles came forward. I think I asked him why he had kept the baby past his time. I don't know what he said then—something about it being his time to have the boy. But I said: 'I want him and I've come to take him.' Then he looked at me and said, 'You can't have him; you can't ever have him.' I saw a look come over his face. I think I was stunned then. I felt a frightful pain in my head."[57] Another of those pauses. Then she said, "I can still hear those words. . . . The next I knew Dr. Wight was bending over me. I suppose it was in the jail. It was the next morning."[58]

A long, pained gap followed. There was perfect silence in the room. Everybody had been sitting on the edge of their seats. At length she murmured, "That's all." There was another pause. "Can I go now?"[59]

"Is that all you know?" asked the judge in kindly tones.

"Yes," came the almost inaudible reply.

"And when did your memory return?"

"I think it was when I found Dr. Wight speaking to me."

"Do you know now when that was—whether it was on the same night or the next day?"

The defendant just sat there, looking bewildered. Justice Manning asked if that was all she could tell the court. With a tired smile she said, "Yes."[60]

It was clear that she had reached the limit of her endurance. Although there were still fifteen minutes of the scheduled session to go, Justice Manning looked at her and said, "You may go now."[61] He banged the gavel. Blanca bowed toward the judge and the jury, stepped down from her chair, and followed the deputy out of the court.

Her ordeal on the witness stand had lasted five hours and she had not put a foot wrong.

FIFTEEN

"Flatter Him to Death"

The Trial, Day 7

Seven days into the trial saw a tightening of courtroom security in an effort to ensure no repetition of the unseemly scramble for seats that had marred the previous day's session. As a result, an orderly procession filled the long corridor that led to the public gallery, with everyone buzzing at the spectacle to come. How would Blanca fare on cross-examination? Would she buckle under the pressure? Would she let slip details of secret lovers? It was all too exciting! Even Blanca, her face more ghostly than ever, looked apprehensive as she entered the court. Several jurors smiled encouragingly at her, and a deathly hush fell over the crowd as she took her place at the defense table, just in front of Señora Errázuriz-Vergara and her other children. As always, Blanca made no attempt to acknowledge their presence. Uterhart whispered a last few words of advice and then she was called to the witness stand. The next few hours would decide the course of her life—in its polar extremes, either freedom or a date with the electric chair.

As Weeks approached, Blanca greeted him with the sweetest smile. He began with general inquiries into the current state of her health, asking how she had fared since she went to jail; for instance, were her nails still brittle?

"They were nearly always brittle."

"And has your hair been falling out?"

She smiled. "All women's hair falls out."

"Yes, but we are confining ourselves to your hair."

"Yes."[1]

Weeks's opening—not so much a salvo, more a gentle salve—had shocked many, as he barely raised his voice above a polite enquiry. And the emollient tone continued. "When did you first find out that your husband had ceased to care for you?"

"I think it was at the time when I went to Europe before the war began."[2]

"When you went to South Bethlehem about the time the baby was born, you were unhappy?"

"Yes, but I was very fond of him [Jack de Saulles],"[3] Blanca said, punctuating her responses with deep, theatrical sighs and a lifting of her shoulders, as if relieving a great weight.

Weeks then reached down for a sheaf of letters that lay on his desk. One day earlier Uterhart had read extracts from the voluminous correspondence that passed between the couple to prove the extent of Jack's cruelty toward Blanca. Jurors had wept openly as defense counsel highlighted those passages that painted Blanca as the devoted but downtrodden wife, waiting at home with the baby while her husband was out raising hell on Broadway. Now it was Weeks's turn to wring some advantage from the correspondence. He began with a letter Blanca had written from South Bethlehem just after the baby was born, in which she addressed her husband as "My precious Dada Boy" and thanked him for all his kindnesses to her. "You have been such a perfect, ideal husband and now you are a sweet father. I want to show my gratefulness to you by being a good wife and a devoted mother."[4]

Weeks peered over the top of his spectacles at the witness. "You meant what you wrote in that?"

"In a way I did."

"He was very kind to you?"

"He was kind because he stayed with me when the baby was born."[5]

Weeks repeated the line about Jack being a "perfect, ideal husband." Was that true?

"Yes,"[6] she said falteringly.

Next came questions about her 1916 visit to London. It was, said Blanca, a miserable time, made worse "because I was away from all my family and friends."[7] This puzzled Weeks. But what about this letter, he asked, written from London on June 29 rhapsodizing about the glittering attractions and social life in Europe? "It is fair for us to assume you were having a pretty good time?"

After considerable hesitation she said, "Yes."[8]

This question appeared to flag a warning signal in Blanca's mind. Thus far, she had answered briskly; henceforth, her replies were shaped more carefully and took much longer to deliver, as she sought to reconcile her alleged unhappiness with the upbeat tone of the letters. Weeks moved it along. "You went to the dances and private theatricals, didn't you?"

"Yes."

"And had a pretty good time?"

"No, I was bored to death,"[9] she said emphatically. "My heart was broken when I wrote that letter."[10]

How, Weeks wondered, if your heart was broken, could you disport herself so gaily at London dances? The answer came back, quick as a rapier. "We don't dance with our hearts."[11] Blanca's long eyelashes fluttered in triumph as the court cooed with delight over her bon mot.

No amount of pretrial coaching from Uterhart could have provoked such good responses from Blanca under cross-examination. She was a natural. And she clearly held the upper hand in the early exchanges. When Weeks, thoroughly flustered, turned to a letter written the next day, June 30, in which she proclaimed her love for Jack, and asked why she had adopted such amorous tones, she smiled, "I thought the surest way to hold a man was to flatter him to death."[12] Weeks immediately asked that this answer be stricken out and Justice Manning agreed, but it was too late. The damage had been done; Blanca had scored yet another big point.

Weeks hurried on to another letter in which Blanca expressed concerns about the influence certain people might be having on Jack. "You spoke of Louise and Maurice; was that Mr. and Mrs. Heckscher?"

"Yes."

"Are they friends of yours?"

"I thought they were."

"Are they now?"

"I don't know."[13]

This allowed Weeks to raise the incident on the Duke of Manchester's boat off Huntington, when, according to Blanca's earlier testimony, she and Louise Heckscher had seen Jack and the duke frolicking with "a lot of girls."[14] Weeks tried to get Blanca to admit that she grossly exaggerated the number of women present. She was unflinching. Weeks continued: "Don't you know that at that time your husband was working on war contracts with the duke?"

"One doesn't work on war contracts at Huntington" was Blanca's sardonic riposte, managing to make the prim Long Island resort sound like a modern-day Sodom and Gomorrah.

"Don't you know that the firm of Heckscher & De Saulles cleaned up $50,000 as a result of this contract?"

"I never knew of it."[15]

Hundreds of killers have talked their way into the electric chair. Blanca de Saulles was not about to make that mistake. This far she had proved to be a textbook witness, never volunteering information, never argumentative, merely answering each question with the fewest words possible.

When Weeks asked about a letter she had written Jack while en route to Chile, Blanca replied that she thought the marriage was "morally ended."[16] Was this an admission, Weeks mused, that she had discontinued sleeping with Jack? "Is it not a fact that since the birth of your boy you had not lived with him as man and wife?"[17]

This sparked a considerable rustling in court, with everyone pressing forward to catch Blanca's reply. "It is not," came the hot response.

"Didn't you tell Mrs. Heckscher that?"

"I did. She was always prying into my married life."[18]

"But didn't you tell Mrs. Heckscher that you didn't mind Jack seeing women, so long as he left you alone?" Again Blanca admitted saying this, but only to fob off Louise Heckscher, who was "constantly prying into her affairs."[19]

Weeks kept up the attack. "Did you tell Mrs. Heckscher that if you had known what married life was you would never have married?"

"No."

"Didn't you tell her that he could run around all he wanted to if he would leave you alone?"

"No."

"And did you not boast of your indifference toward any demonstrations of affection on the part of your husband?"

"No."[20]

"Didn't he write to you that you had never been a wife to him?"

"He wrote me a very long and very rude letter. If he said it, it was a lie."[21]

The "very rude" letter was then introduced. Weeks read from it slowly, "For the last four years you have refused to live with me as my wife."[22] Here, Weeks paused and peered at the witness. All he got back was a contemptuous wrinkling of Blanca's nose.

On balance the correspondence proved damaging to Blanca, especially the time she wrote to Jack: "I got another beastly letter from my mother, so that I have given up trying to bridge the gulf. She is out of her mind."[23] Initially, Señora Errázuriz-Vergara, seated directly facing her daughter, appeared not to hear what had been said, but when everyone suddenly turned and looked in her direction, she asked the person alongside what she had missed. When Blanca's words were repeated to her, tears began trickling down her face. Moments later, unable to control her emotions, she hurried from court. If Blanca saw this interruption—and it's impossible to imagine that she did not—it made no difference. Her implacable expression remained fixed.

Weeks's gentlemanly cross-examination continued. How, he wanted to know, could she pen such endearing communications if her heart were truly broken? "I wouldn't for the world have let him know how offended I was."[24]

Not even after the notorious "which one?" incident at the hotel in London, surely that must have been a gross humiliation?

"I had been offended."

"You wouldn't say humiliated?"

"I would say seriously offended."[25]

Weeks next read out an extract from the Christmas Eve, 1914, letter Blanca wrote to Jack about her arrival in New York. It concerned the incident where she had flirted with the customs man, a Mr. Downey, who had eased her through the immigration formalities, and whose kindness she had repaid by inviting him to visit her family home in New York. "Of course, he was in the seventh heaven of delight," she wrote. "You know better than anyone what saying that means to people of that class."[26] Over sniggers from the public gallery, Weeks continued, saying that, again, this letter gave no indication of the hurt that Blanca claimed she was feeling.

"It wasn't meant to."[27]

In that same letter, Weeks noted, she had mentioned spending a considerable amount of time in the company of Harold Fowler. It was Fowler with whom Blanca dined in London, it was Fowler who accompanied her on the *Lusitania* on the return from London, and it was Fowler whom she met and dined with in New York. The subtext was clear: Weeks was exploring the possibility that Blanca had found solace in someone else's arms. "I should like to ask, was your heart broken at that time?"

"I was miserable."[28]

More sparring followed. Weeks plucked a quote from a letter of February 28, 1915: "When you wrote, 'I don't love anyone more than I do you,' did you mean it?"

"No."

"Your heart was broken then?"

Blanca's eyes flashed. "I answered that before, Mr. Weeks."

"You wrote what you didn't mean?"

"One can smile with a broken heart."[29] Again, Blanca's flair for aphorisms thrilled the public gallery.

Weeks did manage to dent Blanca's sangfroid when he resurrected her comment about so narrowly avoiding passage aboard the *Lusitania,* and her wish to have perished in the tragedy. "Is it not a fact that when you first heard of the sinking you and De Saulles were with Mrs. Mooney and that De Saulles said he wished he had been aboard the Lusitania?"

"I don't remember."[30] This time Blanca's stock answer to so many questions sounded thin and unconvincing. No doubt about it; she had been caught out.

Weeks began to press. After Jack had offered her a divorce if she so desired and she had sailed for Chile, she wrote a letter thanking him for his flowers and kind words. "Do you mean to say that when you wrote that your married life was at an end?"

"At an end, morally."[31]

"Will you please be frank and tell us what you mean by that? Did you mean that you wouldn't live with him as man and wife?"

"I thought that as I was leaving him, I wouldn't."[32]

Blanca was a canny operator. Whenever the questioning became too pointed for comfort, she would look pleadingly at Justice Manning, and he would ease her distress with a few kind words, encouraging her to take her time and not to be nervous. Blanca's palpable effect on the judge was echoed in Weeks's next line of questioning, an attempt to show just how comfortable she was in the company of other men. Blanca reluctantly admitted that she had attended several social functions on her own, but only with a "heavy heart."[33]

Abruptly, Weeks switched to events on the morning after the shooting, when Blanca was in a supposedly dazed state. He asked if she recalled phoning Frederic R. Coudert, asking him to call on her at the jail, that he had done so, and that she had selected, at his recommendation, the firm of Uterhart & Graham to represent her.

"I don't recall seeing him at that time."[34]

Weeks looked incredulous. "You don't recall my walking into the woman's part of the jail that morning and finding you at a table with Suzanne Monteau, your maid, across the table from you and when I found you reading a newspaper?"

"I do not."[35]

"Do you remember reading that Mr. Uterhart said that he would 'acquit this woman' . . . or hand his certificate of admission to the judge?"

"I didn't read that," she said, smiling across at her lawyer, who smiled right back.

Weeks next raised the exhaustive biography that had been delivered to the papers within forty-eight hours of the killing. "Didn't you give all that information to your lawyer in the conference you had with him immediately after the shooting?"

"I don't recollect it. I have no knowledge of any talk with Mr. Uterhart then."[36] Her first claimed memory of meeting Uterhart came on August 13, ten days after the shooting. Nor could she remember phoning Mrs. Roma M. Flint and asking her to bail her maid out. Then Weeks produced a check, payable to the order of Mrs. Flint. It was dated August 4. "Do you recall drawing that check?" Weeks handed her the check. She studied it for several moments.

"No, I do not."

"You know that it was used as the cash bail resulting in the release of your maid, Suzanne Monteau, don't you?"

"I think I heard of it later."[37]

It had been an arduous morning, and as the recess hour drew near, one of the jurors, retired firefighter Alexander Norton, yawned audibly. The crowd tittered and Weeks suggested to the judge that the jury must be getting tired and that maybe it was time to break for lunch. To general astonishment Blanca broke in. "I should think anybody would be tired."[38]

Weeks spun around. It had taken more than two hours, but at long last a flash of emotion colored his face. "Are you tired?" he barked at the witness.

"No, I don't blame the juror for being tired, though."

"Are my questions tiresome to you?"

"Yes."

This brought a gasp in court.

"Do they bore you? Do you think I should not ask you about these things?"

"Oh, no, Mr. Weeks. I know you have to do that."[39]

A couple of exchanges later, Weeks said, "When you said that you didn't mean any disrespect to me, I hope?"

"Oh, no,"[40] she said innocently. On this note, the morning session ended.

During the lunch recess, members of the public gallery exchanged views about the morning's testimony. Reactions were mixed. Some thought Blanca had withstood Weeks's admittedly bland cross-examination with admirable panache. Others were more critical. For the first time Blanca's highly developed sense of entitlement was beginning to grate. The incident with the customs man, in particular, had raised hackles, with one woman marking Blanca down as "a frightful little snob."[41] And then there was the tactless remark that had driven her own mother from the court. All in all, the prosecution had just about shaded the session, but not by much.

After the recess, Weeks sharpened his focus, taking aim at Blanca's finances and defense claims that Jack had been a mercenary predator content to sponge off his wife's inheritance. "Is it not the law in Chile that when a woman marries, her goods and all she owns belong to her husband?"

"Yes."

"I object," interrupted Uterhart, "and ask that the answer be stricken out. When this lady married the American, even down in Chile, she became an American citizen too, and her property was subject only to the American laws."[42] Uterhart was skating on the thinnest of ice, legally, and he knew it, and his objection was swiftly quashed by Justice Manning. When the question was restated, Blanca repeated that such was the case under Chilean law. And was it not also the case, said Weeks, that at the time of the divorce, Jack signed back his interest in your Chilean property? Again Blanca agreed. And what about the diamond stickpin that he gave you? "It belonged to me,"[43] she protested. More dispute over expenses followed, in which Blanca grudgingly admitted that even in her current allegedly impecunious state she was still able to afford three maids.

With these questions about domestic finances, Weeks finally found some chinks in Blanca's armor. Previously, her allegations of Jack's abusive behavior had been largely unverifiable; now they were moving into an area that left paper trails. Her face tightened when Weeks pointed out that in 1916 she had borrowed twenty-five hundred dollars from the New York Trust Company and turned the money over to Jack, who had repaid her with three checks. In another transaction she gave the same trust company a note for three thousand dollars.

"You never paid it, did you?"

"Part of it."

"How much?"

"What he didn't pay."[44]

Weeks showed that all of the checks that cleared the loan were signed by Jack. "Your husband paid all those, did he not?" he said, clinching his point.

"Yes."[45]

There then followed a heated exchange over household expenses, who paid what, and so forth. When Weeks claimed that, on one occasion, Jack had paid bills for Blanca's expenses, amounting to $4,990.80, Blanca just shrugged. Eventually the judge tried to clear the air, "Do you dispute the payment by Mr. De Saulles for these things?"[46]

"Oh, I wouldn't dispute a small amount like that,"[47] she said. A groan from the public gallery showed that, once again, Blanca had misjudged the general mood. Such flippancy might play well at a cocktail party, but in this grim setting her levity succeeded only in setting teeth on edge.

"When you went to Chile in 1915, didn't your husband pay your fare?"

"Possibly."

"Didn't your husband give you $200 for the Chile trip and send you a $2,000 letter of credit?" When Blanca hesitated, Weeks pressed hard, "Do you not remember?"[48]

"I wouldn't deny anything that I don't remember."[49]

Weeks next turned to a ring given to her by August Heckscher, who had been greatly pleased by Jack's work in finding a purchaser for a Manhattan hotel property. Weeks asked if she had not later returned the ring to the jewelry store—Charlton & Co., on Fifth Avenue—for eight thousand dollars and purchased a still more expensive ring? She said, "When I got the divorce I offered the ring back to Mr. Heckscher, and he refused to accept it."

"Then you kept it?"

"Yes."

"And you later turned it in to Charlton's for a still more expensive ring?"

"Yes."

"How much did that one cost?"

"Twenty thousand dollars."[50]

There was a gasp in court. Uterhart leapt to his feet, shouting that his client was being misled, that there were extenuating circumstances regarding the ring. "I'm mixed up," said Blanca, looking puzzled.

"We don't want any mixing up,"[51] soothed Justice Manning, who then took over the questioning himself. He brought out that the ring she had received from Heckscher was appraised by Charlton's at forty-five hundred dollars; that she had turned it in with other money to make up ten thousand dollars; that her brother had added another ten thousand dollars; and that they had bought a twenty-thousand-dollar ring for Blanca to wear.

Weeks ambled through some other general financial transactions for a while and then suddenly his tone hardened. "When did you first learn that you had shot your husband?"

Blanca hesitated for some time. "When Dr. Wight told me."

"When was that?"

"I don't remember."

"Did he give you any details of the shooting? Did he tell you you shot your husband in the back?"

"I do not remember."[52]

Weeks then took her on to the night of the shooting and the arrival of the taxi driver. "When Donner came did you have the revolver in your pocket?"

Another long pause. "I do not remember. I think it was in the pocket of my coat or sweater."

"Was it your habit to carry a revolver?"

"When I was alone."

"You weren't alone this night, were you? Weren't you with the maid Suzanne?"

"Yes." She recalled slipping the revolver into her side pocket when she went upstairs to fetch her hat, prior to the trip

"Do you remember when you were driving across the plains you said to take a shortcut?"

For some reason this question vexed Blanca and she snapped, "Yes, I remember—but not—very specifically."

"You remember that you had the revolver with you?"

"I must have had."

"You remember arriving at The Box?"

"Yes."

"When you went into the house whom did you see first?"

"The baby."

"Do you recall having the revolver in your pocket when you went into the house?"

"I wasn't thinking anything about the revolver."

"I know, but was it in your pocket?"

"I don't remember."

"You remember what pocket it was in?"

"N-n-n-no," she stammered.

Weeks asked if her hands were in her pockets, and Blanca replied that she customarily walked this way.

"You say you saw the baby first at The Box. You didn't speak to him at all, did you?"

"No."

"But you spoke to Mrs. Degener, didn't you?"

"I think I did."[53]

"You made no attempt to take the baby?"

"I don't think so."[54]

Weeks had scored a potent point for the prosecution. If, as she claimed, Blanca came just for the boy, she could have grabbed him then and run. Instead, she went gunning for her ex-husband. "You got into the living room before you saw John De Saulles, didn't you?"

"I think so."

"Do you remember his offering you his hand?"

"No."

"Do you remember his speaking to you . . . his saying that you couldn't have the boy?"

"No," followed by, "I couldn't possibly say."

"What is the last thing you remember—what part of your husband do you remember seeing?"

A long hush ensued, as though Blanca was struggling to recall. Then she said in a barely audible voice, "His eyes."

This was the cue for Nixola Greeley-Smith—a columnist for the *Evening World* and one of the four original sob sisters—to hit purple overdrive: "That silence was masterly. I have known nothing in life or on the stage that equaled it in dramatic tension. Without a word, without a gesture, one frail white girl held the courtroom in her slender hand."[55]

Uterhart, too, played a strong supporting role. All through Blanca's testimony he had sighed, rolled his eyes, and pulled faces at appropriate moments, in an attempt to divert the jury's attention. By the time of the shooting, he had hit full-on sobbing mode, snuffling noisily into a handkerchief that looked far too skimpy for the task in hand. Weeks ignored these interruptions and plowed on. "You remember that he turned his back to you?"

"No."

"You remember he was shot in the back, don't you?"

"Was he?" The reply could not have been more offhand.

"I'm asking you, when did you first know you had shot your husband?"

"When Mr. Ward sat here."

"What! You never knew until Marshall Ward testified in this courtroom? Did you not hear what the doctors said, testifying before Mr. Ward?"

"I paid no attention—I did not see." She explained that her eyes had not been good that day.

"But isn't your hearing good?"

"If I am paying attention I can hear. When the doctors were here I was feeling very badly [*sic*]."

"Any pressure on your head?"

The answer was a cautious "No."

"Were your eyes blurry then?"

"No."

"Nor your tongue large?"[56]

She replied that it wasn't, but that she had never felt worse, despite not having experienced any of the symptoms on the day of the shooting.

"Can't you recall having heard the five explosions, as you turned that revolver on your husband?"[57]

"No."

"You knew you have [*sic*] to press both the trigger and the safety catch to fire it?"

"What do you mean?"[58]

"You heard Captain Jones testify here?"

"Who is Captain Jones?"

"He is a captain in the New York Police Department."

"Oh, I remember."[59]

There then followed a reiteration of Jones's testimony that two separate motions were necessary to fire the gun. Blanca merely shrugged.

"You say you are familiar with firearms?" asked Weeks. Blanca admitted having owned the revolver for some considerable time and knowing about the safety catch. "You want to be frank, don't you, and tell us everything you know?"

"I want to tell everything I know."[60]

She claimed to have no recollection of telling Donner to wait outside The Box, or of Seaman or Thorne arriving at The Box, or telling Donner to drive to her home and get his pay, or being taken in the sheriff's car to the town hall at Hempstead.

"And don't you remember Constable Thorne testifying that you told him, 'I shot my husband because he would not give me my boy, and I hope he dies.'?"

"Is Thorne the one with the nasty voice?" she drawled. "I think I remember him."[61] When the question was repeated, she now claimed not to remember.

Similarly with further questions about the night's events and also the ten days that followed—it was all a total blank.

"You don't remember a single shot on the night of August 3?"

"No."

"But you remember up to the time you walked to the door of The Box?"

"Yes."

"But nothing after your husband's words, which you say are still ringing in your ears?"

"No."

"You remembered that night where Capt. Lydig was in New York, did you not?"

"He always lives at the Ritz, I think."

"And you knew the telephone number?"[62]

Blanca responded with a blank look.

"Did you ever see the inside of the Nassau County Jail?"

"Did I ever see the inside of the Nassau County Jail?" she repeated sarcastically.

"Don't you remember saying when you came in and saw all the bars that it looks like a zoo?"

"It is a very nice jail."

"So you do not remember a single thing that happened until August 13?"[63]

Uterhart was up once again, protesting that she had not so testified. But Justice Manning overruled him and Weeks continued. "Don't you think it strange that all these things have gone from your mind?"

"I think it very strange."[64] She half smiled.

"Then from August 3, 1917, from about a quarter to 9 o'clock until August 13 you have no recollection of a single, solitary thing you did within that period?"

"No—except that someone was hurting me."

"And the hurting was [caused by] the doctors?"

"Yes."

"And you want the court and jury to understand that?"

"Yes."[65]

Under further questioning, Blanca admitted that despite a string of ongoing medical ailments dating from her childhood, she had not needed to consult a doctor since the previous winter. Without pausing for breath Weeks abruptly changed tack. "This is not the first time you have be in a courtroom, is it?"

Blanca admitted that it was not, and he asked if she had attended the Carman trial. "Yes, one afternoon I drove Mrs. Degener over to the trial."

"Did you hear any of the proceedings?"

"Yes. I heard that black thing testify."

Justice Manning looked up sharply. "Did you say you heard a 'black thing testify'?"[66]

"Yes."

"What do you mean?"

"A nigger."[67]

Even in those less enlightened times, Blanca's crude racism sent a shock wave of revulsion through the court, as Justice Manning made plain. "Is that the term you apply to the colored race down in your country?"

"No. We don't have any down there."[68] A little curl of the lip accompanied this remark.

It was an ugly moment, the worst of Blanca's time on the stand, and Weeks, shrewdly, chose this time to close. In truth, though, his cross-examination had been tepid. The district attorney had seemed as much in awe of Blanca as every other male who came within her orbit, treating her with a feathery touch that made a mockery of his judicial obligations. Certainly he made Uterhart's task that much easier as he attempted to coax some damage limitation from Blanca. On redirect he brought out that she had spent just half an hour at the Carman trial, although he skated around the racial slur, knowing that nothing could undo that kind of blunder, and hurriedly moved on to other events. He got Blanca to explain how, on the morning of the shooting, she had phoned Constable Thorne and asked him to come to the house because, on the previous day, she thought she heard someone walking about the property. This had heightened her nervousness and explained why she carried the gun on the night in question. She admitted carrying the gun frequently and having practiced with a target in Chile and on the beach at Huntington. But when Uterhart tried to revive the issue of the expensive ring, Justice Manning cut him off. "In a case as serious as this I shall not bother my head about trumpery like a ring."[69]

And then it was over. Uterhart said he had no further questions, and Blanca bowed graciously to the jury and left the stand at 3:20 p.m. Uterhart led her to his table, where she almost fell into Mrs. Seaman's arms. Along the way she did manage a quick peek back at the judge and smiled. A member of the public gallery, a woman in a cerise hat, was heard to whisper to her neighbor: "She'll get off all right. Look how pretty she is."[70] And this summed up the general view. Although Weeks had landed some telling blows—in particular exposing the uglier side of Blanca's nature—there had been no knockout punch.

When the defense continued, Constable Thorne was recalled to corroborate Blanca's claim that she had seen someone prowling around her Roslyn home. He was followed by Ethel O'Neill (née Whitesides), the nurse employed by Blanca at South Bethlehem in 1913. She talked so faintly, her voice muffled by an ever present handkerchief, that the judge repeatedly asked her to speak up. Her evidence chiefly concerned Jack's infrequent visits to Blanca, and included that heartbreaking incident when Blanca had waited hours for her husband at the railroad station, only to return home alone. She said she had left Blanca in 1913 and didn't see her again until 1916, in Westbury, at which time she noted a great change in her appearance, due, she suspected, to Blanca's tormented domestic life. This transformation was even more apparent the next time she saw Blanca, in September 1917, in the Mineola jailhouse. "I did not know her; I went right past her. She was so white."

"Mrs. De Saulles was always more or less pale, wasn't she?" Weeks asked.

"Not when I first went there."[71]

After Ethel left the stand, Uterhart read out a deposition from Felipe Cortez, who had been unable to attend the trial, confirming the circumstances of the auto accident in Chile. Cortez said he had been driving, and in the passenger seat had been Miss Marie Errázuriz, a cousin of Blanca's. "Mrs. De Saulles was sitting at Miss Errázuriz's feet, holding on to a strap with her right hand. I was going to the club to get some cigarettes. I was going very fast, and suddenly a man on a bicycle came into the path of my car, so I had to stop it suddenly to keep from killing the man. I saw Blanquita fall to the road. I rushed to her. Her head and face were all bloody. Next day I noticed her eyes were all blind black, her face spotted and her chin was cut."[72] (Earlier, Blanca had angrily refuted Weeks's claim that on the night of the accident she had gone to a ball with a bandage on her head.)

Two nurses then took the stand to describe the debilitating effect that marriage had inflicted upon Blanca. One, Miss Isabelle Flaherty, who tended Blanca when Jack Jr. was born, confirmed that at Larchmont in August 1913, Blanca had been the picture of health. "She had color in her cheeks all the time and was extremely pretty."[73] Thereafter, her health had gone into freefall.

A third nurse, Maude Cowan of Glengarry, Canada, who took care of Jack Jr. at the Hotel Gotham for five weeks in 1916, testified to her employer's generosity. She had only asked for twenty-eight dollars a week, but Blanca had insisted on paying her thirty-five as "there was a terrible responsibility in taking care of the little boy."[74] She said that each day the boy was taken away at 3:00 p.m. by his father, and was in "a disagreeable mood"[75] when he came back. Often he was returned late and his clothes were dirty. He told her that "Boobie" (Mrs. Mooney), the nurse at the father's home in Westbury, asked him not to be nice to Miss Cowan. Weeks had just two questions.

"The boy went out with his father and came back somewhat dirty?"

"Yes."

"The fact is, isn't it, that the boy didn't like you and did like Boobie?"[76]

The nurse flushed and did not reply.

After testily warning the lawyers that he might hold a night session the next day, Justice Manning adjourned court until 10:00 a.m. the following morning.

The reporters rushed off to file their copy. That evening or next morning their words would be devoured by millions across America. And no one was paying closer attention or was more anxious about the outcome than a certain aspiring actor in Los Angeles—Rodolfo Guglielmi. According to a highly colored account by Mae Murray, her young friend was utterly distraught. "Through the ten days of the trial he was like a trapped animal. He would come and sit with me beside a burning candle and whisper prayers . . . the prayers of a boy's heart for a mother, the prayers of a man for a woman, a lover begging that a life be spared, asking forgiveness."[77]

All hyperbole aside, Rodolfo had been extremely fortunate. Blanca had survived her ordeal on the witness stand and not once had his name been dragged into evidence. But there was still time for it all to blow up in his face. And there was still that nagging self-doubt, weighing his desire to help Blanca against a personal craving for anonymity. It was a paradox that would tear him apart for the rest of his life.

SIXTEEN

The Medical Evidence

The Trial, Day 8

In court the next morning the public gallery was buzzing. When Amalia and Guillermo took their customary positions one row behind the defendant, their mother was nowhere to be seen, sparking rumors that the stinging humiliation of the previous day had opened an unbridgeable family gulf between mother and daughter. If true, it certainly did not register on Blanca's face. Her sphinxlike imperturbability remained resolutely intact as Uterhart called his first witness of the day, D. Stewart Iglehart. The executive strode assertively to the stand.

Uterhart began: "Do you remember a telephone call you got from her [Blanca] on the night of August 3?"

"Yes, she was very much worried because the boy had not been returned to her, and she had been afraid some accident had befallen him. She had just learned that he was at The Box, and was going to be put to bed, and that his father was going to the club for dinner and would not be back until 9 o'clock." Iglehart's easy fluency on the stand required little prompting from counsel and he continued smoothly. "She asked me to go with her to get the boy and I said I would be glad to do her any service I could, but that I thought this was too delicate a matter for me to intervene. I did ask her to stop and have dinner with us on the way over, but she said she was in a great hurry and would get a taxi and go right over."[1]

Although brief, Iglehart's testimony was crucial to the defense. After all, Uterhart argued, was it really probable that someone with murder in mind would telephone a friend and ask for a ride to the place where she intended to shoot her ex-husband? It was a valid point and one that obviously impressed the jury, to judge from their approving nods.

The next witness caused a genuine stir in court. At long last the public was going to hear from a member of Blanca's family. Amalia, dressed in deep mourning, with a large black picture hat and a close-fitting black dress topped with a high, flaring collar that opened low at the front, oozed confidence as she walked to the witness stand without any hint of embarrassment. Like her sister, she had an obvious English accent as she told how Blanca, when aged eight, had suffered a serious head injury. "I was chasing Blanca through a corridor and as I came close to her she tripped and fell and struck her head on the andirons at the fireplace. . . . I called the nurse, who picked her up unconscious and took her upstairs. She was in bed for several weeks and at times was delirious."[2]

"How long was she unconscious?" asked Uterhart.

"About two or three hours."[3]

"Was she attended by a doctor?"

"Yes. He is dead now."[4]

"Did you notice any change in her after the accident?"

"Yes, she couldn't keep up with us in games and play as well."

"What did she complain of afterward?"

"Her head pained her, and I could feel a hole in the top of her head."[5]

Uterhart then took Amalia forward several years to Paris. "Do you remember some trouble that took place there?"

"Yes . . . De Saulles asked mother to give him a large estate in Chile, and she told him she couldn't. She told him she would give him part of the land at Viña del Mar if he would build on it and settle down. He also asked her to give him complete control of the property and she refused. There was a scene and he was rude to mother."[6]

Uterhart next asked Amalia to describe her sister's appearance upon her return to Chile in 1915, after leaving her husband. "She was emaciated and thin. I was shocked when I saw her."[7] It was during that visit, said Amalia, that Blanca was involved in the automobile accident, sustaining injuries that left the upper part of her face blue for several days. "How long was she in bed?"

"Five or six days."[8]

Amalia next saw Blanca in August 1916, when she visited her in New York while the divorce was pending. "She was so ashy white that I could hardly recognize her. She also complained of pains in the head."[9] After a family discussion, the two sisters and their brother concluded that a trip to Scotland might improve Blanca's health, but that wish failed to materialize.

Constant worry about her domestic plight kept Blanca frail and emotional, a state of affairs that only worsened when she returned to New York and had to get used to the notion of shared custody. "Blanca used to worry a great deal because the boy would return at 8 or 9 o'clock instead of 6," said Amalia. "It made his supper late, and he would come home and misbehave and say that 'Boobie' told him to be bad. He would behave all right, be bright and cheerful, when suddenly he would say, 'I forgot. Boobie told me I had to be bad,' and then he wouldn't talk to his mother."

"Do you remember one time when he wouldn't eat his supper?"

"He became almost hysterical and was kicking in the elevator when we took him upstairs. He said Boobie was downstairs and he had to go down and eat with her. We gave him toast and he wouldn't eat it, and said Boobie was waiting for him and was going to take him away forever."

"What was the effect of this on Mrs. De Saulles?"

"It caused her extreme mental anguish."[10] After Weeks's objection to this characterization of Blanca's mental state, the answer was amended to, "It affected her very much." According to Amalia, Jack Jr. also spoke of visiting barrooms with his father, particularly the Plaza, where the men were "all drinking."[11] Such reports, said Amalia, only exacerbated Blanca's condition, giving her severe headaches.

"Was there any connection between these headaches and the behavior of the child?"

"Yes, they were always much worse after he came back in a temper."[12]

The court stirred as Uterhart picked up the .32 Smith & Wesson and approached the witness. Amalia identified the revolver as the one Jack had bought for Blanca because "she was so much alone."[13]

"Is it customary for a lady to carry a revolver in Chile?"

"Yes."[14]

Amalia took the revolver from Uterhart and was soon handling it like a regular Annie Oakley. Unlike the prosecution, she maintained that only one hand movement was required to fire the gun, not two. "As you press the trigger, the palm of the hand automatically presses and releases the safety catch and the weapon is discharged."[15] In demonstrating this she nonchalantly pointed the revolver at the wall; then once more, this time holding it so that it pointed directly toward Weeks, much to his discomfort.

"Please point that gun the other way," Weeks pleaded. "I know it's not loaded, but—"[16] A burst of laughter reverberated around the court as Amalia lowered the gun, then said that Blanca always carried a revolver when in Chile, because the roads were so lonely.

On cross-examination, Weeks queried Amalia's credentials as a gun expert. She just shrugged. "I've carried one nearly all my life."

"Did you ever hear of Captain Jones?"[17]

Uterhart objected on grounds that *no one* had ever heard of Captain William Jones before the case. Because Jones was the NYPD's foremost firearms expert, and because it was his testimony that had featured so prominently in the sensational and highly publicized campaign to free convicted killer Charles Stielow from death row that same year, this was quite a slur. Justice Manning told Uterhart to sit down and Amalia continued. After more exchanges about the gun, Weeks moved on to Jack Jr.'s comments about his father's girlfriends.

"When did you hear him discuss his father's sweethearts . . . ? What year was that?"

"I think it was 1917."

"Was that not after he had obtained a divorce?"

"I think so."

"What did you ever hear little Jack say about these sweethearts?"

"He spoke of them as his sweethearts as well as his daddy's."

When Uterhart objected, Weeks was ready for him. "The defense opened the door, and I am going to walk through it."[18] The judge agreed. Amalia said that whenever little Jack came back from visits to his father's, bubbling with tales of his sweethearts, it greatly upset Blanca.

"Did the boy act as if he were very fond of Boobie?" asked Weeks.

"Yes, in the evening, but not in the morning before he left."[19]

Weeks was clearly suspicious about Amalia's clarity of recall. He asked how old she had been when Blanca fell and hit her head.

"Twelve years old."

"What was your sister's age at that time?"

"Eight years."

"And you remember all of this now at twenty-seven?"

"Yes,"[20] she answered defiantly. With an incredulous expression Weeks said he had no more questions. As hard as the district attorney had tried, he had failed to unsettle Amalia, who was clearly cut from the same resilient cloth as her sister.

On redirect, Uterhart brought out that the witness's mother, who had not missed a court session until the preceding afternoon, had fallen very ill and that Dr. Wight had been in attendance upon her all night. Amalia feared that she might not testify. A disappointed groan greeted this announcement. The prospect of the haughty señora dueling with the district attorney had been one of the anticipated highlights of the trial and now that expectation had been put on hold. Some wondered if the disgruntled matriarch, drawing on King Lear's observation, "How sharper than a serpent's tooth it is to have a thankless child," had decided to teach her perfidious daughter a lesson.

Things moved briskly along, with Uterhart next calling Suzanne Monteau. The maid was "not the good witness she promised to be."[21] Her heavy accent, faltering English, and terrified demeanor made it difficult for the jury to understand her as she described Blanca's actions on the night in question. "She tell me she like me to go with her to fetch the boy. So I go to wash my hands to go with her. She told the taxi man a short way to go quicker and to drive fast. When we went to the house we saw car there and she said, 'Mr. De Saulles must be in.' She asked Julius where was Mr. De Saulles, and he said in the living room."[22] After a long pause for breath, Suzanne said, "When Mrs. De Saulles went into living room a man in gray suit went upstairs."[23]

The pubic gallery stirred. This could only have been Marshall Ward, whom the defense always maintained had not actually witnessed the shooting. For the second time in this trial the jury heard testimony that branded the dead man's business partner as a blatant perjurer. In her tentative way Suzanne continued: "I saw Mr. De Saulles's face—awful face he make at her."[24] She broke off for a moment and then sobbed, "Oh, it was terrible, terrible."[25] "Mrs. De Saulles said, 'My boy—I have come for him,' and he say, 'You can't have him now or ever.' . . . Mrs. De Saulles's face turn [*sic*] ever so white."

At this point Suzanne had to stop, her mouth opening and closing several times without any sound emerging. She burst into tears. When she had become a little more composed, Justice Manning asked her gently, "Then what happened?"[26]

Eventually she said, "She shooted him. [*sic*] He turned and she fired and he turned and she fired again. She fired three times while he was facing her, then he turned and she fired again twice."[27]

Justice Manning was puzzled. "You say he was facing her?"

"Yes, he was right in front."[28] Suzanne's loyalty might have been commendable but her testimony was directly contradicted by the autopsy findings. As a result, her evidence now came under even closer scrutiny.

After the shooting, said the witness, she and Blanca had retreated to the porch, where the valet approached them. "Julius talked to her, but she did not answer. I heard a woman say, 'Oh, Blanquita, what have you done?' but she didn't answer."[29] Later, as they were leaving the scene, Blanca had asked Donner to take the dog back to Crossways, where he would be paid for his work. Then they drove off. Uterhart interjected, "Did she say on the way over to the jail, 'I hope he dies'?"

"She didn't. I swear she didn't say it."[30]

Suzanne then moved on to events when they reached the town hall office of Judge Jones. Mrs. De Saulles asked if he could get the boy for her. He told her that this would not be possible.

"When she left Judge Jones's office how did she go out?" asked Uterhart.

"She went as if she were going to walk out of the window."[31]

"What did she do when she came to the jail?"

"She was walking with her hands in her pockets, looking up and down, laughing like mad."[32] The last two words were ordered struck out, a decision that caused Suzanne to dissolve in a flood of tears. Uterhart had succeeded in his mission, though, to demonstrate that Blanca had been so disoriented as to be unaware of her surroundings.

Nothing in the trial more vividly demonstrated the brutal social divide of the times than Suzanne Monteau's cross-examination. Weeks "attacked the witness with all the fury of a tornado,"[33] determined not to be "as sparing with her as he had been with her mistress."[34] There was something deeply unpleasant, cowardly almost, about the way Weeks was prepared to browbeat a lowly maidservant, in stark contrast to the cringing deference he had displayed the previous day when cross-examining her upper-class employer. He began by giving Suzanne a contemptuous look. "Are you afraid of testifying here?"

"No, sir."

"Then what are you crying for?"

"I object," shouted Uterhart. "It is a very rude and insulting question. Any woman is likely to cry in such an ordeal."

"Well, another one didn't."

"Some women cannot cry,"[35] Uterhart fired back.

"Perhaps so. Some who did not see it sat and wept,"[36] sneered Weeks, a clear and pointed reference to Uterhart's constant flow of tears during Blanca's testimony.

"Quite right," shouted the big defender. "And some who claim they saw the tragedy did not weep."[37] This was yet another barb aimed squarely at Marshall Ward, who by now had become the defense's chief whipping boy.

After this spat, Weeks turned to face the witness. "Do you say that Mr. De Saulles stood three feet away from his wife, looking at her, and did nothing when she took out the revolver?"

"Yes, he looked as if he were going to jump at her."

"Did he make any motion as if to reach his wife?"

"Yes, he went like this." Suzanne raised her arm as de Saulles might have done if he intended to strike the revolver aside.

"As if to strike her?"

"Yes."

"And you say that because the doctors have said the bullets entered the back of his arm?"

"I don't care what the doctors say."[38]

Weeks's bludgeoning interrogation continued. It was far from pretty, but highly effective as Suzanne slowly disintegrated under the DA's remorseless attack. He read from her contradictory testimony at the coroner's hearing, where she said that Jack did not move or do anything at all when his wife pointed the revolver at him. "Did you say that?"[39] Suzanne agreed that she did. She also admitted that neither Blanca nor herself made any attempt to get the boy, although they both saw Jack Jr. with Caroline on the stairs when they entered the house. "Why did you go into the living room?"

"Because I heard the way Mr. De Saulles spoke to her."

"And you went in to protect your mistress?"

"Yes."

"But she protected herself, didn't she?"

There was no answer from the maid, but Uterhart, from the counsel's table, broke in: "Yes, she did."[40]

Weeks, turning a deaf ear to the interruption, asked Suzanne if she remembered his visiting the jail the day after the shooting.

"I do not remember it at all."[41]

How about the transaction that resulted in her being freed on bail, with Blanca arranging the bail?

"I don't recall it."

"Don't you know that Mrs. De Saulles signed a check for $1,000 and obtained your release?"

"I don't remember."[42]

The numbing frequency of these memory lapses led some in the press box to wonder if the maid was not taking a leaf out of the mistress's book. And there were also grave misgivings about the selective nature of Suzanne Monteau's amnesia. Any scrap of information or incident that might be harmful to her employer was brushed into the "I don't recall" category. On the other hand, those events favorable to Blanca seemed always to kick start her memory back into life. Eventually the young Frenchwoman was put out of her misery and released. She scurried, squirrel-like, from the stand. One headline the next day caught the general mood in court, declaring that the maid had been a "POOR WITNESS FOR THE DEFENSE."[43]

During his opening, Uterhart claimed that a string of physical ailments, most involving head trauma, had caused a mental instability in Blanca de Saulles that led not only to the shooting but also the amnesia that followed, or as some wags were now calling it, "dementia materna,"[44] in joking reference to the Thaw trial. It was now time to produce the medical evidence to back up that claim.

The first expert witness was Dr. J. Sherman Wight, visiting surgeon at the Long Island College Hospital. He told the court how, on August 6, in company with Dr. Johnson and Dr. Cleghorn, he examined the prisoner and found her listless and vague. "I asked her to put her tongue out and at first she didn't. I turned her face to me and I repeated the request, and then she did, and I noticed that the tongue was swollen. . . . Her skin was cold and dry. Her nails were brittle and cracked and her hair was dry and brittle. On the backs of her hands were swellings, her feet were swollen, and her limbs showed elevations of the surface."[45] Her vital signs—blood pressure, temperature, and pulse—were all well below normal and when she tried to move her breathing became labored. "When I touched her abdomen and face she shrank away, and when I touched her head and found a sensitive area, it caused her to shrink away and utter a cry."[46] Further examination led him to conclude that Blanca was suffering from an underactive thyroid. He immediately prescribed a course of thyroid extract.

When Wight reexamined Blanca the next day, he found a concave hollow in the skull—an inch and a half long and three eighths of an inch deep—above the forehead and just behind the scalp hairline. This, he told the jury, was a depressed fracture, most likely the result of Blanca's falling against an andiron when she was a girl. He thought that the bone had been broken a second time during her automobile accident two years previously. Because this problem had never been operated on, if one's finger was pressed on this spot now it caused pain.

According to Wight, "On August 9, I noticed that she was restless and made complaints concerning people in the room."[47] She also began to suffer hallucinations; for example, she asked if her husband could take her baby away from her, then stared vacantly when told that Jack was dead. The following day, Wight decided to X-ray Blanca's skull.

At this point Wight called for a projectoscope—an early form of projector—to be set up beside the witness chair. The jury, which hitherto had veered between bemusement and boredom while listening to Wight's testimony, shifted forward. This looked interesting. They watched as Wight loaded a glass plate showing the X-ray of Blanca's skull in profile. Justice Manning moved from his chair to inspect the X-ray plate more closely, and he invited the jury to join him, but they declined, saying they could see everything clearly from where they sat. Blanca permitted herself one brief glance, then dropped her gaze and looked no more.

Wight pointed to the area he was describing and said that the damaged frontal lobe exerted pressure on that region of the brain "where reason and judgment are seated."[48] Even after beginning treatment, Blanca continued to be depressed and confused, and not until September 4—one month after the shooting—did Wight find her mind "clear and bright."[49] Only then was she able to share with him her family's ill-starred medical history: a father who had succumbed to TB when she was one year old, a sister dead at ten months, and a brother who was thrown from a horse and killed when he was only twelve. None of this, of course, had any bearing on Blanca's alleged hypothyreosis. (Significantly, none of the medical witnesses used this term, only Uterhart.)

It had been an eventful morning and Wight was still on the stand when Justice Manning broke for lunch.

Continuing after the recess, Wight elaborated on Blanca's medical history. In 1913 she had spent thirteen days in the Sloane Maternity Hospital following an operation for a condition caused by sunstroke at Deal Beach (the exact nature of this ailment was not revealed). The following year the headaches returned, then came the car accident in Chile, after which she was laid up for five days. When Uterhart tried to get Wight's opinion of the injuries Blanca sustained in childhood, Justice Manning stepped in. "This is beyond all reason. We want all possible light—but fifteen years ago and a witness who never saw her then? We must remember that what we are trying to find out is the condition of her mind at the time of her act—whether she knew the act was right or wrong."[50]

Wight now dealt with this question. Blanca had told him that her health had declined this past summer; she had suffered stomach pains, neuralgia, and periods of forgetfulness. On the night of the shooting, when she went to The Box, she was "astonished"[51] to find de Saulles there, and that when told she could not have the boy, she felt a great pain in her head. "I questioned her further, but she said she remembered nothing after that."[52]

Weeks rose to cross-examine. "Is it not true that the average person has a depression in his skull?"

"No."

"Is not the location of what you call a fracture at about the same spot as the anterior fontanel?" (The "soft spot" in the skulls of children, which generally closes by eighteen to twenty-four months, can remain soft into maturity in some instances.)

Wight said there could be no mistake.

"Isn't it possible that the mark you call a fracture in the photograph might be the shadow of a vein?"

"It is not; veins do not cast shadows."

"You are sure of this?"

"Yes."

"When did you first give the patient thyroid extract?"

"On the second day after the examination."

"Will not this extract cause headaches?"

"If enough is given, yes."

"Does the condition of the skull you describe still exist?"

"Yes."

"Is there still encroachment and pressure on the frontal lobes of the brain?"

"Yes."

"But not sufficient to cause any great harm?"

"No."

"That's all."[53]

The next witness provided a textbook example of why medical evidence struggled to gain a foothold in early twentieth century courtrooms. Dr. Louis C. Johnson, who lectured at the Long Island College Hospital, seemed utterly oblivious to the fact that he was addressing a jury of laymen and not some postgraduate class. He was pompous, used incomprehensible medical jargon, and had an irritating habit of lapsing into Latin whenever the mood struck him, which was far too often, judging from the glazed expressions on jurors' faces. In the end Justice Manning, as baffled as anyone, halted the witness and told him to tell the court what he had found in "plain English."

"May I say—" Johnson began.

"Don't say anything except what I have told you."

Visibly smarting from the rebuke, Johnson continued. "Mrs. De Saulles was in bed in the jail when I saw her. I felt at the time that the general body processes—metabolism—were at a very low ebb. It was such a condition as I believe might arise from a severe disease of the blood—anemia, or a condition where toxic substances ordinarily secreted by the kidneys might be stored up in the body. She was a typical picture of hypothyroidism."[54]

Oddly enough, unlike most in court, Blanca paid close heed as Johnson droned on. Various bloods tests, coefficients, Johnson provided lengthy coverage of them all, and he was just about to favor the jury with extracts from a speech delivered by some obscure French scientist when Weeks butted in: "How do we care about that?"[55]

Justice Manning agreed. "We don't care anything about the lecture. Let us hear just what were your conclusions about this particular patient."

"I concluded she was a typical picture of hypothyroidism."[56]

The judge sighed in relief. "That's what we want."[57]

After deciphering Johnson's Latin-laced verbiage, this diagnosis emerged: Mrs. de Saulles was anemic, with a low blood count, and suffering from an underactive thyroid. He was happy to report that since treatment began, her thyroid complaint had improved markedly.

Finally, to the relief of everyone—especially those journalists who were struggling to turn this labyrinthine testimony into usable copy—Johnson was excused and replaced by Dr. Smith Ely Jeliffe, a Manhattan-based specialist in nervous disease and an experienced expert witness. Unlike his predecessor, Jeliffe used short punchy sentences and simple words that the jury could understand. He explained that Wight gave him no advance knowledge of Blanca's condition, but merely asked for a second opinion. Jeliffe first saw Blanca on August 11. "She saw well and did not hear well. Her hair broke easily, her skin was scaly . . . thick and rubbery."[58] He pinched his own skin by way of demonstrating what ordinary skin should be like. "Her skin was cold and more or less like marble. Her pupils dilated and then contracted; instead of getting smaller rapidly when a light was brought close to her eyes, they were sluggish. The tongue was swollen to twice normal size."[59]

Like Wight, Jeliffe had found the patient unusually sensitive. "She winced when the nerve trunks were touched. . . . When a fingernail was drawn across her skin the white line that ought to fade away did not, but was followed by a deep red line, showing marked instability of blood vessels. There were bumps on the lower and upper extremities."[60] Blanca, he said, had refused to cooperate in the medical examination on August 11. She became fatigued, had a dreamy look, and asked him not to bother her. He also diagnosed a distinctly hypothyroid condition.

On November 9 he saw her again. The swellings or bumps had subsided; she was extremely weak but getting stronger; mentally she was normal. "She was bright and could cooperate."[61] Justice Manning asked if the X-ray showed the skull accurately and he said it did. Rather than proceed at the current time, Weeks said he would defer cross-examination of the witness until after the hypothetical question to be asked by the defense. At this point Uterhart said he wasn't ready to ask the question today.

Justice Manning sighed. Uterhart's announcement guaranteed that the trial would now run into the following week. The hypothetical question would be read to each of the expert witnesses and would probably consume an entire session. In the Thaw trial, the hypothetical question took three and a half hours to read, a record for length. Uterhart refused to speculate on how long his estimated twenty-thousand-word epic would last. All he was prepared to say at the moment was that it would end with the query: "If you knew such evidence had been introduced and if such were the acts of the defendant, would you hold that she was of sound mind when the act was committed."[62] Because the medical experts were all on the defense payroll, it was a foregone conclusion that their answer would be "No."

It was also a monumental waste of time, as Justice Manning made clear. Wearily, he turned to the jury. "I had hoped that we could make this proceeding move with such celerity as to close it up here. I thought of sitting tonight and tomorrow, but that is beyond you and me. We shall have to give the people and the defendant more time in which to handle the medical situation in an effort to get at the true situation. . . . They hope to get the medical evidence in such condition that it can be presented on Friday. In the end we may save time by wasting a little time now. I now have to tell you to take the day off."[63]

After the usual admonishments to the jury against discussing the case among themselves or with outsiders, he wished them a happy Thanksgiving and then adjourned the hearing until 10:00 a.m. Friday.

SEVENTEEN

The Hypothetical Question

As promised, Blanca provided Thanksgiving Day dinner for the other inmates of Mineola jail, and a truly splendid affair it turned out to be. Fifty-five prisoners sat down to the most extravagant banquet ever given in this most exclusive section of Long Island real estate. Amalia and two of the sheriff's daughters, Ethel and Ellie, took up their positions in the jail kitchen, alongside the chef, Arthur Benton, basting the turkeys, testing the cranberries until they jellied, making the coffee, and jabbing forks into the browning sweet potatoes. "Let everybody forget their troubles for just this one day,"[1] said Blanca that morning as the turkeys were pushed into the jail's brick oven. A long pine table had been moved into the corridor that led to the "thirty day room"[2]—ordinarily used to house those prisoners serving a month or less—and covered with a linen tablecloth.

Even on so egalitarian an occasion as this, a strict jailhouse hierarchy was observed, with head of the table slots being reserved for the most serious offenders. Pride of place among these went to Dominick Damasco, already convicted of killing a man in a fight and awaiting sentence the following day. Next came Frank Sniegoski, a moody Polish immigrant from Great Neck accused of killing his wife after a long, drawn-out domestic dispute. It was a charge he bitterly denied and the merriment cut no inroads into his sullen nature as he remained taciturn throughout the entire meal. Alongside him sat Thomas O'Brien, who had shot his wife with a rifle and was awaiting trial. By a peculiar coincidence, O'Brien had gunned down his wife at almost exactly the same time as Blanca pulled the trigger on her ex-husband. And his defense was uncannily similar, too—a claim that amnesia had erased any memory of the event, which had been provoked by jealousy (his wife had been sleeping with a younger man).

When the main doors of the kitchen were thrown open and fifteen steaming-hot brown fowls had been brought through and placed upon the table, the men bowed their heads in silent prayer. The cast list of "thirty dayers"[3] who were delegated to serve the food read like the characters from a Damon Runyon short story. There was pickpocket "Blinky the Dip," who ladled cranberries, while Austin Riley, otherwise known as the "Educated Bartender,"[4] took charge of the sweet potatoes. By all accounts Riley earned his moniker from the fact that on those weekends when he wound up in the DD cells—drunk and disorderly—he would sober up by reading thick books. The food was delicious, especially to men fed an unvarying daily diet of stew and brown bread, and they showed their approval by clapping their hands and passing their plates for second and third helpings. For dessert there was ice cream and coffee, and every prisoner was given a box of cigarettes.

Elsewhere in the jail, the institution's two lesser-known female inmates—one charged with arson, the other a habitual drunk—were served a turkey of their own, while Blanca was allowed to dine in her own room. She had a special guest. Jack Jr. had arrived that morning at eleven o'clock in one of the Heckscher limousines and was escorted into the jail by private detective Harry Dougherty. As soon as Jack saw his mother, he ran into her arms. "They said you had turkey," he cried. "Where is it?"[5] He was led to the ovens and given a glimpse of the birds crackling in their pans.

While little Jack stared wide-eyed at the feast to come, Blanca took Dougherty to one side and asked his opinion of how the trial was going. He hedged. "Well, there may be a disagreement."

"Oh, don't say that. Anything but that. I don't want to go through this again."[6]

Suzanne Monteau, who had arrived with Amalia, looked on horror-stricken. "Would I have to testify again?" Told that she would, she exclaimed, "I could not stand it, to have that district attorney talk to me again."[7]

One person increasingly likely to be spared a confrontation with Weeks was Señora Errázuriz-Vergara. Reports had her still reeling from the humiliation of hearing Blanca mock her on the stand, and they also said that she had returned to Crossways in a hysterical state, with a recurrence of her reported heart condition. For this reason, Uterhart had delayed calling her. According to Dr. Wight, who remained in close attendance, the señora's condition was slightly improved, but he doubted that she would be up to the strain of a courtroom appearance. Nor was she fit enough (or willing) to visit her daughter in jail.[8]

Now, though, it was time for Blanca to set family and court worries aside as the fowl made its appearance. Blanca carved the golden-brown turkey and piled her son's plate high. Her own portion was much smaller. She had never had much of an appetite and merely picked at her food, sitting back for the most part and watching her little boy wolf his dinner down hungrily, until they reached the wishbone, which they pulled together amid much mystery as to their hopes. At the same time, from another quarter of the building, came a rarely heard jailhouse sound—loud roars of laughter, as the other prisoners made the most of this unexpected treat.

In the improvised banqueting hall, the "Educated Bartender" lived up to his nickname by producing a piece of paper and announcing that decorum demanded some written expression of gratitude to Blanca. "All right, scratch it off and we'll sign it,"[9] yelled one. Eight prisoners signed the following:

"Mrs. Blanca De Saulles, Mineola, L.I.

Dear Madam: We desire to thank you sincerely for your kindness and thoughtfulness toward us today. It is impossible to put into words our kindly thoughts toward you. However, it is our earnest wish that your next Thanksgiving will be spent with your dear family and your noble little boy."[10]

As Riley was looking around for someone to bear this note to Blanca, the door opened and the "White Mother,"[11] as she had been affectionately dubbed by the other prisoners, entered, hand in hand with little Jack. Her appearance triggered a raucous round of applause and cheers.

Blanca stood at the head of the table and smiled down at the inmates. One prisoner, accused of stabbing a fellow workman, feeling that some words of gratitude were necessary, fumbled with his fork, overturned his coffee, and succeeded in getting to his feet with what was intended as a courtly bow. "We're all mighty thankful to you—for what you've done for us."[12] Blanca rewarded him with a broad smile and a deprecating wave of her hand. "I'm mighty glad I could have this little dinner with you today."[13] Jack, too, added his good wishes, in a grave voice that belied his tender years, before proudly brandishing a brass sheriff's badge that had been presented to him as a gift and saying, "I am a policeman and I can arrest any of you."[14] The unintended irony was not lost on the audience, most of whom convulsed with laughter as they held out their hands and complied with the lad's attempts to take them into "custody."

All too soon the levity was over and it was time for Jack to be returned to his guardians. Blanca gave her son one last crushing embrace before Dougherty led him out to the waiting automobile.

Although a few favored journalists had been given access to the dinner to record Blanca's Thanksgiving generosity—Uterhart's PR skills were as sharp as ever—outside the jail an even bigger press scrum awaited Dougherty as he emerged with Jack Jr. And for the first time they learned that the private detective had been on the de Saulles family's books for more than a year. "During the divorce proceedings De Saulles said to me: 'My wife is getting a divorce from me. We can't get along together. I haven't anything to say against her at all, but if the boy should ever be taken to Chile there would be no chance on earth that I could get him back again.'"[15] To ensure that Blanca did not attempt to flee the country, Dougherty had operatives watching the boy whenever he was with his mother, either in the city or at Roslyn. According to Dougherty, even after de Saulles was killed other family members were fearful that Jack Jr. would be kidnapped, hence their insistence that Dougherty accompany the lad everywhere. He also noted that on little Jack's first visit to the jail, the boy and his mother had seemed very distant, but since that time they had become increasingly affectionate. His media duties over, Dougherty joined Jack Jr. in the auto, which sped them back to the Heckscher household, where the Thanksgiving festivities were, understandably, muted.

Others, too, had a blighted holiday. Uterhart, assisted by his co-counsel Lewis J. Smith and Cleveland Runyan, had labored into the small hours of Thanksgiving morning on the much vaunted "hypothetical question." The lawyers had worked in relays in their rooms at the Garden City Hotel, framing the question and exhausting four stenographers in the process before calling a halt.

The question—a formidable document rumored to be fifteen-thousand words in length and getting longer with every revision—would begin with Blanca's birth, summarize the accidents in her life, recount a string of humiliations inflicted by her husband, and conclude by requesting an opinion as to whether the defendant was capable legally of understanding her act when she shot Jack de Saulles. One newspaper acidly suggested that all that wordiness could be condensed thus: "Do you believe this lady was sufficiently crazy to justify a kind-hearted jury in acquitting her for the murder of a brutal husband?"[16]

A general sinking of hearts greeted reports that Weeks, not wanting to be outdone, was preparing a hypothetical question of his own, though what form this would take was not revealed. Far more certain, and far more interesting circulation-wise, was the DA's bitter and continuing antipathy toward

Sheriff Seaman. Weeks said that because the sheriff had "seen so much of the defendant,"[17] he feared that her charm had clouded his judgment, and for that reason, he would not be recalling Seaman to the stand on rebuttal.

The Trial, Day 9

November 30, 1917

When court reconvened after the holiday, the first order of business was sentencing Dominick Damasco. Originally charged with murder, he was ultimately convicted of manslaughter and could count himself lucky to be so, according to Justice Manning, who sentenced him to eleven years. In a daze, Damasco rose from the same chair that Blanca would occupy and made his way slowly to the door. As he exited the court, he passed Blanca in the corridor. She smiled and looked as if she were about to speak, but Damasco, totally preoccupied, passed by without raising his head and the door closed behind him. Blanca stood for some time just staring at the spot where Damasco had been, and then she took her seat. Unlike previous days she did not wear an outfit that emphasized the frailness and girlishness of her figure, but instead wore a suit of heather mix. She was very pale. And she looked anxious. For the first time since the trial began, she would glance at the jury to see how various strands of evidence had struck them.

In the morning the by now notorious "hypothetical question" was read out by Lewis J. Smith to the two defense doctors. He began at 10:20 with "Assume, doctor, that Blanca Errázuriz De Saulles was born near Santiago, Chile, April 29, 1894, that in her childhood . . ."[18] and kept on going for another eighty-five minutes. During the question's reading, Juror No. 4 fell asleep (he was elbowed awake by the juror to his left), while some of his colleagues watched airplanes through a window. Others, with closed eyes, nodded in their chairs.

The hypothetical question was a popular (with lawyers) legal strategy at the turn of the century, especially in high-profile trials where the defendants had deep pockets and could afford all those extra billable hours. No court-appointed attorney was going to squander this time-consuming option on some indigent prisoner.

It first appeared at length during the trial of Carlyle Harris, a New York medical student who poisoned his wife in 1891. On that occasion, several times during its reading a juror was heard to snore loudly, impervious to nudges and kicks from his comrades. Finally, the judge's patience snapped. If any juror fell asleep, he boomed, he would order the entire question to be read out again. At this, the dozing juror was now almost kicked out of the jury box by his indignant colleagues. Their prompting worked; the question did not, and Harris died in the electric chair. A similar somnolence befell jury members subjected to hypothetical questions in the Molineaux[19] and Thaw cases.

And it was the same here. As one paper commented slyly, "When Juror No. 4 at Mineola decided that his mind was made up and he had heard enough he was merely following a precedent as old as the hypothetical question itself."[20]

In essence the question dealt with Blanca's early life, the fall in childhood, meeting Jack and marrying him, his use of her money and his adultery, all the events that culminated in the shooting on August 3. Weeks objected to the question being put to Wight, as he was a surgeon, with no background in psychology, but he was overruled. When the question was complete, Uterhart asked Wight, "Assuming all the forgoing facts and having in mind your personal examination of the defendant, in your opinion was the defendant mentally sound at the time of the shooting?"

Wight turned very deliberately to the jury. "She was not," he said, laying heavy emphasis on each word.

"In your opinion did the defendant know the nature and quality of the act she was committing?"

"She did not."

"In your opinion did the defendant know the act was wrong?"

"She did not."[21]

Wight then fell back on his claim that Blanca's condition had been caused by hypothyroidism. He compared her mental state with the type of shell shock—much in the news at the time—in which soldiers obey orders and afterward remember nothing of them. In summary Wight thought that Blanca had suffered an "edema or swelling on the night of August 3,"[22] and that this caused her amnesia. However, having not examined her at the time he couldn't be sure. He said there was no danger of a relapse into her former lethargy because the thyroid treatment had been successful, a prognosis that brought obvious signs of relief to Blanca as she sat listening.

On cross-examination, Weeks delved further into the X-ray of Blanca's skull that Wight had taken. "Your plate is a good one, is it, doctor?"

"A very good one."[23]

"Of course it was," chipped in Justice Manning dryly. "He made it himself."[24]

"You wouldn't feel hurt if anyone said your plate was a poor one?"

"He would be wrong,"[25] snapped Wight.

"Doctor," said Weeks. "Isn't it possible you were mistaken about that open fracture? Don't you ever make mistakes?"

"I have been mistaken at times, but not now. In this case I'm absolutely sure."

"You have been a witness many times in court?"

"A number of times."

"And you have testified a great many times for clients of Uterhart & Graham, haven't you?"

"No," Wight said, adding after a pause, "only five times."

"That's all."[26]

Succinct and effective, Weeks's cross-examination had exposed Wight as Uterhart's "go-to" expert medical witness, a pliable doctor who could be relied upon to provide any diagnosis that his paymaster requested.

Dr. Smith Ely Jeliffe came next. His answers to the hypothetical question echoed those of Wight, as did his belief that the so-called fracture had contributed to Blanca's actions on the night in question. Blanca, he said, "was in an automatic state"[27] when she shot her husband. With Jeliffe standing firm and unshakable on this part of his testimony, Weeks changed his line of attack by asking the witness if he considered himself an expert in insanity. Jeliffe replied in the affirmative. Weeks asked, "Dr. Jeliffe, you testified at the trial of Hans Schmidt.[28] Do you remember that after his conviction for murder, he said he had 'faked' the experts and wasn't insane at all?"[29]

After a prodigious bout of ducking and dodging, eventually Jeliffe mumbled that he *might* have seen reports to that effect. An angry Justice Manning intervened. "There is no doubt about it; the court so stated on appeal."[30]

More sparring followed. Jeliffe was under the gun and although he admitted being one of the experts whom Schmidt had duped, he angrily denied that his was the deciding voice. And as he became more agitated, reason flew out the window. Suddenly he exploded. "Schmidt was a crazy man, no matter what the jury said. I knew it."

"What!" said Weeks. "You mean to say that the State of New York executed a crazy man?"

"It did," retorted Jeliffe. "I know it."[31]

After this bizarre outburst, Jeliffe stepped down from the stand and, staring straight ahead, left the courtroom. Although neither he nor Wight had performed well, nor had they been budged from their stated belief that at the time of the shooting, Blanca de Saulles had been unaware of her actions.

In a surprise move, Uterhart recalled garage owner Raymond D. Hamilton to the stand. Hamilton had contacted Uterhart because he wanted to correct his previous statement that the first telephone call was received by him at 7:30 p.m. on the night in question. He now thought that the call came through shortly after the arrival of the 7:11 train from New York. With this evidence, Uterhart hoped to show that Blanca was making all possible haste to reach The Box before Jack returned home; instead, it merely muddied the already murky waters as the garage owner, under cross-examination, became confused over whether the call had succeeded the arrival of the 7:11 train or the train arriving half an hour later.

With the defense winding down, all it needed now, in the opinion of most courtroom observers, was for the imperious Señora Errázuriz-Vergara to make her much anticipated appearance. Sadly, Uterhart advised the court that Blanca's mother was too ill to testify, an announcement that caused "keen disappointment among the spectators,"[32] and at 2:30 p.m. the defense rested.

It was now Weeks's turn to fight back. His first rebuttal witness was Dr. Lewis Gregory Cole, a fifteen-year X-ray specialist and professor of Roentgenology at Cornell Medical College who currently held the rank of major in the army, where he was training X-ray operatives for the military. The major presented a picture of uniformed rectitude as he marched briskly to the stand. Uterhart conceded that Dr. Cole was a qualified witness. "He photographed one of my teeth once, so I guess he's all right."[33]

Cole sat patiently while the radiograph of Blanca's skull was set up beside the witness stand. Weeks asked him to study the plate. "Does the skull of Mrs. De Saulles show any evidence of fracture?"

"It does not."

"In your opinion, what is that depression at the top of the skull?"[34]

"The plate shows neither a depression nor a fracture, where the frontal bone has united with the bone about it."[35]

Cole was scathing about the quality of Wight's workmanship, describing the X-ray plate as "poor."[36] Even so, he offered to clear up the confusion about the so-called fracture and invited the jury to take a closer look. As before, jurors who hitherto had shown scant interest in any of the medical testimony eagerly gathered around the projectoscope. Cole pointed to the plate. "You will see, instead of a fracture, the typical saw-toothed edges of bone that have failed to knit together."[37] All through Cole's demonstration, Uterhart emitted a series of heavy sighs, interspersed with theatrical dissenting gestures. Weeks glowered across at him.

"I wish you wouldn't shake your head in the sight of the jury."

"Pardon me, I did not mean it,"[38] Uterhart replied innocently.

In a heated, at times bad-tempered cross-examination, Uterhart attacked Cole on his interpretation of the indentation. "It is a place where there is no bone, isn't it?"

"None in infancy."

"Eventually it heals over, so it forms a perfect curve with the skull, doesn't it?"

"Not necessarily."[39]

Uterhart then asked if the witness was expecting to be paid for his testimony.

"I don't know. I came at the State's call. Dr. Kirby[40] called me. No arrangement was made."

"But you expect to be paid, don't you?"

"Yes, I presume I shall be."

"Why are you wearing that uniform today?"

"Because it is an army rule. I have been in the service of the United States since last January, sir."[41]

When Uterhart persisted in this line of attack, the judge cut him off abruptly. "Let's have no more questions of this kind. This man has a perfect right to wear his uniform. That is not to be questioned at all."[42] This was a rare miscalculation by Uterhart. Criticizing the military during times of national emergency was hardly likely to endear him to the jury, and he hurriedly retreated.

Weeks, caught off guard by the comparative brevity of the medical evidence, now asked for a twenty-minute recess in which to prepare his further rebuttal witnesses. During this hiatus angry words were heard at the prosecution table. One of the physicians sat there, outraged by Uterhart's impertinence, and urged Cole to go across and "smash"[43] the defense counsel. No smashing was done and, instead, Weeks presented a string of rebuttal witnesses to refute defense assertions that Blanca had been *non compos mentis* on the night of the shooting and in the subsequent days.

The first, Mrs. Helen McLaughlin Martin, who lived in Manhattan, told of having known Blanca for three years and visiting her on or about August 6 in the jail. She had asked the prisoner if there was anything she could do, and Blanca requested her to "give my love to the little boy if you see him,"[44] and also to remember her to Mrs. Heckscher.

"Did her acts impress you as being rational?"

"They did."[45]

Uterhart kept his cross-examination brief, merely getting Mrs. Martin to admit she was a friend of the Heckschers.

Then it was the turn of Caroline Degener. She confirmed that on the night of the shooting, no one passed her on the stairs when she came down with little Jack as Blanca entered the hallway. This directly impugned Suzanne Monteau's claim that Marshall Ward did not witness the shooting, but instead went upstairs just before it occurred. Caroline also said that prior to the shooting, she had not seen Blanca for more than a year. "When you saw her a year before this did she complain of headaches?" asked Weeks.

"No."[46] And in her opinion, on the night in question, Blanca seemed "quiet and rational,"[47] before and after the incident.

A lively interlude was provided by Miss Jean Mallock, a "peppery little governess from London,"[48] who told the court that she had been employed by Blanca from December 15, 1916, to July 5, 1917. During that time her employer had never complained of headaches. She also portrayed Blanca as a neglectful mother, who, in early July, shipped Jack Jr. off to Roslyn, ostensibly to escape the heat in the city, while she remained in Manhattan living the high life.

Uterhart gave the witness a skeptical glare. Wasn't it true, he asked, that she had been fired by Blanca? Grudgingly, Miss Mallock admitted that she had been discharged by Blanca and that she was "angry with both of them."[49]

"Isn't it a fact, that you frequently offered her your own headache remedies?"

"I don't remember. I may have done so,"[50] she said. "I have suffered from intense headaches myself and I have a very fine remedy."[51] Under more abrasive questioning, she admitted an initial reluctance to get involved in this sordid case because she had "a grievance against Mrs. De Saulles, and . . . a still larger one against De Saulles."[52] She volunteered to give the court the reasons for her anger, a tantalizing prospect that caused an expectant rustle in court, only for Justice Manning to decline the offer. Bitter disappointment on the face of the witness was matched only by frustration in the public gallery.

Constable Thorne was then recalled to the stand. He expressed his belief that Blanca acted rationally at the time of her arrest. "I did not think she was insane."[53] Justice Manning ordered this remark struck out.

After this the court recessed for the day. There was much to mull over. As the trial unfolded, it became apparent that sympathy for Blanca had definitely cooled, both in court and especially in the press. Edith Cornwall, one of the sob sisters, who earlier in the trial had dished up glowing accounts of the defendant, now turned on her savagely, claiming, "It was jealousy that filled the heart of Blanca De Saulles when she drove to The Box that night."[54] Wounded pride, as much as anything else, provided the impulse that sent Jack de Saulles to his death, wrote the acerbic Ms. Cornwall. Blanca had been twice stung by fear and rejection; first, by a husband who preferred other women to her, and then by a fear that her baby was preferring his father's company to that of herself. "Who can doubt that when Blanca De Saulles shot her husband as he turned from her it was one mad final outburst of jealousy that guided her hand and blinded her eyes?"[55]

Certainly this echoed the prosecution's view. In their eyes Blanca was a cold-blooded killer and a scheming manipulator whose high-priced legal team was threatening to subvert the American judicial system with a phony plea of amnesia. But, as Weeks well knew, verdicts aren't delivered by prosecutors, they come from the minds of impressionable jurors, and judging from what Weeks had seen, this avuncular panel had taken the demure and vulnerable "white widow" to its collective heart.

EIGHTEEN

The Verdict

The Trial, Day 10

Because it had been heavily trailed that today would see a verdict in the trial, the crush on the steps of the ivy-walled courthouse was heavier than ever and not even a slanting, icy drizzle could dampen the crowd's enthusiasm. When the doors were thrown open, they surged forward, along the narrow corridor and into the court where this "sensational trial"[1] would reach its denouement.

At a few minutes before ten o'clock, Blanca was led in. Although her face had a little more color than in previous days, her listless expression was unaltered and so was her outfit. The sailor collar of her white blouse peeked demurely over the oft-worn sweater of heather mix. Several in the jury gave her encouraging smiles as she sat at the defense table.

As soon as Justice Manning took his seat on the bench, Weeks rose and called his first witness. Judge Walter R. Jones had seen the defendant within a couple of hours after the shooting, and her actions had impressed him as rational. Chief Jailer George H. Hoffman thought so, too. He swore that early on the morning of August 4, he heard Blanca on the phone, using the name of Henry Uterhart. Significantly, Uterhart chose not to cross-examine this witness.

Mrs. Anna Mooney, employed by Blanca from March 1914 until November 1916 and currently living in Yonkers, was the next witness. "You are the nurse they call 'Boobie'?" asked Weeks.

"I'm Boobie."

"Do you know Mrs. De Saulles?"

"I ought to know her."[2]

Mrs. Mooney was asked about Blanca's European trip, when she had claimed to be brokenhearted. Nothing of the kind, scoffed the witness. Blanca "went to dances, dinners and balls and had a very good time in London,"[3] culminating in her presentation to the king of England at Buckingham Palace. On another occasion Blanca went up in an airplane and frequently took trips to Paris "to buy finery."[4]

The judge intervened, "Oh, all ladies do that when they have money,"[5] a comment that brought much laughter. Mrs. Mooney said that in her experience, Blanca had always seemed very happily married. The witness had also been present in Chile when Blanca was thrown from the automobile. It was a trivial accident, she said; her mistress "took three stitches"[6] in her chin and that same evening attended a concert, countering defense claims that Blanca had been confined to bed for several days.

Mrs. Mooney was also able to shed some light on that *Lusitania* incident. Blanca's tale of having canceled her ticket on the stricken liner at the last minute was total fiction, said the witness, as both she and her husband were in New York when the ill-fated ship was torpedoed. In fact, Mrs. Mooney distinctly remembered both persons saying they wished they had been aboard. In a puzzling and rare oversight, Uterhart failed to ask the witness how she squared this revelation with her earlier testimony that Blanca had been happily married. He did, however, ask if she had ever seen Blanca cry, and the nurse replied that her former mistress never shed tears. How about during that long, lonely voyage to Chile? Not once, said Mrs. Mooney; nor did Blanca seem at all depressed.

Frederick. R. Coudert, a prominent lawyer, made no secret of where his sympathies lay, pausing en route to the stand to shake hands with Blanca. Weeks had called him to demonstrate that Blanca was sufficiently rational at about eight o'clock on the morning after the shooting to telephone him at his Oyster Bay home and seek his advice concerning counsel to defend her. Coudert dug in his heels. Yes, a call had come through, but he now claimed that the voice was unrecognizable. His obduracy incensed Weeks, who was forced to produce office slips from the local telephone exchange, confirming that Blanca had indeed made the call. Only then did Coudert reluctantly concede that the defendant had, indeed, phoned him.

Weeks saved the best till last—Countess Maud Salm, wife of Count Otto Salm, the tennis player. Throughout the trial the jury had heard talk of kings and dukes, but this was the first time that a genuine royal was produced in the flesh and they paid close heed to her evidence. According to the countess, when she visited Blanca shortly after her arrest, the prisoner had joked, "It is awfully nice of you to come and see a murderess."[7] A little while later, as they discussed various matters, Blanca leant forward and urged caution in what they said, "as there might be a Dictaphone about."[8] If true, this statement was clear evidence that Blanca's claims of amnesia since the time of the shooting were a sham, and that she was patently aware of her actions and the danger she was in.

Uterhart had only one question for the witness: "Are you not a cousin of De Saulles?" When she answered in the affirmative, he dismissed her with a curt, "That's all."[9] It was a reasonable riposte, but did little to dent the perception that the countess had "administered one of the hardest blows the defense had sustained."[10]

Then it was the state's turn to read out one of those dreaded hypothetical questions. Assistant prosecutor Charles J. Wood was given the task. It lasted twenty-seven minutes and was addressed to Dr. Isham Harris, superintendent of the Brooklyn Hospital for the Insane. Like the defense hypothetical question, it boiled down to a single query—did the witness think that Blanca was sane? Uterhart objected on grounds that the question had not been properly framed but the judge waved him to his seat. Harris began, "She knew what she was doing and was responsible—" until the judge cut him off and asked him to answer the question, "Was she in sound mind?"

"She was."

"Did she know the nature and quality of the act she was committing?"

"She did."

"Did she know that her act was wrong?"

"She did."[11]

Uterhart then cross-examined, attempting to show that Harris had seen few cases of hypothyroidism. "No, I haven't, because they do not often reach insane asylums, and that is where I have had most of my experience,"[12] was the terse reply,

Dr. Charles Pilgrim, a longtime specialist in mental illness and president of the State Lunacy Commission, had also listened to the question and his answer was broadly similar to his predecessor. His only concession on cross-examination came with an admission that a full examination of a patient was necessary for a sure determination of mental soundness, together with observation covering a period of a week or more.

George H. Kirby, director of New York State's Psychiatric Institute, who had been advising the prosecution throughout the trial, concurred in the opinion of the other two mental health professionals: When Blanca shot her husband, she had been in sound mind. After Kirby left the stand, Weeks announced that the state had completed its case. Justice Manning checked his watch. The time was 11:40 a.m. Rather than begin the final addresses now, he decided to adjourn early, thereby allowing the defense to present their plea to the jury without interruption.

Blanca, who had shown more animation during the testimony dealing with her sanity than at any other time of the trial, stood and walked steadily from the court, attended by her constant companions, Mrs. Seaman and Dr. Wight.

The court was heaving at one o'clock when Justice Manning took the bench. Moments later, Blanca was led in. As she passed the jury box, there was the customary nod to the jury, several of whom bowed graciously in return. Five minutes later, Uterhart began the most important speech of his life. He sensed that in recent days sympathy for his client had been waning, certainly since her performance on the witness stand, and he now embarked on a mission to rebuild Blanca's character in the eyes of the only people who really mattered—the jury.

He leant toward the twelve men, one hand on the counsel table, the other resting on his hip, and said, "I want to thank the district attorney for the fair way he has presented this case, though I am going to say many mean things about him."[13] He then delivered an all-out assault on the so-called promises that the DA had made at the trial outset and had not been able to fulfill. As he spoke, Uterhart punctuated his words by pounding the defense table, an action that instinctively drew the jury that bit closer. The testimony of Julius Hadamek, he said, was critical. "The prosecution's case starts with a lie. John De Saulles told his valet to say he was not at home when he really was."[14] Indeed, "had it not been for that lie, Jack De Saulles would have been alive today."[15] Uterhart sighed. "What did Mrs. De Saulles do? She said to the valet, 'Don't say anything about my ringing up, for I'll be right over.' Gentlemen, is that premeditation?"[16] A general shaking of heads in the jury box suggested that Uterhart had successfully made his point.

Blanca was, said Uterhart, everything a doting wife could be. In a voice trembling with emotion, he spoke of her youthful love for her husband and with a flourish produced a picture of a smiling Blanca taken in Paris, the day before her wedding. "Gentlemen, I want you to keep the picture of this defendant before you as you deliberate this case. I want you to keep in mind the way she looked the day she married De Saulles."[17] Then he invited them to compare this joyous photograph to the downcast defendant they now saw before them. Blanca's forlorn expression was perfectly judged.

On the night of the shooting, Blanca had been "a distressed and distracted mother expecting her boy, worrying because he did not come, setting out to get him."[18] And she was scared. That was why she grabbed the revolver. "It is uncontested that her husband bought the pistol for her in Larchmont in 1912 for her to carry because she was alone and unprotected. On August 3 she had to drive through one of the loneliest spots on Long Island and in a strange taxi cab with a strange man. Was it extraordinary that she would put a revolver in her pocket? Would you jurors think it strange if your daughters did the same thing under such circumstances?"[19] More nods of agreement in the jury box. "Every act and move she made that night shows her dominating thought was to get over to The Box before De Saulles returned and get her boy. She offered the driver $1 if he would get her there on time. 'On time' means nothing except before De Saulles got back."[20]

Advocacy is all about persuasion and few could rival Uterhart at this masterly art. Slowly and inexorably, he bent the jury to his will. "No matter how the district attorney may twist the facts, the evidence all shows that the dominant purpose in her mind was not murder, but to get her child and bring him home and put him to bed."[21]

All through this speech, Justice Manning listened alternately from his chair and on his feet, framed by the large Stars and Stripes, hands clasped behind his back, taking in every word. A few feet to his left, the jurors sat transfixed as Uterhart blasted prosecution claims of premeditation. "If she had gone there to kill him what reason would she have for stopping 200 feet away from the house? She did that because she thought he was away and she could slip in and get the boy and hurry away undetected. Isn't that more reasonable?"[22] Nor did he see anything peculiar in her asking "Where is Mr. De Saulles?" if she had just seen his car in front of the house. When de Saulles told her, "You will never get your boy," a great silence settled over her. Blanca, he said, fell victim to "the maternal instinct, the strongest thing in the world,"[23] and she had acted according to her instincts. Mercifully, the mind's protective mechanism meant that the horror of that dreadful night had now been scrubbed clean from her memory.

It wasn't all smooth sailing for Uterhart, especially when he had to explain those troublesome letters exchanged between husband and wife. He knew they were a double-edged sword. In some Blanca came across as a sympathetic victim, scarred mentally by her crumbling marriage; in others—the majority—she was the embodiment of gaiety, a fun-loving society belle, prepared to abandon her own son in New York so that she might gad about Europe, indifferent to everything except her own pleasure. Ignore this latter impression, said Uterhart; it had all been a subterfuge. "The letters of 1914 indicated a tremendous change. She had been neglected and deserted. She was trying to be the kind of woman that he liked—the frivolous Broadway type. . . . She feared he was drifting from her. She was trying to pretend she was not the same girl who rejoiced over the appearance of baby's first tooth. But other letters showed she hadn't really changed. She was pouring out her love, changing her character even, to hold the man's love—and he was away from her practically the whole time. That's what the district attorney has proved by putting in these letters. Do you jurors think she was a vain, frivolous woman, or a loving wife who wanted nothing but her husband by her side?"[24]

The best gauge of Blanca's genuine state of mind, said Uterhart, lay in the "Dinky Boy" letters, one in particular. "At the time it was written De Saulles was selling her house and pocketing $7,500. It was a case of a woman's heart against a man's cold, calculating mind. Her saying in a later letter that their unhappy married life was due to her, is merely the letter of a noble woman and a loyal wife." He paused to glance across at Blanca. "She had come to the parting of the ways. It takes a big person to say they are in the wrong and yet feel they are in the right. That's exactly what she did in this magnanimous letter she wrote her husband when she went to Chile in 1915."[25]

Uterhart dwelt on the letters at length, contrasting the district attorney's "theory that De Saulles was a wonderful husband" with the fact that "he didn't give her five cents in their early married life and got from her $18,000. . . . And yet, we find this woman . . . writing to her husband and asking him to forgive her."[26] By this time Uterhart's cajoling was having a plainly visible effect on the jury, most of whom sniffled back tears or dabbed at their eyes with handkerchiefs.

Uterhart's voice rose and rasped as he outlined Jack's misuse of Blanca's fortune, buying and selling property using her money and putting the title in his own name. Any ordinary real estate man who acted in so cavalier a fashion would be "up in Sing Sing now,"[27] roared Uterhart. Jack de Saulles, he insisted, didn't want the boy, he wanted Blanca's money. It was "fraud and deceit and larceny, only this time he capitalizes not only her wifely love but her mother love [*sic*]. There's a little vignette of John De Saulles's character—a man who swindles his own wife and cashes in on the love of her child.

That's John De Saulles."[28] He spat the name out like he was trying to get a bad taste from his mouth.

He even vilified de Saulles for daring to keep a copy of the letters he wrote to his wife. There had to be some underlying motive at work; after all, Uterhart said, "No man ever keeps a copy of a letter to his wife."[29] This was the action of a scheming husband who was "making a record for future use."[30] And what nerve! Why, at the very time he wrote this letter, Jack was enmeshed in "a low, coarse love affair"[31] with the Broadway dancer Joan Sawyer. Uterhart's look of disgust was more eloquent than a thousand insults. And as for de Saulles's complaint that she had not lived with him as a wife, "Why, good God, gentlemen, she chased him all over the world to live with him."[32]

All through Uterhart's speech, Blanca had watched intently, hands folded in her lap, but, as always, the only real signs of animation came when Uterhart dealt with the medical evidence. Then Blanca's eyes, usually so dull and glazed, took on a new sharpness. "No matter what Dr. Cole, the X-ray man, says, you saw a depression in that woman's skull, and we say it is not a fontanel but an unclosed fracture."[33] Uterhart glossed over the X-rays, aware that his trio of expert witnesses had fared poorly when compared to Dr. Cole, whose vast experience in radiology had given his testimony an unbreachable authority. Instead, he quickly turned to the shooting itself. "If she had wanted to kill him she easily could get him to Crossways on some pretext and kill him when nobody else was around. She could have shot him from behind, yet the bullets sprayed all over his head like a machine gun. You can't get away from the fact that the first bullet hit the front knuckle."[34]

As no evidence had been adduced during the trial to substantiate this outlandish claim, Weeks's failure to object was astounding. But the district attorney remained glued to his seat, a legal eunuch, seemingly content to give Uterhart his head. What followed next was pure pantomime, as Uterhart offered his version of how the shooting had occurred. Twisting his bulky frame this way and that, he insisted—again without an iota of evidence—that the bullet to the back had been fired last. And he dismissed Marshall Ward's account of the shooting as "a fabrication,"[35] because Ward had not even been in the room at the fateful moment.

After a fleeting and curt review of the prosecution's medical witnesses, Uterhart lacerated the state for not calling Dr. Guy Cleghorn, the county physician and the first medical man to examine Blanca and who kept her under constant surveillance in the jail. "Is it not plain why the district attorney has discarded the testimony of a competent medical man on his own staff"[36] to tell the court of Blanca's mental state? Instead the state chose to rely on the testimony of witnesses such as the Countess Salm, whom Uterhart branded as nothing more than a spy "sent over to the jail by members of the De Saulles family to frame up this little woman."[37] This was sharp enough, but like Weeks one day earlier, Uterhart reserved his most venomous attack for someone lower down the social scale. Anna Mooney—"that hard faced, vicious harridan"[38]—was condemned as a vengeful ex-servant "trying to swear her former mistress's life away."[39]

Uterhart had been on his feet for more than two hours and not a word had been wasted or ignored. The climax of his speech saw him stand before the jury, arms spread wide, like some preacher before his congregation. "I say to the defendant who sits there that she can trust you gentlemen. She is looking into the faces of the strong, true American gentlemen who are going to give her full and ample justice by acquitting her."[40] He then turned to Blanca and declared his belief that the jury would acquit her. She returned his gaze without smiling. Uterhart faced the jury one more time. "I feel now that there is a spirit in this room that is going to fill your hearts—the spirit of the Man who stood on the Mount and said, 'Blessed are the merciful for they shall receive mercy.'"[41] Then Uterhart slumped down at the defense table, utterly drained by his effort.

Some in the press box thought that, for the first time in the trial, the ice princess had been moved to tears, with one reporter noting that when Justice Manning announced a fifteen-minute recess, "she went out weeping and leaning on the arm of her physician."[42] Blanca's red-rimmed emotion was mirrored in the jury box and the public gallery. For those few moments the courtroom was awash with maudlin sentiment.

After the break Weeks took center stage. The jowly, bespectacled district attorney stood up knowing that he faced a thankless task. Uterhart's address had been adrenaline-charged, jammed full of emotion, and he had a copybook defendant, beautiful, vulnerable, almost schoolgirlish. All Weeks could offer in response was cold, hard facts; thin gruel, indeed, for the task ahead. He began by reminding the jury that it was Blanca de Saulles who was on trial, not her former husband. "The only issue—the only thing for you to determine—is whether this defendant knew what she was doing that night."[43] He noted that Uterhart had spent forty-five minutes trashing a dead man's reputation. "I don't care how base a man may have been, how much he may squander his wife's money, that does not give a woman the right to shoot him down like a dog,"[44] he said. "John De Saulles is dead, and his faults, they say, were many, but it has seemed to me that this trial has changed from a trial of Mrs. De Saulles to a trial of John De Saulles."[45]

And what about the defendant's character? Weeks wondered. Was she really as angelic as she would have everyone believe? He reminded the jury of her patronizing, often grossly insulting references to other people: There was "the little man" who had helped her at the steamship pier; Constable Thorne, with his "nasty voice"; and "the black thing"[46] who had testified at the Carman trial. These were not the utterances of a kindly nature, argued Weeks, but rather the products of a warped and narcissistic disposition, disdainful of any perceived underling. "Has one word of pity or one of regret come from the defendant, or from her witnesses or counsel?" Weeks asked. "Has even decent respect been shown to his relatives? No, it seems that even the family of the dead man cannot be mentioned without a snarl or a hiss, even the aged mother must be referred to discourteously as 'Old Mrs. De Saulles.'"[47]

Weeks cited the letters written by Blanca as proof that Jack really was the "perfect husband"[48] that she had once called him. The defendant's courtroom performance had been a sham, delivered by "one of the keenest minds that ever faced a jury."[49] At this point Blanca shook off her apathy for an instant and speared the district attorney with a withering glare as he continued. Regardless of Jack's marital shortcomings, this was a murder trial and the defendant had killed her husband with premeditation. "What was the first sight this distracted mother saw when she opened the door? Her own child. Did she grasp him to her bosom or speak to him? No, she did not, but she did speak to Mrs. Degener. If she had grasped the child and held him, and then said, 'Come on, Jack De Saulles, you committed grand larceny' and then had shot him she would never have been held by the Grand Jury of this county."[50]

Weeks ridiculed Uterhart's reenactment of how the shooting had unfolded, and he was similarly scathing about Suzanne Monteau's evidence that Jack had been only three feet from his wife and facing her, saying that if such had been the case Jack would have knocked the gun aside. "No one contends that he was not a brave man."[51] Weeks also mocked Blanca's claims of amnesia. All her actions after the shooting, he said, were those of someone in full possession of her faculties. "Do you remember when I was cross-examining and a juror yawned, and, quick as a flash, that woman said, 'Do you blame him, Mr. Weeks?' Quick to see her opportunity and keen enough to turn it to her own advantage."[52]

The DA maintained that any shock Blanca suffered came not when she shot Jack, but later in the jail when the full realization of what she had done sank in. The so-called amnesia, he said, was a convenient ruse to wipe out the time for which she should be held to account. She was entirely sane, as evidenced by her words to Countess Salm just days after the shooting. "Could anything be more rational than her warning to a visitor at the jail to be careful what she said, as there might be a Dictaphone in the cell?"[53] And even before this, just seconds after the shooting, she had calmly instructed the eyewitnesses to call the police. Again, this was powerful evidence of sanity, said Weeks. He looked directly at the jury. "I wouldn't care if the experts stood in one long line from here to New York. . . . I would take the evidence of my own eyes—the commonsense evidence that you jurors must consider. Mrs. De Saulles knew what she had done, and this calling for the police showed that she knew her act was a crime."[54] Weeks reminded the jury that they had taken a solemn oath to render a fair and impartial verdict on the evidence alone and not to permit themselves to be swayed by sympathy. After this plea, Weeks sat down. He had been speaking for eighty-five minutes.

Justice Manning began his charge without any pause. First, he told the jury, they needed to dismiss from their minds Blanca's social status; also, he warned them to banish any prejudice they might feel about divorce. He referred to Blanca's story as one "graphically, if not dramatically told,"[55] and he reminded the jury that this was a woman on trial for her life. "On the people is placed the responsibility of determining her sanity at the time of the crime," he said, "and if there is any reasonable doubt as to her sanity you must acquit her. That is the law. The condition of this woman's mind on that day is the vital one."[56] As for the medical experts, Justice Manning said it was impossible for them to determine whether the defendant was sane or insane when the tragedy occurred. He quoted several opinions as to what constituted insanity in the eyes of the law, then said that one of the oldest authorities—the M'Naghten defense—gave lack of knowledge of the crime as an excuse. "If . . . the defendant did not know the quality of her act and did not know that it was wrong, you will find her not guilty. If, on the other hand, she was in possession of her faculties, and did know that her act was wrong, you will find her guilty."[57]

What followed next was extraordinary. Inexplicably, Justice Manning tossed out the law books and decided to invoke the scriptures as an aid to determining insanity, repeating the cry of Jesus on the cross—"Father, forgive them, for they know not what they do."[58] Such an utterance might have been excusable on the part of some counsel pleading for his client's life, but coming from the bench it was breathtaking. Justice Manning went on, "Don't decide this case on the addresses of either counsel, but keep your minds strictly on the evidence. No favors, no sympathy, no prejudice should be weighed against either those who are here seeking to enforce the laws or she who comes here accused of an infraction of the laws and who has denied her guilt."[59] After a reading on "reasonable doubt" that was heavily skewed in the defendant's favor, he defined the varying degrees of homicide:

1. *Murder, first degree, the result of deliberation and premeditation.*
2. *Manslaughter, second degree, killing without deliberation or premeditation.*
3. *Excusable homicide.*
4. *Justifiable homicide.*

He explained that in this case, the last two degrees were not at issue; this was either murder or manslaughter, whereupon Uterhart leapt up and reminded the judge that he had omitted to include the possibility of "not guilty," which oversight was amended. Forget everything else, Justice Manning told the jury, except one thing—"Did this woman know the nature and the quality of her act at the time of the commission of her act? This is the sole, important consideration of you gentlemen at this time."[60] And with this, he asked the jury to consider its verdict.

The twelve men dutifully trooped out of court at 6:00 p.m. Before the commencement of deliberations, they adjourned to the Garden City Hotel for supper. Justice Manning said he would allow them two hours to eat, and he wanted them back at court by eight o'clock. Twenty minutes before that deadline the jury returned and retired to their room on the second floor. The fact that most jurors carried their hand baggage with them suggested a quick verdict. They called for all the exhibits in the case—maps, photographs, including the X-ray of Blanca's skull, pictures of The Box, and letters written by Jack and Blanca. And then the door shut behind them.

It had closed on a courtroom still heaving with activity. Upward of one hundred spectators had decided to either delay or forgo their evening meal rather than surrender hard-won seats in the public gallery. Outside, in the corridor, officials, attorneys, and gossipers huddled in small groups, all trying to predict the outcome. The shrewd money, those who'd seen this kind of thing countless times before, was on a verdict of manslaughter or, at worst, insanity. No one was expecting a clear-cut conviction of murder in the first degree; after all, who on that jury could live with the responsibility of having consigned this fragile flower to the electric chair?

The bets were still being struck at 9:15 p.m. when a bailiff shouted out that the jury was rapping at their door, a sign that they had reached a decision. This announcement caused a stampede for the courtroom, led by Weeks and two assistants. A few steps behind, Uterhart made his way more sedately, and certainly with more panache, back to his place at the defense table. Moments later, Sheriff Seaman brushed aside a few stragglers who were blocking a doorway to clear a path for Blanca. She was followed by quite an entourage: Amalia and Guillermo, Mrs. Seaman and Suzanne, a nurse, and members of her legal team. As Blanca reached the table, she bit her lip but was otherwise unmoved until Uterhart gave her a triumphant grin. When she leant across the table toward him, he nodded his head, and a faint smile lit her features. She turned and looked at the door expectantly and for a moment rested her head in her hands on the table.

The door opened and the jury filed in. They looked uniformly solemn. Blanca, seated just a few feet away, scanned their faces. Some smiled at her, others looked away, but once they were seated, Juror No. 5, William Jones of Freeport, a jovial looking man with snowy white hair and a mustache to match, gave Blanca a broad wink.

Moments later the door to the judge's chambers swung open. Everyone stood as Justice Manning swept in, black robe trailing behind him. He took his seat at the bench and issued a warning to everyone present. "There must not be the slightest expression of approval or disapproval, regardless of the verdict. If anyone so offends, I will commit him to jail."[61]

Clerk Daniel E. Sealey then asked the jury if they had agreed upon a verdict, and they said they had. "Jury, rise and look upon the defendant," he said. "Defendant, rise and look upon the jury."[62]

Blanca stood, the tips of her fingers resting on the table, and waited calmly.

"Gentlemen, what is your verdict, guilty or not guilty."[63]

The foreman, John C. Bucken, said loudly, "Not guilty."[64] Simultaneously his fellow jurors joined him and a chorus of "Not guilty" reverberated up and down the double row of jurors.

Blanca beamed at the jury. Her lips moved as if she were saying "Thank you," but apart from that there was no other sign of emotion. Elsewhere, the court was eerily quiet, with barely a sound. Blanca sat back down. Uterhart leant across the table and shook her hand.

Justice Manning took a moment to gather his thoughts and then addressed the jury. "Gentlemen, the case of Blanca De Saulles is over forever. I assume you have discharged your duty according to your consciences, and with my best wishes for your future, I bid you good night."[65] He then turned toward Blanca. "The verdict of the jury is not guilty and you are therefore free. You may go."[66]

The court now burst into life. Telegraph messengers dashed from the reporters' table, desperate to get their copy back to the newsrooms before the final deadline, as a surge of well-wishers surrounded Blanca, all eager to add their congratulations. One of the jurors, Philip H. Ohm, a retired grocer with two sons, pushed his way through the crowd and shook hands with Blanca. His gray head wagged with joy as he looked down upon her. "I want to say that we are all pleased that you are going to get your boy. 'We' means all of us. I came to say it for them. It was the boy that was in our minds most of all."[67]

He withdrew his hand and Blanca's placid wanness of the trial gave way to a radiant smile as she turned toward Uterhart, "I hope you will get my boy for me now."[68]

Uterhart answered quickly. "Yes, I'll see to it."[69]

As the jury dispersed, Blanca shook hands with each and exchanged a few words. One said, "We're your friends, little girl."[70]

Even the judge wanted to add his best wishes. In an unusual gesture, Justice Manning returned to court and held out his hand to Blanca. "I hope you will be happy now."

"Thank-you, Judge, oh, thank-you."[71]

Almost unnoticed on the far side of the court, Charles de Saulles, the only family member in court to hear the verdict, sat with his back to the wall and did not show by even a blink of his eyelids that the verdict affected him in any way. For a long time he appeared too stunned to move. Eventually, he left court, head bowed and without saying a word.

As Blanca walked from the court, a woman ran up and kissed her on the forehead. Bailiffs sprang forward to thrust the woman back but Blanca only laughed. Then, releasing the arm of her counsel, she skipped down the stairs, through the basement, and out into the drizzling rain. Hatless and coatless, she grinned and took a deep draught of the air of freedom. A volley of flashbulbs greeted her as she kissed her brother and sister.

Moments later she disappeared behind the iron gate of the jail for the last time. The sheriff's dog bounded down the steps to greet her. She patted him and continued to her room, which had been bedecked with flowers. News of her acquittal had preceded her and all the inmates cheered as she entered. Mrs. Seaman, weeping with joy, threw open her arms in a welcoming embrace. Suzanne had already packed her belongings and these were bundled downstairs and into an automobile.

On the street outside the court, a crowd of well-wishers sought to grasp Blanca's hand. Men and women were driven back by a home guardsman, who brandished a rifle that he loudly declared to be "well loaded."[72] Blanca turned to Uterhart and laughed: "It will seem strange to wake up anywhere but in the jail."[73]

In the brief press conference that followed, Blanca was radically different to how she had appeared throughout the trial. The transformation was incredible. The lethargy was jettisoned, her cheeks were flushed, her eyes were aglow, and she beamed nonstop. "I'm so happy," she said. "And I thank you with my whole heart for being so glad for me."

"Does your mother know of the verdict?" asked one female reporter.

"Oh, yes," said Blanca. "I telephoned myself."[74] She stressed the personal pronoun. Then Blanca, accompanied by her brother and sister, climbed into a car and, with Amalia at the wheel, raced off.

Uterhart was left to handle the press, who wanted his reaction to the greatest victory of his career. "It's a good clean verdict," he said and smiled, "there being no restrictions as to insanity."[75] He said he would be asking the family to deliver the boy into Blanca's custody the next day.

Weeks was, understandably, more subdued. Deep in his heart, he had not expected a verdict of guilty in the first degree, but he was shocked by the absence of any mention of insanity, temporary or otherwise. "I feel that we could not do any more than present the case. The responsibility lay with the jury and that's all there is to it."[76]

Others, too, were uneasy. At the beginning of the trial, there had been almost universal press support for the "White Widow," but as the evidence unfolded, much of the cheerleading had died down, and now, with the verdict in, a palpable sense of unease afflicted the fourth estate. Had they in some way helped to undermine the judicial process? Did their hyperbolic coverage of this wealthy, glamorous defendant contribute to this perverse verdict? Or was there something deeper in the American psyche, a disturbing refusal on the part of all-male juries to apportion serious criminal blame to any member of the fair sex (provided, of course, that she was white, rich, and beautiful)? One newspaper that evening went even further, posing the question: "Is it worthwhile to put women on trial for murder?"[77]

NINETEEN

A Courtroom Bernhardt

OTHER NEWSPAPERS WERE EQUALLY HORRIFIED BY THE VERDICT. Complainer-in-chief was the *New York Times,* with a blistering editorial, unable to fathom how Blanca had beaten the charge. "On a certain night last August this woman, having armed herself with a revolver, traveled . . . to the residence of her divorced husband and there shot him dead. She took the life of a human being, an act which the law forbids and makes punishable. The fact of the killing undisputed, the law was declared to the jury by the court. Yet the verdict was 'not guilty,' absolute acquittal. The jury, by that verdict, found that the woman in killing De Saulles had done no wrong; if they had some lingering doubts about the righteousness of her act, they declared that she should not be punished for it. It need not be pointed out that it is not the intention of the law that a person who takes the life of another shall go scot-free."[1]

Thousands of taxpayer dollars had vanished down the drain on a case that looked open and shut. So who was to blame? The *New York Times*'s indignant lather spared no one. "Probably there was never a flimsier insanity plea presented in any court. It was surpassed, however, by the pitiful feebleness of the prosecution's efforts to combat it." And the judge, too, was roughly handled for his bizarre biblical reference. "In countless cases new trials have been granted—not possible in this case—on grounds far less substantial than that utterance. If it was not an impropriety to put that thought into the minds of the jurymen, then we do not know what would constitute impropriety in a judge's charge."[2]

One thing was certain, it was another victory for the unwritten law. In Chicago—that hotbed of perverse verdicts when the defendant was female, attractive, and preferably young—one newspaper sighed, "An American jury again made its own laws when it gave a verdict of 'not guilty' and set Mrs.

John De Saulles free. . . . The American mind seems convinced that law is an imperfect remedy."[3]

While the leader writers fulminated, the object of all this ink and ire was sitting for press photo shots in her living room at Crossways. Blanca smiled easily and affably. Her large dark eyes gleamed with life and happiness as she posed, wearing a fetching winter outfit of tan and white, complete with brown checked stockings. The zombielike stupor present from the day of her arrest had been consigned to history, leading one reporter to wryly observe: "The interim has wrought a marvelous change in the central figure of the most remarkable murder trial which Nassau County has ever witnessed."[4]

The morning had been tension-filled. From an early hour Uterhart and George Gordon Battle had been locked in negotiations over the custody of Jack Jr. Eventually, at 1:30 p.m., Uterhart heard that if he went to Maurice Heckscher's home at 35 East 49th Street at 2:30 p.m., the boy would be returned. Uterhart immediately called for his car.

An hour later, he knocked at the Heckscher's door. As promised, Jack Jr. was ready, wearing a sailor suit and proudly displaying the badge given him by Sheriff Seaman. Uterhart stood to one side as the boy kissed the two little Heckscher girls good-bye; then came a poignant moment as Louise leaned down, kissed Jack Jr., and said "good-bye forever."[5] On the return journey Uterhart kept Jack Jr. amused by recounting fairy tales. The lad seemed particularly thrilled by "Jack the Giant Killer."

Out on Long Island, as the shadows lengthened and the clock edged close to four o'clock, Blanca became anxious; Jack Jr. should have been here by now. She implored the reporters, "Can't you do something to help me get him back?"[6] The words had barely left her mouth when she heard the crunching of wheels on gravel, a honk on a car's horn, and the slamming of a car door. Moments later Jack Jr. came scampering into the room and threw himself into his mother's arms.

"I'm so glad to be back, Bumby," he said. "I would rather be with you than all the world."

"And I would rather be with you than all the universe."

"What's that, Bumby?"

"The universe is all there is."

"Well, I would rather be with you than twice that,"[7] he said, and a hug from his pudgy arms completed the pronouncement. Asked about his father, the boy replied, "He tried to take me away from my mother."[8] Jack Jr. gave her a loving smile, then said that Uterhart told him that when Jack the Giant Killer slew the giant he stuck a sword in his head. This had puzzled the youngster. "Feel my head," he said to his mother. "It's hard and you can't stick anything in it."

"Well, giants may have heads like Dr. Cole,"[9] was his mother's sardonic reply, and she dutifully grabbed hold of her son to accommodate the clamoring photographers. After another fusillade of flashbulbs had recorded the mother and son reunion, Amalia called from the dining room for Jack Jr. to come and have a cup of chocolate.

Blanca turned back to the audience of eager pressmen. The questions came in a flurry and she fielded them like a seasoned pro. Asked if the boy had been told of the tragedy, she said yes, but that she regretted him having his head filled with stories of her being a murderer. So what do you think of American courts? "They are wonderful," she said. "I shall always have the kindest feelings for Americans."[10] Asked what she thought was the most impressive thing about the trial, she gave the questioner a pitying look. "The verdict, of course."[11]

So what about the future, do you intend taking Jack Jr. to Chile? "I do not know that I shall ever leave North America," she said. "I love North America. I think it is just fine. Probably we shall remain right here for a time at least, as I believe the country is the place for a child."[12]

Did you see the juror wink at you when he came back into court? "Of course I did. I would not have missed that for the world."[13]

But the revelation that really jolted those reporters present was Blanca's frank admission that her catatonic demeanor during the trial had been a charade, a ruse calculated to deceive the court and win over the jurors. "I schooled myself in repression,"[14] she announced in matter-of-fact fashion. It took a moment or two for such candor to sink in, but when someone pointed out that such self-control was unusual in a murder case, her response was a knowing smile. "Well, one can do anything if one has to."[15] She expanded on her technique. "I knew that I would have to use every faculty of which I was possessed. I knew every amateur psychologist and 'sob sister' would be studying my features, my expressions and my every movement. I studied all the time, the judge and the jury, the lawyers and the newspaper men."[16]

This was no idle boast, as it became clear that she really had absorbed every last courtroom detail. For instance, there was the reporter who wrote with his left hand; he had really irked her. So too had the telegraph messenger who kept brushing against her chair every time he ran out of court with copy from the reporters. Nor was she pleased with certain members of the press. "I didn't like what two of the women writers said about me. Oh, those women—"[17] Before she could elaborate, her words were broken off by Jack Jr., who came charging in from the dining room and launched himself onto his mother's lap. Blanca smiled, but then those dark eyes gave that familiar flash of anger as she mentioned another female journalist's comment that her plight "was the more pitiful because she had never read a book and was short of intellectual resources, which might have kept her brooding over the trial."[18]

Overall, though, she had been delighted by the coverage. "I didn't mind the publicity at all—I liked it," was her surprising admission. She also made it plain that she would make no attempt to recover any money from her husband's estate, nor to recover any of the money she allegedly gave him. "I would not touch a penny of it under any circumstances," she said. "I do not wish to have anything to do with the De Saulles family,"[19] even if it meant finding a job, because "I need money."[20] A glance at the luxurious setting in which these words were uttered made the reporters chuckle. "The way she said it didn't carry any conviction," wrote one. "She gave the impression that she was still practicing repression."[21]

When asked if she had been impressed by Mr. Uterhart's closing speech, Blanca replied, "It was wonderful, but his opening address was greater."

"Did he make you cry?"[22]

The eyes blazed once again. "Do you think I would go through what I did at the trial and then cry over myself?"[23] And while on the subject of counsel, she also thought Weeks had "not been very nice" to her, in spite of her attorney's praise for the district attorney's "gentlemanly"[24] conduct of the trial.

Blanca's attention began to wander. There was nothing more to be said. The reporters had their quotes and their photographs, and it was obvious that she now had no further use for them. A few minutes later she instructed Jack Jr. to say good-bye and excused herself, saying it was time for tea. She vanished into the dining room, with Guillermo closing the door behind her. Her flirtation with the American press was over.

But they were far from being done with her. Nobody likes to be hoodwinked—least of all the press—and one newspaper that early on had been a staunch supporter now rounded on their former heroine. Under a blaring headline, Mrs. De Saulles . . . Admits Role of Actress at Trial, the paper dubbed her a "greater actress than Bernhardt,"[25] and wondered sarcastically if, in light of her alleged financial difficulties, she might find employment on the stage. The bile continued: "While psychologists . . . were studying her in court, analyzing her apathy and likening her to the canvas painted dreams of dead and gone genius, the beautiful guileless child was playing a part."[26] The role, the paper suspected, had been cooked up by Uterhart and Blanca together, though it had little doubt that Blanca's had been the controlling hand. "Those who saw her through the trial little dreamed the great help she was to her attorney in getting her verdict of acquittal. Hidden behind the face of a child was the mind of a master, a mind which grasped everything going on about her, while the spectators were convinced that that mind was a blank."[27]

Whatever the motivation, it worked. One juror, who only spoke under condition of anonymity, revealed that the verdict had been reached on just the second vote. He hinted that on the first ballot two jurors had favored temporary insanity, but they were soon won over to the majority view. Then came the surprising revelation that the jury had been particularly impressed by Hadamek and Ward, both of whom, they thought, had told the truth! Dr. Wight was also singled out for his testimony—"he did not smother facts with long words and medical terms"[28]—and they accepted without demur Blanca's explanation of the contradictory letters. "She had tried to be a good, old-fashioned wife," said the juror, "and had failed to keep her husband. Then she tried to play the part of a butterfly, because she believed that would bring him back to her."[29] One aspect of the trial that did upset the jury was the courtroom conduct of certain members of the de Saulles family. The juror remarked that one of these relatives "kept smiling in a sardonic way"[30] whenever the district attorney scored against the defense.

There was still plenty of work for the lawyers. Because he had died intestate, Jack's entire estate would go to his son. It was thought that Charles would be appointed administrator and that to prevent any possible complications, Blanca would, by formal decree, have herself made the guardian of her son. While under indictment and in jail, Blanca had been "civilly dead,"[31] which left her son subject to no legal control. Even now her path to full guardianship of Jack Jr. was likely to be rocky, with rumors persisting that the de Saulles family was ready to use the court testimony to show that Blanca was an unfit mother.

Given this development it did not come as a shock when, next day, Blanca suffered a relapse and was ordered to bed by Dr. Wight. Rich litigants—be they in criminal or civil court—seem unusually prone to illness when confronted by legal adversity. It would be several days, said Wight, before she would be permitted to leave her room or meet friends. This left Amalia and Guillermo to deal with the scores of congratulatory letters and telegrams that were flooding into Crossways. On Blanca's specific instructions, none were made public.

Press bewilderment over the verdict rumbled on. Another Pretty Woman Has Been Acquitted[32] ran one newspaper headline above an article that rounded up incredulous reaction from journals from as far afield as Savannah, Philadelphia, and Kansas City. A cartoon reproduced from the *New York Herald,* depicting an attractive young woman skipping through a jailhouse door, beneath a caption that read "Of Course!" caught the general mood of weary resignation over the jury's decision.

Even the *New York Law Journal,* mouthpiece of the New York County Supreme Court, took issue with Uterhart over the defense. When the verdict came in, the *Law Journal* took the same view as the *New York Times:* "Probably there never was a flimsier insanity defense presented in any court." Uterhart bridled under the attack from his peers and denied that he had made any reference to the "unwritten law." He had, he insisted, followed precepts laid down in the recent Malcolm murder trial in England,[33] in which defense counsel expressly disclaimed any and every suspicion of an appeal to the unwritten law.

Others simply wanted to set the record straight. John E. Bruce, president of the Negro Society for Historical Research, in a letter to the *New*

York Tribune, blasted Blanca for her racist remarks on the stand, in particular her assertion that "we don't have them [blacks] in my country." Bruce then delivered a history lesson of the colonization of Chile by African Americans dating from as early as 1515. Other references to African Americans in Chile were to be found in the works of Charles Darwin, said Bruce. Perhaps, he concluded, Blanca's ignorance of her own country's history owed much to "her long residence outside of it."[34]

Sadly, this case had one more victim to claim. On Christmas Eve, just three weeks after he had seen his son's killer walk free, Major Arthur Brice de Saulles died at age seventy-seven. By common consent, the tragedy and the strain of testifying at the trial had hastened his end. One of his last acts was to order a generous assortment of Christmas gifts for the grandson whom he loved so much, and who had been the reason for his fateful visit to The Box on the night of the shooting.

Two days later, Señora Errázuriz-Vergara and Guillermo returned to Chile, leaving Amalia with Blanca. The sisters spent New Year's together and then on January 11, 1918, with a blizzard bearing down on New York, they left, with Jack Jr., for California. With them was the ever-loyal Suzanne. While in San Francisco, Blanca instructed her lawyers to draw up the necessary documents in her action to obtain the sole legal right to her son's custody.

Being in California gave Blanca time to relax. If she ever intended seeing Rodolfo again, now would have been the time. But Blanca was not interested. Rodolfo Guglielmi had served his purpose; she had no desire to share her triumph with some insignificant nightclub performer. It was time to move on.

Rodolfo was not so fortunate. His life since moving to Los Angeles had been one of perpetual disappointment. He spent his days tramping around agents' offices, and at night he retreated to his tiny apartment on Sunset Boulevard to find the mailbox stuffed with letters from Italy warning that his mother's health was failing fast. Then came the black-bordered letter that he had dreaded. It told him that on January 18, Gabriella had died. He tried to keep his grief private, but friends noticed a new desolation in his face. At night, locked away alone in his room, he sobbed bitterly. Within a matter of weeks he had lost the two most important women in his life, one to mortality, the other to fate. It was a terrible wrenching away of all that he held dear.

In the meantime, Blanca was long gone. On January 21, the woman who just over one month earlier had told reporters she had no intention of leaving North America arrived in Honolulu. Even there she was hounded by reporters. She told them that she and her son only wanted some rest and that, in hopes of stifling any further press intrusion, she intended reverting to her maiden name.

Back in Manhattan, more details of Jack de Saulles's financial arrangements were beginning to emerge, and they didn't make pretty reading for those who claimed that the dead realtor had no need of his wife's fortune. At the time of his death, he was neck-deep in debt. Most of his money problems had been caused by improvements he lavished on The Box. To clear some of these debts, it was thought that Jack's string of international-class polo ponies would have to be auctioned off in the spring.

Blanca didn't have long to wait for the courts to clarify her custody concerns. On March 11, after two months of deliberation, Surrogate Fowler rejected claims that as an American citizen, Jack Jr.'s interests would be best served by his being raised by the de Saulles family and instead awarded permanent custody to Blanca. The nomadic mother and son were notably absent when the verdict was announced, and not until three days later did reporters track them down, this time in Japan, at a villa a few miles outside of Tokyo that Blanca had rented for the summer. She intended to stay there, she said, until the notoriety surrounding her name died down.

Not that there was much chance of that. Within weeks of the custody issue being decided, a "quickie" movie called *The Woman and the Law* opened at the Lyric Theatre in New York before hitting screens nationwide.

Miriam Cooper in *The Woman and the Law* (1918), based on the de Saulles murder case

LYCEUM

TONIGHT, TOMORROW & SATURDAY

You have a slight veneer of civilization gleaned through the ages of man

BUT

if the man you married and to whom you were all that loving, faithful wife could be, and he in turn subjected you to every humiliation, every insult his mind could conceive, and then when the courts had given you back your name, your freedom and the right to look the whole world in the face

HE
TRIED
TO STEAL
YOUR
BABY

would the veneer of civilization stand the strain?

Woman and the Law

Based on the internationally sensational De Saulles case, which so shocked the United States and South America and which was discussed in every home in the country, it is said, the thrilling moment when the woman who had slain for the sake of her child faces the jury which is to decide her fate, depicts a situation to hold the most hardened playgoer spell bound.

Are women but the scum of man to be scraped off on the edge of man's unfaithfulness?

Contemporary newspaper advertisement for *The Woman and the Law*

Written and directed by Rauol Walsh, and based on the de Saulles case, it starred Walsh's wife, Miriam Cooper, as Blanquetta La Salle. Because of Cooper's strong resemblance to Blanca, it was rumored that the distributors, Fox, originally wanted to leave Cooper's name off the credits to create the impression that Blanca had played the part herself. According to the press releases, the film posed such moral conundrums as: "Are there provocations which justify a woman to kill?"[35] and, "Has the law the right to deprive a mother of her child?"[36] These questions, it said, were decided by the jury "in a scene that will live long in the memory of every one who sees it."[37] Because of its controversial subject, the meaty drama was rated as suitable only for audiences older than age twenty-one. One reviewer proclaimed it "the greatest woman's picture ever staged."[38] Sadly, this film has been lost to history.

After this flurry of publicity, interest in Blanca waned, leaving her free to resume her globe-trotting lifestyle in peace, with Jack Jr. at her side.

The Jack de Saulles estate was proving even more troublesome than originally thought, as attorneys wrestled to unravel the financial mess left by Jack's intestacy. An initial valuation assessed his total estate at $68,380, made up of $53,380 in bonds, securities, and cash, and realty worth $15,000. Under the law Blanca was entitled to her dower interest in the realty, while the remainder of the estate went to Jack Jr. in trust until he reached majority. The estate was administered by Charles de Saulles in conjunction with the Nassau County Trust Company, and getting to the bottom of how much Jack really owned and, more important, how much he owed, was a financial headache that would drag on for another eighteen months.

To ease the burden, the administrators decided to offload The Box. When it came on the market, its star-crossed history repelled most buyers, and it was eventually sold on August 5, 1918, to Thomas H. Bowles of Kansas—the only bidder—for the knockdown price of $19,348. Documents and receipts showed that Jack had spent close to fifty thousand dollars on renovations. This didn't surprise anyone. What did raise eyebrows in the financial community was the revelation that Jack didn't even own the house. It had been purchased in September 1916 by his longtime business associate, Stephen S. Tuthill, for twenty-eight thousand dollars, using an eighteen-thousand-dollar mortgage held by prominent local landowner Mrs. Emily Ladenburg. Tuthill had then leased The Box to Jack. When held up to the light, the deal turned out to be considerably less sinister than first appeared. With his marriage on the rocks and a divorce pending, Jack wanted as few assets in his own name as possible, and the likelihood is that he transferred ownership of The Box to Tuthill's name to keep it out of Blanca's clutches should any settlement go against him. When the mortgage matured without anything having been repaid on the principal, Mrs. Ladenburg foreclosed.

As the months passed, and with the principals either dead or else scattered around the globe, memories of that awful night at The Box began to fade. But they were brought back into sharp relief on January 11, 1919, when fifty-one-year-old millionaire sugar baron and notorious eccentric Jacques Lebaudy, known as the "Emperor of the Sahara,"[39] was shot and killed at The Lodge, in Westbury, just a stone's throw from where Jack had been gunned down. A string of coincidences connected the two killings. First, there was the location; second, Lebaudy died from five gunshot wounds; third, the weapon used was a .32 revolver; fourth, the arresting officers were Sheriff Seaman and Constable Thorne; and fifth, the confessed shooter was the dead man's wife.

"Yes, I shot him," Augustine Lebaudy admitted. "He deserved it. But I will go free. Look at Mrs. Carman and Mrs. De Saulles."[40] Once again responsibility for the prosecution fell to the long-suffering Charles Weeks, and this time the case didn't even make it to trial. Ten days after the shooting, the grand jury refused to indict, saying that Mrs. Lebaudy had clearly acted in self-defense. Because there were no witnesses to the shooting, the verdict caused a degree of surprise, although many cynics attributed the grand jury's leniency to its belief that anyone with Lebaudy's bizarre habits—among other peculiarities, he liked to ride cows bareback, though he was unsuccessful in his attempts to make them hurdle—probably would benefit from a bullet in the back.

So, once again a wealthy female defendant had escaped the electric chair after killing her husband. Such homicides were now becoming a national epidemic. And, once again, Chicago had spearheaded this courtroom bias.

When, in April 1918, Ruby Dean became the twenty-fifth women in barely ten years to be acquitted of murder in Cook County, prosecutor Justin McCarthy wearily observed that the shooting of a man by a woman had become "the king of indoor sports."[41]

Christmas 1918 saw the final winding-up of Jack de Saulles's estate, and a very messy affair it turned out to be. When the numbers were finally calculated, they showed that Jack had died heavily in debt. Renovating The Box had ruined him financially. At the time of his death, he owed $53,881 and had assets of just $29,932. Creditors got less than fifty cents on the dollar. Jack Jr. got nothing.

Not that he needed it. The youngster was now being raised in the grand style on his mother's estate in Viña del Mar, enjoying all the trappings of wealth that the vast Errázuriz-Vergara family fortune could bestow. After her return from Japan, Blanca had declared that she would never remarry, but it was hard to imagine this fun-loving society butterfly signing up to a life in widow's weeds. Just like a decade earlier, there was no shortage of suitors beating a path to her front door, and this time the victor in the contest for Blanca's hand was a wealthy Chilean engineer named Fernando Santa Cruz Wilson. The couple married in Santiago on December 22, 1921, just three days shy of Jack Jr.'s ninth birthday. According to one paper, Blanca chose Fernando because her "little son is such an ardent admirer of Sénor Wilson and has long been anxious to have him for a stepfather."[42] It was reported that Wilson and the boy were inseparable companions, and he took the youngster hunting.

But calamity never strayed far from the blighted Errázuriz-Vergara family. Just a few months later, on May 1, 1922, Blanca's brother, Guillermo, blew his brains out in a Parisian hotel after being rejected by the American actress and world-class gold digger Peggy Hopkins Joyce. Added irony derived from the fact that Peggy had played the role of Josie Sabel (based on Joan Sawyer) in the movie *The Woman and the Law.*

While Blanca struggled to come to terms with this latest tragedy, her erstwhile savior, Rodolfo Guglielmi, was making headlines all on his own. After

Rudolph Valentino—formerly known as Rodolfo Guglielmi—in his most famous role as *The Sheikh*

several false starts in the stage-name department, he had finally settled on Rudolph Valentino. It had the right ring to it, exotic, but not too foreign-sounding; and under this guise, the former gardener from Castellaneta had taken Hollywood and the world by storm. In just four short years he had gone from uncredited extra—usually in roles that featured his dancing ability—to being one of the most famous actors alive. His breakthrough movie, *The Four Horsemen of the Apocalypse,* had become the highest grossing film of 1921 and made him the heartthrob of millions. But what few knew at the time was that just two years earlier, his career had teetered on the brink of disaster. All thanks to Blanca de Saulles.

His problems surfaced at a party thrown in September 1919 to celebrate the completion of *Stronger Than Death,* the latest movie of temperamental Russian-born stage star Alla Nazimova. For Valentino it was an unmissable opportunity to network, and he managed to wangle himself an invite. It just so happened that among those sitting at Nazimova's table was Dagmar Godowsky, an old friend of Valentino's from New York, and as she saw Valentino dancing past, she raised a hand and beckoned him over. Nazimova's face was thunderous as he approached and when Dagmar attempted to introduce the upcoming actor to the rest of the party, Nazimova snubbed him cold. She lowered her head and refused to even look at Valentino. Soon, she was joined in this act of public humiliation by the rest of her guests. Valentino, face flushed red with embarrassment, withdrew without saying a word. Nazimova glared at Godowsky. "How dare you bring that gigolo to my table?" she hissed. "How dare you introduce that pimp to Nazimova?"[43] She then regaled everyone with a raunchy—and wholly fictitious—account of how Valentino had fled New York to avoid being dragged into a sordid society murder. Blanca de Saulles, she said, had shot her husband out of love for that pimp!

When news of Nazimova's outburst reached Valentino, it shook him to his core. Naively, he thought that that dark interlude in New York had been left far behind. Was there nowhere he could escape his past? Despair grabbed hold and then squeezed tighter still as his already chaotic life grew even messier. Among the other guests at Nazimova's table that night was a beautiful actress recently signed to Metro Pictures named Jean Acker, and she was also beset with a potentially career-threatening problem. But in Valentino she saw a possible remedy. Jean was blessed with the same ethereal quality as Blanca, the pale skin and dark hair, so that when she secretly sought out Valentino, it was déjà vu of the heart for the impressionable young actor. A whirlwind romance followed—or so it was reported in the movie journals—in truth, theirs was a platonic relationship, because what Valentino had failed to realize was that Jean was a lesbian. And, just lately, her most ardent lover had been the fiery Alla Nazimova.

With the Hollywood gossip mill on full production, Jean, desperate to keep her career on track, turned to Valentino for help. She begged him to marry her. The streak of hopeless naivety that had shaped so many of his romantic decisions was indestructible. Always a sucker for a damsel in distress, Valentino duly obliged, and the couple tied the knot on November 6, 1919. They spent their wedding night at the Hollywood Hotel, where they danced into the early hours, but when Valentino tried to join his bride in the honeymoon suite, he found the door locked against him. The frustrated groom pounded on the door with his fists—loud enough to wake the other guests, some of whom stumbled out in pajamas and dressing gowns to see what all the ruckus was about—but Jean refused to budge. Disconsolately, Valentino trudged back on foot to his own apartment. The marriage never was consummated. Just like Blanca before her, Jean Acker had exploited the gullible young man for her own ends and then thrown him to the wolves.

In no time at all, details of Valentino's humiliation whistled around the Celluloid Village. For someone hoping to carve out a career as a romantic lead, such a rejection was not just deeply embarrassing, but profoundly worrying. Hollywood tittle-tattle was bad enough, but what if people went digging even deeper for dirt? Valentino's nerves began to fray, especially as his career was finally beginning to show signs of taking off. He had been hired by Universal Studios and his name was starting to figure in the film credits. If news of his involvement in the de Saulles divorce action and his subsequent arrest on vice charges leaked out into the public domain, he knew Universal would drop him like a lump of red-hot coal.

So he came clean and told his bosses everything. In the early days of silent films, movie moguls were wondrously adept at covering up scandals, and Universal wasn't about to see its latest golden goose get cooked. Although there is no proof of bribes being paid to officers, what is certain is that at some time in the early 1920s, all details of Guglielmi's arrest mysteriously disappeared without trace from the NYPD records office. And the press, too, was targeted. On May 17, 1920, the *New York Sun* published a strange clarification under the headline Rodolfo Guglielmi Was Not Accused, explaining how it had earlier reported Guglielmi's arrest over the Thym affair and now took "pleasure in stating the articles were not intended to reflect upon

Mr. Guglielmi's character . . . and [he] was speedily released from custody." On the same day, the *New York Tribune* published a similar retraction, saying, "Mr. Guglielmi was not taken into custody upon any criminal charge. The *Tribune* did not assert or intend to assert the contrary and it neither made nor intended to make any reflection upon him."

Significantly, neither apology mentioned that Guglielmi had gone on to enjoy success in the movies, and nowhere did it mention the name by which he was becoming increasingly known—Rodolpho de Valentina (the full and final transition to Rudolph Valentino would not come until the following year). Universal had ensured that if anyone did decide to go digging for dirt in some dusty newspaper morgue, Valentino was covered. With the really damaging evidence buried forever, Valentino was safe, at least for the time being.

It's reasonable to assume that Blanca was aware of Valentino's extraordinary success—remaining ignorant of his global superstardom would have taxed the reserves of a Trappist monk—but after the trial she washed her hands of him. As for Valentino, he never did get over the lady from Chile. Speaking privately he once said, "For years I had cherished a picture in my mind of how the perfect woman would look, a picture composed of the many things I had read and some of the great paintings I had seen. When Mrs. De Saulles stood before me it was as though the picture had come to life."[44]

This obsession haunted Valentino for the remainder of his short life. Mae Murray tells of a strange incident that happened in December 1925. Valentino was in Europe to publicize his latest film *The Eagle,* and Mae Murray was along for the ride. After being mobbed by thousands of ecstatic fans in London, the Hollywood superstar escaped to Paris, only to receive the bombshell news that his second wife, stage designer Natacha Rambova—who could have passed for Blanca's sister—had filed for divorce.[45] To combat his despair, Valentino was desperate for diversion, and it came in the form of gossip that his beloved Blanca happened to be in Paris at the same time. This, he figured, was his big chance. After all, he was now the world's premier sex god, lusted after by millions of women around the globe, a far cry from the humble tango dancer that Blanca had once known. Surely now she would respond to his advances?

Valentino found out where Blanca was staying and bombarded her with requests for a reunion. She rejected him cold. In desperation Valentino turned to Murray and begged her to act as an intermediary, to tell Blanca that he craved one more chance to see her. Murray approached the elusive Blanca and pleaded Valentino's case. After considerable hesitation Blanca agreed to meet Valentino on one condition: no speaking or touching. The bizarre assignation reportedly took place in a Paris hotel.

From all accounts, the Great Lover arranged himself on a sofa in the foyer and waited like a skittish teenager for the woman he had not seen in nine years. At some point, Blanca glided into view. Their eyes met and nothing more. Blanca sashayed by Valentino and out of his life for good. Shortly after this, she returned to Chile and Valentino caught a liner back to New York City. But nothing could efface the memory of Blanca. According to Murray, even when Valentino fell in love with other women, he could never escape "the shadow that Blanca De Saulles had cast over his heart."[46]

Less than a year after this alleged meeting, tragedy struck. On August 15, 1926, at the height of his fame, Valentino collapsed at the Hotel Ambassador in New York City. He was rushed to the Polyclinic, where an examination revealed him to be suffering from appendicitis and gastric ulcers that required surgery. The operation was not a success and Valentino developed peritonitis. At first his doctors were optimistic, but six days after surgery, and still very weak, Valentino was stricken with severe pleurisy in his left lung. This time the prognosis was lethal. As was customary at the time, Valentino was spared the details of what awaited him, and for a while he remained quite cheerful, even chatting with doctors about his plans when he left the hospital. The end came on August 23. Suddenly, the Great Lover fell into a coma and died. He was just thirty-one years old.

In a coincidence that might have been lifted from a Hollywood screenplay, his body was taken to Campbell's Funeral Church, the same undertakers that eight years earlier had attended to Jack de Saulles's bullet-riddled corpse. At the time people had marveled at the ceremony lavished on the former Yale football star, but those scenes paled into insignificance compared with the frenzy that attended Valentino's death. More than one hundred NYPD officers—most on foot, some on horseback—were drafted in to keep control of a crowd that numbered in excess of one hundred thousand people. A full-scale riot ensued, with distraught fans smashing windows and fighting to gain access to the funeral parlor, desperate for a final glimpse of their idol. Around the world, it was rumored, some women were so overcome by grief that they committed suicide. Everyone wanted a slice of the Valentino pie. Polish actress Pola Negri, claiming to be Valentino's fiancée—this was never confirmed—collapsed in hysterics while standing over the coffin, while the studio hired four actors to impersonate a Fascist Blackshirt honor guard, allegedly dispatched by Italian dictator Benito Mussolini.

After a funeral service in New York, Valentino's body was taken by train cross-country to California, where, after a second service, it was interred in the Hollywood Memorial Park Cemetery. To this day, fans of the actor gather at his tomb on the anniversary of his death, to celebrate his life, to pay their respects to a life that was tragically brief, and to worship at the shrine of the silent movie era's greatest romantic male lead. Like those other great sex gods, Marilyn Monroe and James Dean, Valentino died at the right age, his beautiful image preserved forever on celluloid. He would forever remain the Great Lover.

For the millions of adoring women who swooned over Rudolph Valentino, the 1920s brought huge societal changes. The most obvious of these was ratification of the 19th Amendment in 1920, which granted women the right to vote. Elsewhere, the newfound liberties kept on coming. Fashion, sex, partying, gals and guys were now on a much more level playing field, and nowhere was this more noticeable than in the American courtroom. As noted earlier, in the "Golden Age," from the start of the twentieth century and up to Blanca's trial, just four women were executed in the United States. In the two decades following female suffrage, that number jumped to fourteen. Equality had come at a price. Gone were the rose-tinted views of womanhood that placed attractive females on pedestals. Almost overnight the American courtroom became a far more pragmatic, hardheaded workplace. The rich of either sex remained unaffected, of course—to this day they receive a discount on justice that lesser mortals can only dream about—but for the female killer, American jurisprudence had undergone a seismic shift. The days of the unwritten law were over.

Arguably the greatest beneficiary of this judicial quirk never did manage to find the happiness she was seeking. When she wearied of the incessant globe-trotting, Blanca de Saulles retreated into semiseclusion in Chile, and, fittingly, it was here where the final act in this tragedy unfolded. In 1940, Viña del Mar was still home to the Errázuriz-Vergara dynasty and Blanca was still the resident princess. And once again "The Flower of the Andes" was alone. Her problems with men had continued. Her second marriage had failed and even Jack Jr.—the son she had killed for—was no longer around. At the first opportunity, several years previously, he had severed all connection with the mother who had killed on his behalf and returned to the United States and welcome obscurity. For Blanca, life was irredeemably miserable, made worse by failing health. On March 21, 1940, careworn and exhausted, the woman who had once been "The Richest and Most Beautiful Girl in All South America," the woman who had won the heart of the silent screen's greatest lover, and the woman who some believed got clean away with murder, lay down on her bed, swallowed a handful of barbiturates, and slowly died. She was just forty-five years old.

Acknowledgments

I am greatly indebted to several people and several organizations that have assisted in the preparation of this book. These are, in no particular order: Tom Tryniski; the Library of Congress; the British Newspaper Library; the British Library; James Jayo and Lauren Brancato at Lyons Press; Kate Hertzog; Kris Patenaude; David Andersen; Greg Manning; and Roger Williams at New England Publishing Associates. A very special vote of thanks goes to those often unnamed and unheralded reporters who daily produced thousands of words about this extraordinary case. How they did it I will never know. But it's thanks to them that this story can finally be told. The usual caveat applies, however; any errors or omissions are entirely the responsibility of the author. As always, the final thank-you goes to Norma.

Notes

Prologue

1 *New York Herald,* November, 23, 1917.

2 Ibid.

One

1 Today the family name is best known for the highly regarded winery founded in 1870 by Maximiano Errázuriz in the Valle de Aconcagua.

2 *New York Times,* July 28, 1916.

3 *Los Angeles Times,* August 4, 1916.

4 Other alumni include the movie stars Vivien Leigh and Maureen O'Sullivan, as well as numerous daughters of European royal houses.

5 *Chicago Daily Tribune,* August 5, 1917.

6 *New York Sun,* December 14, 1913.

7 *New York Times,* November 24, 1901.

8 *Evening World,* November 23, 1917.

9 Much later, in 1920, Heckscher would establish the Heckscher Museum of Art in Huntington, New York, with 185 paintings from his own collection. That same year he also donated four million dollars to the Society for the Prevention of Cruelty to Children.

10 *New York Times,* November 24, 1917.

11 Ibid., January 19, 1907.

12 The incident obviously had no lasting impact on Miss Moore's social standing. On August 15, 1907, she married into the Italian royal family and became the Duchess of Torlonia. (Among her great-grandchildren is the actress Brooke Shields.)

13 *Los Angeles Times,* February 17, 1910.

14 *Atlanta Constitution,* August 27, 1916.

15 *New York Times,* January 12, 1912.

16 Ibid.

17 *Chicago Daily Tribune,* February 4, 1912.

18 Ibid., February, 4, 1912.

19 (Tonawanda, New York) *Evening News,* March 4, 1912.

20 Ibid.

21 *Atlanta Constitution,* September 2, 1917.

22 *Washington Times,* December 3, 1912.

23 (Tonawanda, New York) *Evening News,* March 4, 1912.

24 *New York Sun,* January 9, 1912.

Two

1 This situation in Chile persisted until 1994.
2 *New York Times,* November 24, 1917.
3 Roughly equivalent to $2.5 million in 2013.
4 *Chicago Daily Tribune,* March 5, 1913.
5 *New York Tribune,* August 31, 1912.
6 Pope would go on to design the National Archives building and the Jefferson Memorial, both in Washington, DC.
7 *New York Sun,* September 12, 1912.
8 Balmaceda had an unusual end to his political career, choosing, on September 1, 1891, to put a bullet in his brain rather than surrender to the new government.
9 *New York Times,* September 29, 1912.
10 Ibid.
11 *New York Times,* January 17, 1913.
12 The year 1905 also saw the first running of the Belmont Stakes, the third leg of horse racing's Triple Crown, at the newly built racetrack. Previously the race, which was named after the Belmont brothers' father, had been contested at Morris Park.

Three

1 *New York Evening Telegram,* November 28, 1917.
2 *Washington Times,* November 28, 1917.
3 *New York Times,* November 27, 1917.
4 Although the identity of this "well-known actress" was never revealed, subsequent events suggest she might have been stage and screen star Mae Murray, who was known to be very friendly with Jack de Saulles around this time.
5 *Washington Times,* November 28, 1917.
6 *New York Times,* November 27, 1917.
7 Ibid.
8 *Brooklyn Daily Eagle,* November 26, 1917.
9 *New York Evening Telegram,* November 26, 1917.
10 *New York Sun,* November 27, 1917.
11 Ibid.
12 In later years this position would be retitled the White House Chief of Staff.
13 *New York Evening Telegram,* November 26, 1917.
14 Ibid.
15 *New York Herald,* November 27, 1917.
16 *New York Sun,* November 27, 1917.
17 Ibid.
18 Ibid.
19 Ibid.
20 Ibid.
21 Ibid.
22 Ibid.
23 *New York Times,* November 24, 1917.

24 Ibid., November 27, 1917.
25 Ibid., November 24, 1917.
26 Malone had one of the more unusual careers in American public life. A liberal activist who campaigned vociferously for female suffrage, he was also a noted lawyer who, in 1925, assisted Clarence Darrow during the infamous "Scopes Trial." After this he resumed his successful divorce practice, this time in Paris, until moving to Hollywood and taking up a career as a movie actor. His most notable roles were playing the part of Winston Churchill—to whom he bore a strong physical resemblance—in three films. He died in 1950.
27 *New York Evening Telegram,* November 23, 1917.
28 *New York Sun,* December 14, 1913.
29 Home to the Philadelphia Athletics and Philadelphia Phillies until 1970.
30 *New York Sun,* December 14, 1913.

Four

1 When presented to the US Immigration authorities, the ship's manifest continued to show Rodolfo Guglielmi as a second-class passenger.
2 The column on Ellis Island where new arrivals were traditionally greeted by relatives and friends already resident in America.
3 This version of events comes from Valentino's own life story, which was published in three parts by *Photoplay Magazine* in 1923. Others have claimed that he was actually "sponsored" by Frank Mennillo, a successful Italian businessman and old family friend who made his fortune importing olives to the United States, earning him the nickname of the "Olive King." It was Mennillo, they say, who showed Valentino the ropes in New York City.
4 Rudolph Valentino, "My Life Story," part 255. *Photoplay Magazine,* 1923.
5 The current Chilean minister, Henry Prather Fletcher, a career diplomat, had held the office since 1910 and President Wilson was disinclined to rock the boat, especially in light of Washington's intention to elevate the post to the rank of ambassador. This occurred in September 1914.
6 *Washington Herald,* March 11, 1914.
7 Ibid.
8 Allan R. Ellenberger, *The Valentino Mystique,* 113.
9 Ibid.
10 *New York Times,* March 31, 1957.
11 Before being converted into a hotel, 21 Pont Street was also the residence of Lily Langtry, the famed "Jersey Lily" who became the mistress of the Prince of Wales, later Edward VII. She continued to live there for two years after the transition. The hotel still has a restaurant named Langtry's in her honor.
12 *New York Tribune,* November 24, 1917.
13 *New York Sun,* June 2, 1914.
14 Ibid., November 28, 1917.
15 *New York Herald,* November 28, 1917.
16 Ibid.

17 Ibid.
18 Ibid.
19 Viscount Grey of Fallodon, *Twenty-Five Years 1892–1916* (Frederick A. Stokes Co.: New York, 1925), 20.
20 President Wilson had already confirmed America's neutrality.
21 *Milwaukee Sentinel,* May 24, 1942.
22 Ibid.

Five

1 Adela Rogers St. Johns, "Valentino: The Life Story of the Sheik," *Liberty,* September 18, 1929, 66.
2 By 1918, more than one million horses were in use in all theaters of war. Two thirds of these came from North America.
3 *Daily Mirror,* February 10, 1947.
4 *Washington Post,* November 24, 1917.
5 *Time,* November 19, 1965.
6 In 1935, once again living in England, the duke was sentenced to nine months' imprisonment for fraud, but after four weeks behind bars his conviction was quashed and he was freed to lead a life of unabashed hedonism—usually at someone else's expense—until his death in 1947.
7 *New York Sun,* November 27, 1917.
8 Ibid.
9 *Syracuse Herald,* November 26, 1917.
10 *New York Sun,* November 27, 1917.
11 *Brooklyn Daily Eagle,* November 26, 1917.
12 *New York Times,* October 22, 1914.
13 An early type of listening device that allowed one to eavesdrop on a conversation.
14 *New York Times,* November 24, 1917.
15 Although born in Liverpool, Fowler (1873–1943) was raised in the United States. After attaining the rank of colonel during the Great War, he later became First Deputy Commissioner in the New York Police Department.
16 *New York Times,* November 24, 1917.
17 Ibid.
18 Ibid.
19 *New York Sun,* November 24, 1917.
20 Ibid.
21 Paris did suffer artillery bombardment from March–August 1918.
22 Schwab didn't return entirely empty-handed. By his estimation, American companies, including his own, had already secured contracts worth three hundred million dollars to provide goods to Europe.
23 *New York Herald,* November 28, 1917.
24 Ibid.
25 Ibid.
26 *New York Sun,* November 28, 1917.

Six

1 *New York Times,* November 24, 1917.
2 *New York Evening Telegram,* November 23, 1917.
3 *New York Sun,* November 27, 1917.
4 *New York Times,* April 25, 1915.
5 Ibid., May 9, 1915.
6 She returned to live with her husband at their house on Merrick Road, Freeport, and the couple was still living there in 1929 when Dr. Carman was convicted of performing abortions, placed on probation, and removed from the medical register.
7 *New York Sun,* November 27, 1917.
8 *New York Times,* November 24, 1917.
9 Divorce only became legal in Chile in 2004.
10 *New York Sun,* November 24, 1917.
11 *Brooklyn Eagle,* December 1, 1917.
12 Ibid.
13 *New York Tribune,* November 24, 1917.
14 *New York Times,* November, 24, 1917.
15 Ibid.
16 *New York Tribune,* November 27, 1917.
17 *New York Herald,* November 27, 1917.
18 *Evening World,* November 26, 1917.
19 *New York Times,* September 4, 1910.
20 *Los Angeles Times,* August 4, 1916.
21 *New York Tribune,* July 28, 1916.
22 *New York Sun,* November 24, 1917.
23 Emily W. Leider, *Dark Lover,* 71.
24 *Washington Times,* August 12, 1917.
25 Emily W. Leider, *Dark Lover,* 71.
26 Ibid.
27 Ibid.
28 Ibid.
29 *New York Times,* August 12, 1917.
30 Ibid.
31 Emily W. Leider, *Dark Lover,* 72.
32 *New York Sun,* November 24, 1917.
33 Ibid.
34 The seamen, oilers, and firemen aboard the *St Paul* had refused to sail unless they received a 25 percent war bonus. Their employers, the International Mercantile Marine Company, agreed to this increase.
35 *New York Sun,* November 27, 1917.
36 *New York Evening Telegram,* November 27, 1917.

Seven

1 *New York Tribune,* September 6, 1916.
2 Ibid.
3 Ibid.
4 Ibid.
5 *New York Sun,* September 6, 1916.
6 *Syracuse Herald,* September 8, 1916.
7 *New YorkTimes,* September 6, 1916.
8 *Evening World,* September 6, 1916.
9 *New York Times,* September 6, 1916.
10 *New York Tribune,* September 6, 1916.
11 Ibid.
12 Allan R. Ellenberger, *The Valentino Mystique,* 119.
13 On January 30, 1917, Swann agreed to drop all charges against Enright and Foley. Both detectives returned to active duty.
14 Emily W. Leider, *Dark Lover,* 72.
15 *New York Times,* November 24, 1917.
16 Colin Evans, *SuperLawyers* (Detroit: Visible Ink, 1998), 228.
17 Ibid.
18 *Chicago Daily Tribune,* August 12, 1917.
19 *Washington Times,* August 12, 1917.
20 Coincidentally, Rudolph Valentino would hire Steuer in 1922 to try to untangle his tortuous financial affairs.
21 *New York Times,* November 24, 1917.
22 Ibid.
23 *New York Times,* August 11, 1915.
24 *Chicago Daily Tribune,* March, 15, 1917.
25 *New York Times,* November 24, 1917.
26 (Ogden City, Utah) *Ogden Standard,* May 12, 1917.
27 *New York Evening Telegram,* May 3, 1917.
28 *New York Times,* June 3, 1917.
29 *New York Herald,* November 27, 1917.
30 *Brooklyn Daily Eagle,* August 4, 1917.

Eight

1 *Evening World,* August 5, 1917.
2 *New York Sun,* November 23, 1917.
3 Ibid.
4 *New York Tribune,* November 23, 1917.
5 Ibid.
6 *New York Times,* August 6, 1917.
7 *New York Sun,* November 24, 1917.
8 Ibid., November 23, 1917.
9 Ibid.

10 Ibid.
11 *Evening World,* August 5, 1917.
12 *New York Tribune,* November 23, 1917.
13 Ibid.
14 *New York Sun,* November 23, 1917.
15 *New York Tribune,* November 23, 1917.
16 *New York Sun,* November 23, 1917.
17 *New York Tribune,* November 24, 1917.
18 *New York Sun,* November 24, 1917.
19 *New York Tribune,* November 23, 1917.
20 *New York Sun,* November 24, 1917.
21 Ibid., August 5, 1917.
22 Ibid., August 10, 1917.
23 *New York Tribune,* November 23, 1917.
24 *New York Sun,* August 5, 1917.
25 *New York Times,* August 5, 1917.
26 *Evening World,* August 5, 1917.
27 *New York Times,* August 5, 1917.
28 Ibid., November 23, 1917.
29 *New York Sun,* August 9, 1917.
30 *Syracuse Herald,* August 5, 1917.
31 *New York Sun,* November 23, 1917.
32 Ibid.
33 *New York Herald,* August 5, 1917.
34 *New York Sun,* November 23, 1917.
35 *New York Herald,* November 23, 1917.
36 *New York Sun,* November 24, 1917.
37 Ibid.
38 On another occasion Seaman faced accusations of allowing prisoners to roam freely through the jailhouse and permitting inmates to attend the movies. There were also rumors of jailhouse orgies. In 1919, Seaman was fired after his laxness allowed Dr. Walter Wilkins to commit suicide one day after Wilkins had been convicted of murdering his wife.
39 *New York Tribune,* August 5, 1917.

Nine

1 *Syracuse Herald,* August 5, 1917.
2 *Milwaukee Sentinel,* June 14, 1942.
3 *Syracuse Herald,* August 5, 1917.
4 *New York Evening Telegram,* August 5, 1917.
5 *Brooklyn Daily Eagle,* August 5, 1917.
6 *New York Evening Telegram,* August 5, 1917.
7 *New York Herald,* August 5, 1917.
8 *New York Evening Telegram,* August 5, 1917.

9 Ibid.
10 *New York Times,* August 6, 1917.
11 *Odgensburg (NY) News,* August 7, 1917.
12 *New York Times,* August 6, 1917.
13 Ibid.
14 *Brooklyn Daily Eagle,* August 5, 1917.
15 *Syracuse Herald,* August 5, 1917.
16 *Evening World,* August 6, 1917.
17 *New York Sun,* August 5, 1917.
18 *New York Times,* August 6, 1917.
19 Ibid.
20 Ibid.
21 Ibid.
22 *New York Sun,* August 6, 1917.
23 Other celebrities who have taken their final curtain call at Campbell's include Enrico Caruso, Joan Crawford, Judy Garland, Jacqueline Onassis, Heath Ledger, and John Lennon.
24 *New York Times,* August 6, 1917.
25 *New York Sun,* August 6, 1917.
26 *New York Tribune,* August 7, 1917.
27 *New York Evening Telegram,* August 6, 1917.
28 *Evening World,* August 6, 1917.
29 *New York Times,* August 7, 1917.
30 Ibid.
31 Ibid.
32 *New York Evening Telegram,* August 7, 1917.
33 *Brooklyn Daily Eagle,* August 7, 1917.
34 *New York Evening Telegram,* August 7, 1917.
35 *New York Herald,* August 7, 1917.
36 *New York Times,* August 7, 1917.
37 *New York Herald,* August 7, 1917.
38 *Brooklyn Daily Eagle,* August 7, 1917.
39 Ibid.
40 *New York Times,* August 7, 1917.
41 Ibid.
42 *New York Evening Telegram,* August 6, 1917.
43 *New York Sun,* August 7, 1917.
44 *Syracuse Herald,* August 8, 1917.
45 *Milwaukee Journal,* August 7, 1917.
46 *New York Herald,* August 7, 1917.
47 Ibid.
48 *New York Sun,* August 8, 1917.
49 Ibid.
50 *New York Herald,* August 8, 1917.

51 Ibid.
52 *Washington Times,* August 8, 1917.
53 *New York Evening Telegram,* August 7, 1917.
54 Ibid.
55 *New York Sun,* August 8, 1917.
56 *Syracuse Herald,* August 9, 1917.
57 *New York Tribune,* August 10, 1917.
58 Ibid.
59 *Syracuse Herald,* August 8, 1917.
60 Ibid.

Ten

1 *Pittsburgh Press,* August 10, 1917.
2 *New York Times,* August 9, 1917.
3 *New York Herald,* August 9, 1917.
4 *New York Times,* August 9, 1917.
5 Ibid.
6 *Syracuse Herald,* August 8, 1919.
7 *New York Evening Telegram,* August 8, 1917.
8 Ibid.
9 Ibid.
10 *Syracuse Herald,* August 9, 1917.
11 Ibid.
12 *Tacoma Times,* August 8, 1917.
13 *Chicago Daily Tribune,* August 9, 1917.
14 *New York Sun,* August 9, 1917.
15 *New York Times,* August 9, 1917.
16 *New York Sun,* August 9, 1917.
17 *New York Times,* August 9, 1917.
18 *Atlanta Constitution,* August 10, 1917.
19 *New York Times,* August 10, 1917.
20 Ibid.
21 Ibid.
22 *New York Herald,* August 10, 1917.
23 Ibid.
24 *New York Evening Telegram,* August 9, 1917.
25 *Brooklyn Daily Eagle,* August 10, 1917.
26 *New York Times,* August 10, 1917.
27 Ibid., August 11, 1917.
28 *New York Sun,* August 11, 1917.
29 *New York Times,* August 11, 1917.
30 *New York Herald,* August 11, 1917.
31 Ibid.
32 Ibid.

33 *New York Sun,* August 11, 1917.
34 *New York Times,* August 11, 1917.
35 Ibid.
36 *New York Herald,* August 11, 1917.
37 *New York Evening Telegram,* August 11, 1917.
38 *New York Sun,* August 11, 1917.
39 *New York Times,* August 11, 1917.
40 Ibid., August 12, 1917.
41 *New York Tribune,* August 12, 1917.
42 *New York Sun,* August 12, 1917.
43 *Washington Times,* August 12, 1917.
44 Ibid.
45 *New York Evening Telegram,* August 12, 1917.
46 *New York Tribune,* August 12, 1917.
47 *New York Herald,* August 13, 1917.
48 Ibid.
49 *New YorkTimes,* August 14, 1917.
50 *New York Evening Telegram,* August 13, 1917.
51 Ibid.
52 *Washington Times,* August 14, 1917.
53 After an abortive attempt at the movies, Joan Sawyer faded into obscurity.
54 *Ithaca Daily News,* August 14, 1917.
55 *Washington Times,* August 14, 1917.
56 *New York Times,* August 15, 1917.
57 *Daily Mirror,* August 27, 1917.

Eleven

1 A judge in some states (notably New York) responsible only for probates, estates, and adoptions.
2 *New York Herald,* September 5, 1917.
3 *New York Times,* September 6, 1917.
4 Ibid.
5 *Ogdensburg (NY) News,* September 13, 1917.
6 Ibid.
7 *New York Times,* September 19, 1917.
8 Ibid.
9 Ibid.
10 Ibid.
11 *Brooklyn Daily Eagle,* October 2, 1917.
12 *New York Sun,* October 18, 1917.
13 *Brooklyn Daily Eagle,* October 18, 1917.
14 Elizabth Fry (1780–1845), an activist who did much to reform England's prison system.

15 *New York Evening Telegram,* October 28, 1917.
16 *New York Tribune,* November 9, 1917.
17 Ibid.
18 *New York Herald,* November 13, 1917.
19 *New York Evening Telegram,* November 14, 1917.
20 Ibid.
21 *New York Herald,* November 19, 1917.
22 *New York Evening Telegram,* November 14, 1917.
23 *New York Tribune,* November 17, 1917.
24 *Evening World,* November 16, 1917.
25 Although the 19th Amendment extended the vote to women in 1920, it left the subject of jury service up to each state. In New York it was 1937 before women were made eligible for jury service on the same terms as men.
26 The term had been coined during the Thaw murder trial of 1907 to describe four female writers, Winifred Black, Dorothy Dix, Nixola Greeley-Smith, and Ada Patterson, who sat at their own special press table in the crowded courtroom, dispensing highly emotive coverage to their various employers.
27 *Rome (NY) Daily Sentinel,* November 22, 1917.
28 *Washington Times,* November 19, 1917.
29 Ibid.
30 *New York Times,* November 20, 1917.
31 Ibid.
32 *New York Tribune,* November 20, 1917.
33 Almost a decade later, this hotel would be where Charles Lindbergh spent his last night on American soil before his historic transatlantic flight.
34 *New York Evening Telegram,* November 19, 1917.
35 Ibid., November 20, 1917.
36 *Evening World,* November 20, 1917.
37 *New York Evening Telegram,* November 20, 1917.
38 *New York Herald,* November 21, 1917.
39 Ibid.
40 *New York Evening Telegram,* November 20, 1917.
41 *New York Herald,* November 21, 1917.
42 *Brooklyn Daily Eagle,* November 22, 1917.
43 Ibid.
44 Ibid.
45 Ibid.
46 *New York Herald,* November 22, 1917.
47 Ibid., November 23, 1917.
48 *Atlanta Constitution,* September 2, 1917.

Twelve

1 *New York Evening Telegram,* November 22, 1917.
2 *Brooklyn Daily Eagle,* November 22, 1917.
3 *New York Tribune,* November 23, 1917.
4 *New York Sun,* November 23, 1917.
5 Ibid.
6 *New York Evening Telegram,* November 22, 1917.
7 *New York Sun,* November 23, 1917.
8 Ibid.
9 *New York Evening Telegram,* August 22, 1917.
10 *New York Sun,* November 23, 1917.
11 *Washington Times,* November 22, 1917.
12 Ibid.
13 *New York Herald,* November 23, 1917.
14 Ibid.
15 *Lockport (NY) Union-Sun,* November 22, 1917.
16 *New York Times,* November 23, 1917.
17 *New York Herald,* November 23, 1917.
18 *New York Tribune,* November 23, 1917.
19 Ibid.
20 *New York Herald,* November 23, 1917.
21 *New York Times,* November 23, 1917.
22 *Rome (NY) Daily Sentinel,* November 23, 1917.
23 *New York Tribune,* November 23, 1917.
24 Ibid.
25 Ibid.
26 Ibid.
27 *New York Herald,* November 23, 1917.
28 Ibid.
29 *New York Sun,* November 23, 1917.
30 *New York Sun,* November 23, 1917.
31 Ibid.
32 *New York Sun,* November 23, 1917.
33 *Washington Herald,* November 23, 1917.
34 *New York Herald,* November 23, 1917.
35 *New York Sun,* November 23, 1917.
36 Ibid.
37 Ibid.
38 Ibid.
39 *New York Tribune,* November 23, 1917.

Thirteen

1 *Brooklyn Daily Eagle,* November 23, 1917.
2 *New York Evening Telegram,* November 23, 1917.

3 *Washington Times,* November 23, 1917.
4 *New York Sun,* November 24, 1917.
5 Ibid.
6 *New York Evening Telegram,* November 23, 1917.
7 Ibid.
8 *New York Sun,* November 24, 1917.
9 Ibid.
10 Ibid.
11 *New York Times,* November 24, 1917.
12 *New York Evening Telegram,* November 23, 1917.
13 Curiously, Rector's was the upmarket restaurant where Rodolfo Guglielmi once worked.
14 *New York Sun,* November 24, 1917.
15 *New York Times,* November 24, 1917.
16 *Brooklyn Daily Eagle,* November 23, 1917.
17 *New York Evening Telegram,* November 23, 1917.
18 *Brooklyn Daily Eagle,* November 23, 1917.
19 *New York Herald,* November 23, 1917.
20 *New York Times,* November 25, 1917.
21 *New York Evening Telegram,* November 23, 1917.
22 Ibid.
23 *Evening World,* November 23, 1917.
24 *New York Tribune,* November 24, 1917.
25 *New York Evening Telegram,* November 23, 1917.
26 Ibid.
27 *New York Sun,* November 24, 1917.
28 Ibid.
29 *New York Evening Telegram,* November 23, 1917.
30 Ibid.
31 Ibid.
32 *New York Herald,* November 24, 1917.
33 *New York Sun,* November 24, 1917.
34 *New York Evening Telegram,* November 24, 1917.
35 Ibid.
36 *New York Times,* November 24, 1917.
37 *New York Herald,* November 24, 1917.
38 *New York Sun,* November 24, 1917.
39 *New York Herald,* November 24, 1917.
40 *New York Sun,* November 24, 1917.
41 Ibid.
42 Ibid.
43 *Amsterdam Daily News,* November 23, 1917.
44 *Brooklyn Daily Eagle,* November 23, 1917.
45 For a full account of this landmark case in the history of forensic science, see *Slaughter on a Snowy Morn* by Colin Evans (London: Icon Books, 2011).

46 *New York Sun,* November 24, 1917.
47 *New York Herald,* November 24, 1917.
48 *New York Sun,* November 24, 1917.
49 Ibid.
50 Ibid.
51 It was two days after agreeing to these terms, on May 5, 1917, that Blanca filed an affidavit to have the travel restrictions lifted, only to withdraw her action that same day.
52 In 1913 Thaw escaped from Matteawan State Hospital and fled to Canada. He was later extradited back to the United States. A third trial found him not guilty and no longer insane, and he was set free.
53 *New York Sun,* November 24, 1917.
54 *New York Herald,* November 24, 1917.
55 *New York Sun,* November 24, 1917.
56 *New York Tribune,* November 24, 1917.
57 *New York Sun,* November 24, 1917.
58 Ibid.
59 *New York Herald,* November 24, 1917.
60 Ibid.
61 *New York Sun,* November 24, 1917.
62 Ibid.
63 Ibid.
64 *New York Herald,* November 24, 1917.
65 Ibid.
66 *New York Sun,* November 24, 1917.
67 Ibid.
68 Ibid.
69 Ibid.
70 *Brooklyn Daily Eagle,* November 24, 1917.
71 Ibid.
72 *New York Herald,* November 24, 1917.
73 *New York Sun,* November 24, 1917.
74 Ibid.
75 Ibid.

Fourteen

1 *Washington Times,* November 24, 1917.
2 *Brooklyn Daily Eagle,* November 25, 1917.
3 *New York Herald,* November 25, 1917.
4 Ibid.
5 *New York Tribune,* November 25, 1917.
6 Ibid.
7 *New York Times,* November 25, 1917.
8 Ibid.

9 Salm and his brother would represent Austria in the 1924 Davis Cup.
10 *New York Sun,* November 26, 1917.
11 Ibid.
12 *New York Herald,* November 26, 1917.
13 Ibid.
14 *New York Sun,* November 26, 1917.
15 *New York Times,* November 26, 1917.
16 *New York Herald,* November 26, 1917.
17 *Brooklyn Daily Eagle,* November 26, 1917.
18 *New York Sun,* November 27, 1917.
19 *New York Tribune,* November 27, 1917.
20 Ibid.
21 *Brooklyn Daily Eagle,* November 26, 1917.
22 *New York Times,* November 27, 1917.
23 *New York Evening Telegram,* November 26, 1917.
24 *Brooklyn Daily Eagle,* November 26, 1917.
25 Ibid.
26 *New York Herald,* November 27, 1917.
27 Ibid.
28 *Brooklyn Daily Eagle,* November 26, 1917.
29 *New York Evening Telegram,* November 27, 1917.
30 *Brooklyn Daily Eagle,* November 26, 1917.
31 *New York Sun,* November 27, 1917.
32 *Brooklyn Daily Eagle,* November 26, 1917.
33 Ibid.
34 *New York Sun,* November 27, 1917.
35 Ibid.
36 *New York Evening Telegram,* November 26, 1917.
37 *Syracuse Herald,* November 26, 1917.
38 *New York Sun,* November 27, 1917.
39 *Syracuse Herald,* November 27, 1917.
40 Ibid.
41 *Brooklyn Daily Eagle,* November 26, 1917.
42 *New York Tribune,* November 27, 1917.
43 Ibid.
44 *New York Sun,* November 27, 1917.
45 *New York Times,* November 27, 1917.
46 *New York Sun,* November 27, 1917.
47 Ibid.
48 The estranged wife of James Wilson Woodrow, a cousin of the president.
49 *Washington Times,* November 26, 1917.
50 Ibid.
51 *New York Tribune,* November 27, 1917.
52 *New York Sun,* November 27, 1917.

53 Ibid.
54 Ibid.
55 *New York Tribune,* November 27, 1917.
56 *New York Herald,* November 27, 1917.
57 Ibid.
58 *New York Tribune,* November 27, 1917.
59 Ibid.
60 *New York Sun,* November 27, 1917.
61 *New York Herald,* November 27, 1917.

Fifteen

1 *Evening World,* November 27, 1917.
2 *New York Herald,* November 28, 1917.
3 *New York Sun,* November 28, 1917.
4 Ibid.
5 Ibid.
6 Ibid.
7 Ibid.
8 Ibid.
9 Ibid.
10 Ibid.
11 Ibid.
12 Ibid.
13 Ibid.
14 Ibid.
15 Ibid.
16 Ibid.
17 Ibid.
18 Ibid.
19 Ibid.
20 *Syracuse Herald,* November 30, 1917.
21 *New York Sun,* November 28, 1917.
22 *New York Evening Telegram,* November 28, 1917.
23 *New York Times,* November 28, 1917.
24 *New York Sun,* November 28, 1917.
25 Ibid.
26 *New York Herald,* November 28, 1917.
27 *New York Sun,* November 28, 1917.
28 *Washington Times,* November 28, 1917.
29 *New York Sun,* November 28, 1917.
30 Ibid.
31 Ibid.
32 Ibid.
33 *New York Evening Telegram,* November 28, 1917.

34 *New York Tribune,* November 28, 1917.
35 *Syracuse Herald,* November 27, 1917.
36 *New York Tribune,* November 28, 1917.
37 Ibid.
38 *New York Herald,* November 28, 1917.
39 *Brooklyn Daily Eagle,* November 27, 1917.
40 *New York Sun,* November 28, 1917.
41 *Syracuse Herald,* November 30, 1917.
42 *Brooklyn Daily Eagle,* November 27, 1917.
43 *New York Sun,* November 28, 1917.
44 Ibid.
45 Ibid.
46 Ibid.
47 *Evening World,* November 27, 1917.
48 *New York Sun,* November 28, 1917.
49 Ibid.
50 *New York Times,* November 28, 1917.
51 *New York Sun,* November 28, 1917.
52 Ibid.
53 *New York Tribune,* November 28, 1917.
54 *Brooklyn Daily Eagle,* November 27, 1917.
55 *Evening World,* November 27, 1917.
56 *New York Sun,* November 28, 1917.
57 *New York Tribune,* November 28, 1917.
58 *New York Sun,* November 28, 1917.
59 *New York Evening Telegram,* November 27, 1917.
60 *New York Sun,* November 28, 1917.
61 Ibid.
62 Ibid.
63 Ibid.
64 Ibid.
65 Ibid.
66 This was a reference to Celia Coleman, who had been a prosecution witness.
67 *New York Times,* November 28, 1917.
68 *New York Sun,* November 29, 1917.
69 *New York Sun,* November 28, 1917.
70 *Tacoma Times,* November 28, 1917.
71 *New York Sun,* November 28, 1917.
72 *Washington Times,* November 28, 1917.
73 *New York Sun,* November 28, 1917.
74 Ibid.
75 Ibid.
76 Ibid.
77 *Milwaukee Sentinel,* June 14, 1942.

Sixteen

1 *New York Sun,* November 29, 1917.
2 Ibid.
3 *New York Evening Telegram,* November 28, 1917.
4 *Brooklyn Daily Eagle,* November 28, 1917.
5 *New York Sun,* November 29, 1917.
6 Ibid.
7 Ibid.
8 *New York Evening Telegram,* November 29, 1917.
9 *New York Sun,* November 29, 1917.
10 Ibid.
11 Ibid.
12 Ibid.
13 Ibid.
14 Ibid.
15 *New York Herald,* November 29, 1917.
16 *New York Sun,* November 29, 1917.
17 *New York Evening Telegram,* November 28, 1917.
18 Ibid.
19 *New York Sun,* November 29, 1917.
20 *New York Evening Telegram,* November 28, 1917.
21 *Evening World,* November 28, 1917.
22 *New York Sun,* November 29, 1917.
23 Ibid.
24 Ibid.
25 *Washington Times,* November 29, 1917.
26 *Evening World,* November 28, 1917.
27 *New York Sun,* November 29, 1917.
28 *New York Herald,* November 29, 1917.
29 *New York Sun,* November 29, 1917.
30 *Brooklyn Daily Eagle,* November 28, 1917.
31 *New York Sun,* November 29, 1917.
32 Ibid.
33 *Syracuse Herald,* November 28, 1917.
34 *Evening World,* November 28, 1917.
35 *Brooklyn Daily Eagle,* November 28, 1917.
36 *Syracuse Herald,* November 28, 1917.
37 Ibid.
38 *New York Sun,* November 29, 1917.
39 Ibid.
40 Ibid.
41 *New York Tribune,* November 29, 1917.
42 Ibid.
43 *New York Herald,* November 29, 1917.

44 *Washington Times,* November 20, 1917.
45 *New York Sun,* November 29, 1917.
46 Ibid.
47 Ibid.
48 Ibid.
49 Ibid.
50 Ibid.
51 Ibid.
52 Ibid.
53 Ibid.
54 Ibid.
55 Ibid.
56 *New York Tribune,* November 29, 1917.
57 *New York Sun,* November 29, 1917.
58 Ibid.
59 Ibid.
60 Ibid.
61 Ibid.
62 *Syracuse Herald,* November 28, 1917.
63 *New York Sun,* November 29, 1917.

Seventeen

1 *New York Tribune,* November 30, 1917.
2 Ibid.
3 Ibid.
4 Ibid.
5 Ibid.
6 *New York Times,* November 30, 1917.
7 Ibid.
8 Señora Errázuriz-Vergara died in 1955 at the age of eighty-nine.
9 *New York Times,* November 30, 1917.
10 Ibid.
11 *New York Herald,* November 30, 1917.
12 *New York Tribune,* November 30, 1917.
13 Ibid.
14 Ibid.
15 *New York Times,* November 30, 1917.
16 *Washington Times,* November 30, 1917.
17 *New York Times,* November 30, 1917.
18 *New York Herald,* December 1, 1917.
19 In 1899 Roland B. Molineaux, a Brooklyn chemist, was accused of poisoning Katherine Adams. After two trials he was acquitted.
20 *New York Herald,* December 1, 1917.
21 *New York Sun,* December 1, 1917.

22 Ibid.
23 *Evening World,* November 30, 1917.
24 *New York Times,* December 1, 1917.
25 *Evening World,* November 30, 1917.
26 *New York Sun,* December 1, 1917.
27 Ibid.
28 In 1913 Hans Schmidt, a Roman Catholic priest, was charged with killing his housekeeper, Anna Aumuller, whom he had secretly married. At his first trial he feigned insanity, leading to a hung jury. Tried a second time, he was convicted and executed at Sing Sing on February 18, 1916, the only priest put to death in the United States.
29 *New York Sun,* December 1, 1917.
30 Ibid.
31 Ibid.
32 *Washington Times,* December 1, 1917.
33 *New York Sun,* December 1, 1917.
34 Ibid.
35 *New York Tribune,* December 1, 1917.
36 *New York Herald,* December 1, 1917.
37 *New York Tribune,* December 1, 1917.
38 *New York Times,* December 1, 1917.
39 *New York Sun,* December 1, 1917.
40 Dr. George H. Kirby, president of the Manhattan State Hospital for the Insane, who was sitting at the prosecution table.
41 *New York Sun,* December 1, 1917.
42 *New York Times,* December 1, 1917.
43 *New York Sun,* December 1, 1917.
44 Ibid.
45 Ibid.
46 Ibid.
47 Ibid.
48 Ibid.
49 *Atlanta Constitution,* December 1, 1917.
50 *New York Sun,* December 1, 1917.
51 *New York Times,* December 1, 1917.
52 Ibid.
53 *New York Sun,* December 1, 1917.
54 *Syracuse Herald,* November 30, 1917.
55 Ibid.

Eighteen

1 *New York Times,* March 22, 1914.
2 *Evening World,* December 1, 1917.
3 *New York Herald,* December 2, 1917.

4 *Evening World,* December 1, 1917.
5 *New York Times,* December 2, 1917.
6 *Los Angeles Times,* December 2, 1917.
7 *New York Times,* December 2, 1917.
8 Ibid.
9 Ibid.
10 Ibid.
11 *Evening World,* December 1, 1917.
12 *New York Tribune,* December 2, 1917.
13 *New York Herald,* December 2, 1917.
14 *New York Sun,* December 2, 1917.
15 *Evening World,* December 1, 1917.
16 *New York Evening Telegram,* December 1, 1917.
17 Ibid.
18 *New York Sun,* December 2, 1917.
19 Ibid.
20 Ibid.
21 *New York Herald,* December 2, 1917.
22 *New York Sun,* December 2, 1917.
23 Ibid.
24 Ibid.
25 Ibid.
26 Ibid.
27 *Brooklyn Daily Eagle,* December 2, 1917.
28 *New York Sun,* December 2, 1917.
29 Ibid.
30 Ibid.
31 Ibid.
32 *Syracuse Herald,* December 2, 1917.
33 *New York Sun,* December 2, 1917.
34 *Syracuse Herald,* December 2, 1917.
35 *New York Sun,* December 2, 1917.
36 *New York Times,* December 2, 1917.
37 *New York Herald,* December 2, 1917.
38 *Atlanta Constitution,* December 2, 1917.
39 *New York Sun,* December 2, 1917.
40 Ibid.
41 Ibid.
42 *New York Herald,* December 2, 1917.
43 *Atlanta Constitution,* December 2, 1917.
44 *New York Herald,* December 2, 1917.
45 *New York Sun,* December 2, 1917.
46 *New York Times,* December 2, 1917.
47 Ibid.

48 *New York Sun,* December 2, 1917.
49 Ibid.
50 Ibid.
51 Ibid.
52 Ibid.
53 *New York Tribune,* December 2, 1917.
54 Ibid.
55 *New York Sun,* December 2, 1917.
56 Ibid.
57 Ibid.
58 Ibid.
59 *Brooklyn Daily Eagle,* December 2, 1917.
60 *New York Tribune,* December 2, 1917.
61 *New York Times,* December 2, 1917.
62 *New York Sun,* December 2, 1917.
63 Ibid.
64 Ibid.
65 *Brooklyn Daily Eagle,* December 2, 1917.
66 *Washington Times,* December 2, 1917.
67 *New York Sun,* December 2, 1917.
68 *Brooklyn Daily Eagle,* December 2, 1917.
69 *New York Sun,* December 2, 1917.
70 *New York Times,* December 2, 1917.
71 *Syracuse Herald,* December 2, 1917.
72 *New York Tribune,* December 2, 1917.
73 Ibid.
74 *Syracuse Herald,* December 2, 1917.
75 *New York Tribune,* December 2, 1917.
76 *New York Sun,* December 2, 1917.
77 *Evening World,* December 1, 1917.

Nineteen

1 *New York Times,* December 3, 1917.
2 Ibid.
3 *Chicago Daily Tribune,* December 4, 1917.
4 *Evening World,* December 3, 1917.
5 *New York Times,* December 3, 1917.
6 Ibid.
7 *New York Sun,* December 3, 1917.
8 *Evening World,* December 3, 1917.
9 *New York Herald,* December 3, 1917.
10 *New York Sun,* December 3, 1917.
11 Ibid.
12 *Washington Post,* December 3, 1917.

13 *New York Times,* December 3, 1917.
14 *New York Tribune,* December 3, 1917.
15 *New York Sun,* December 3, 1917.
16 *Evening World,* December 3, 1917.
17 *New York Tribune,* December 3, 1917.
18 *New York Times,* December 3, 1917.
19 *Syracuse Herald,* December 3, 1917.
20 *New York Times,* December 3, 1917.
21 *Evening World,* December 3, 1917.
22 Ibid.
23 *New York Times,* December 3, 1917.
24 Ibid.
25 *Evening World,* December 3, 1917.
26 Ibid.
27 Ibid.
28 *Washington Times,* December 4, 1917.
29 *New York Times,* December 4, 1917.
30 *Washington Times,* December 4, 1917.
31 Ibid.
32 *New York Tribune,* December 9, 1917.
33 In July 1917, Lieutenant Douglas Malcolm, an officer serving on the Western Front, returned to England on furlough and caught his wife in bed with Anton Bamberg. Malcolm thrashed Bamberg severely, but he could do nothing to prevent the affair. On August 17, he surprised the couple in a London hotel, and this time he shot Bamberg dead. An inquest returned a verdict of "justifiable homicide," and he was subsequently acquitted at trial. The senior defense lawyer, Sir John Simon, had told the jury that he was not going to appeal to the "unwritten law." In his summation the judge stressed that the so-called unwritten law did not exist in England.
34 *New York Tribune,* December 9, 1917.
35 *Chicago Defender,* April 4, 1918.
36 *Atlanta Constitution,* April 15, 1918.
37 *Chicago Defender,* April 4, 1918.
38 *Amsterdam Evening Recorder,* August 21, 1918.
39 *New York Times,* January 12, 1919.
40 *New York Times,* January 13, 1919.
41 *Chicago Daily Tribune,* April 23, 1918.
42 *Syracuse Herald,* January 5, 1922.
43 Emily W. Leider, *Dark Lover*, 99.
44 Adela Rogers St. Johns, "Valentino: The Life Story of the Sheik, Part 2," *Liberty,* September 18, 1926, 66.
45 Valentino had divorced Jean Acker in 1922. In a typically impulsive gesture, that same year he married Natacha Rambova before his divorce decree was absolute, leading to him being briefly jailed on charges of bigamy.
46 *Milwaukee Sentinel,* June 14, 1942.

Bibliography

Because this is the first full-length book dealing with the de Saulles case, and because the court records and a trial transcript were lost in a fire, the main sources of research, by necessity, have been contemporary newspapers. Thanks to the high caliber (and exhaustive length) of crime reporting in the early twentieth century, there was no shortage of material. The following newspapers were consulted at length:

Amsterdam Daily News
Atlanta Constitution
Brooklyn Daily Eagle
Chicago Daily Tribune
Evening World
Ithaca Daily News
Lockport Union-Sun and Journal
Los Angeles Times
Nassau Post
New York Evening Telegram
New York Herald
New York Sun
New York Times
New York Tribune
Rome Daily Sentinel
South Side Messenger
Syracuse Herald
Washington Herald
Washington Post
Washington Times

In addition, the following books provided background information:

Baden, Michael, with Judith Adler Hennessee. *Unnatural Death: Confessions of a Medical Examiner.* New York: Ballantine, 1989.

Botham, Neil. *Valentino: The First Superstar.* New York: Metro, 2002.

Capuzzo, Michael. *Close to Shore: A True Story of Terror in an Age of Innocence.* New York: Random House, 2001.

Cuthbert, C. R. M. *Science and the Detection of Crime.* London: Grey Arrow, 1962.

Dearden, Harold. *Death under the Microscope.* London: Hutchinson, 1934.

Ellenberger, Allan R. *The Valentino Mystique: The Death and Afterlife of the Silent Film Idol.* Jefferson, NC: McFarland, 2005.

Hocking, Denis. *Bodies and Crimes.* London: Arrow Books, 1994.

Leider, Emily W. *Dark Lover: The Life and Death of Rudolph Valentino.* New York: Farrar, Strauss and Giroux, 2003.

Morland, Nigel. *Science in Crime Detection.* London: Camelot, 1958.

Morris, Michael. *Madam Valentino: The Many Lives of Natacha Rambova.* New York: Abbeville Press, 1991.

Saferstein, Richard. *Criminalistics: Introduction to Forensic Science.* Upper Saddle River, NJ: Prentice Hall, 2003.

Index

Note: Page numbers in *italics* indicate illustrations.